Enduring Legacy

Enduring Legacy

Rhetoric and Ritual of the Lost Cause

W. Stuart Towns

The University of Alabama Press

Tuscaloosa

The University of Alabama Press
Tuscaloosa, Alabama 35487-0380
uapress.ua.edu

Hardcover edition published 2012.
Paperback edition published 2023.
eBook edition published 2012.

Typeface: Minion and Goudy Sans

Cover design: David Nees

Paperback ISBN: 978-0-8173-6070-2

A previous edition of this book has been cataloged by the Library of Congress.
ISBN: 978-0-8173-1752-2 (cloth)
E-ISBN: 978-0-8173-8581-1

To Helen Ruth, who shares my love of the South.
My deepest thanks for all these years as
my best editor, critic, and friend.

Contents

Introduction

In the mid-1990s, while working on an anthology of speeches from the civil rights movement, I began to have the feeling of déjà vu. A few years earlier, I had edited a two-volume collection of speeches by southern orators from the nineteenth and twentieth centuries, and many of the themes, attitudes, values, and perceptions sounded familiar in the speeches I was reading from some of the civil rights protagonists. Segregationists like George Wallace and Ross Barnett were expressing thoughts and feelings similar to southern speakers from sixty to eighty years earlier such as Charles C. Jones Jr. and John Brown Gordon. About the same time, the debates over the public display of the Confederate flag (whether on T-shirts or flying from state capitol buildings), the singing of "Dixie" at football games and other public venues, the erecting of an occasional Confederate monument or the repairing of one damaged by time or storm, the surging popularity of Civil War reenactments, the growth of chapters of the Sons of Confederate Veterans, and the continued strength of the United Daughters of the Confederacy all reflected some of those same themes from the late nineteenth and early twentieth century. I kept returning to a central question as I read more and more of the mid-twentieth-century segregationist speeches: what was the rhetorical foundation for these themes, appeals, and values?

I have long believed that historical study of public address and an understanding of what speakers were communicating to their audiences in years gone by can help us better understand the present. My belief in the importance of the study of public communication was reinforced when I began teaching a seminar on rhetoric in the civil rights movement and my students asked, after reading some of the speeches by Orval Faubus and Senator James Eastland, why intelligent white southerners continued to oppose racial justice and the civil rights movement and to defend segregation and racial discrimination. Part, at least, of the answer I gave them lies in the enduring legacy left by the rhetoric of the Lost Cause. The proverbial lightbulb went on over their heads after they read some of the Lost Cause speeches we will be examining here. I was intrigued the more I thought about it and wanted to see if there really were connections between Lost Cause oratory, those who fought so hard to maintain segregation and racial discrimination at midcentury, and those at the end of the twentieth century and beginning of the twenty-first who continued to defend the public use and display of Confederate memorabilia and memories of the Civil War. Of course, there were connections, as I quickly found out; hence this volume on the rhetoric of the Lost Cause.

I contend that twentieth-century white southerners learned much of how they were going to think about race, about the North, about the Civil War and Reconstruction, and about themselves from the rhetoric of the Lost Cause. The twentieth-century South would have been vastly different had the oratory of the Lost Cause not prevailed. My intent is to examine how the ceremonial orators of this era created the fabric of public memory, how to understand their words as their listeners understood them, and how to see their values and themes echo in contemporary debates and speeches many decades after they created their vision of the Old South, the Civil War, and the Reconstruction and Redemption eras. David Goldfield reminds us that "how white Southerners remembered the Civil War and its aftermath defined and distinguished the South for the next century."[1] I contend that much of "how they remembered" comes from the rhetorical foundation we call the Lost Cause.

This body of Lost Cause oratory provides an excellent example of Robert Hariman's reminder that "the analysis of a canon of public speeches can identify crucial elements of understanding and action that are likely to be overlooked by historians."[2] These speeches arose out of the remembered smoke and blood of the Civil War, and the orators painted a verbal picture of that war as they and others recalled it with the goal in the early postwar years of restoring and strengthening the confidence of the defeated South and the shell-shocked former Confederates. Lost Cause ritual and oratory created a sense of order and community out of the chaos, uncertainty, and despair of defeat. The ceremonial events and the speeches were designed to redeem the honor of white southern men and rebuild their egos and confidence. The ceremony, ritual, and oratory worked together to help the defeated southerners have something to recall and cherish in the midst of turmoil, change, poverty, stress, desolation, and defeat.

The stories of the Old South and the Confederacy, the Reconstruction,

Redemption, and Reconciliation years, the images they portray, the reality as the orators saw it—all helped Lost Cause orators explain to their white southern audiences the postwar world. The war was over, the defeated soldiers were home, but it was not really home. It was a new world, a changed world, a vastly different world. The veterans and their fledgling nation had failed. How could former Confederates and their region be made whole again? The strategy was to create through their oratory a narrative about a larger-than-life Old South and Confederacy and about how heroically their fellow soldiers had fought and lost—not to better soldiers and certainly not to a more correct version of truth, but to overwhelming military might, materialism, and sheer numbers.

The communication goals of these Lost Cause speakers involved creating a unified front in the white South regarding the region—an "us against them" mentality that created its own set of heroes and myths, just as the new American nation did after the Revolutionary War. It was almost as if the South had won the Civil War and successfully established a new nation. The various monuments, reunions, Memorial Day celebrations, and the oratory that went with them had an element of thumbing the region's collective nose at the North: "Yes, the war is over, but it is worth remembering forever—indeed, it is our duty to recall that heroic effort." There are many shared memories we Americans cherish: Paul Revere's ride, Washington crossing the Delaware, Jackson at New Orleans, Custer at Little Big Horn, and Teddy Roosevelt charging up Kettle Hill in the San Juan Heights all come quickly to mind. The mythology and memories of Jefferson Davis, Robert E. Lee, Stonewall Jackson, Gettysburg, Shiloh, Pea Ridge, and countless other battles and skirmishes, gallant leaders, heroic soldiers, faithful slaves, and staunch women on the home front form a similar mosaic of legend for many white southerners.[3] That mosaic was created in large part by the public address of Lost Cause orators.

After the Civil War, southern orators established a rhetorical narrative of their view of the region's past, present, and future that conformed to how white southerners wanted to see their world. The high-water mark of the Confederacy had passed decades before, and Appomattox marked the end of the war, but in a sense, white southerners kept fighting by other means. In hundreds of speeches presented at three ceremonial and ritualistic events occurring all over the region—Confederate Memorial Day, Confederate veterans' reunions, and Confederate monument dedications—these speakers built a public memory of the Old South, the Confederacy, the Civil War, Reconstruction, Redemption, Reconciliation, the New South, and race relations. By virtue of continued and frequent repetition and astute audience analysis, this public memory formed the foundation of white southerners' perception of the world and how they should respond to that world. This perspective remained viable in the public consciousness at least through the civil rights movement of the 1950s and 1960s. As we will see, in some respects and to some degree it continues even in the first decade of the twenty-first century in the minds of some southerners, perhaps much more than one might expect.

This rhetorical story about the Lost Cause created for white southerners after the Civil War the feeling that they better understood their world after it had been turned upside down; they understood, or thought they did, why they had lost the war and how to live with that defeat. The orators of the Lost Cause, speaking from the stages created for them by scores of chapters of Ladies' Memorial Associations and military unit reunions, and later, the United Daughters of the Confederacy and the United Confederate Veterans, and even later, the Sons of Confederate Veterans, reinvented the past and their vision of what they recalled and how they wanted to remember it. As we will see, this paradigm still influences the lives and sense of history of countless southerners and even many outside the boundary of the old Confederate States of America.

Lost Cause defenders helped define and configure the defeated South in ways that grew out of the Civil War experience and the tradition and history of their states and region. Lost Cause oratory created the grand narrative story of the Civil War and what had preceded it and what came after Appomattox with the goal of shaping the present and guiding the future. This narrative provided a road map and a set of glasses through which to view the world for most southern whites for well over one hundred years; some are still following that road map, using those glasses in 2012 and will be likely to continue doing so for years to come. The sesquicentennial of the Civil War (2011–15) will provide a new stage on which to follow this road map, as many southerners doubtless will.

In many cases, these Lost Cause orators I have surveyed are not well-known speakers of their era. To be sure, some were in the regional or even national spotlight, such as Wade Hampton or John B. Gordon, but many are known only as footnotes in southern history—or even less notable. But they, too, reflected and shaped the mode of thinking, the perceptions, and the attitudes of their auditors, just as much as the better-known former Confederate generals or governors. These speakers surveyed were the "keepers of the flame" for the small communities that featured them in their festivities around monuments, at reunions, and at special days like Confederate Memorial Day. They were seen as elder statesmen, as military heroes in the eyes of their local infantry company, as the bulwarks of the Confederate culture they were celebrating. Their credibility as former Confederate soldiers or sons of soldiers gave the narrative its strength, vitality, and enduring power—and what they told their listeners is exactly what most white southerners wanted to hear and believe. Katharine Du Pre Lumpkin wrote about her father's oratory at various reunions and monument dedications: "He spoke such things as his audience wanted to hear, and in the way they wanted—feelingly, eloquently."[4] These values, themes, ideas, and stories were all deeply held by the speakers and their listeners and passed on through the generations by this Lost Cause oratory. I cannot imagine a Lost Cause orator from the nineteenth century or a segregationist governor of the 1950s or even a Confederate flag enthusiast of the twenty-first century needing to rely on public-opinion polls or focus groups to tell him or her what to say about the Old South, the Confederacy, the Civil War, or Reconstruction!

A thoughtful exploration of southern public address, rituals, and symbols of the decades immediately following the Civil War reveals many of the premises on which twentieth-century southern culture was based and shows the still-persisting values and memories of much of that culture as we move forward into the twenty-first century. Anyone seeking to understand the present South, the civil rights movement South, the Dixiecrat South, or the Sunbelt South must come to these speeches, which built the foundations of all the Souths that have existed in postwar memory and reality. When southerners—either black or white—engage with or relate to the Civil War, often their feelings or understandings about the war have a direct relationship to the rhetoric we will be examining. If we listen carefully to these Lost Cause orators, we will perhaps understand better the disparities between how various groups and individual southerners and other Americans see our Civil War, as these perceptions of the Confederacy and the Civil War have been shaped for modern minds by the rhetoric and ritual of the Lost Cause.

At the sesquicentennial of the Civil War, perhaps our understanding of the results and lasting effects of that conflict will be deeper if we understand how the rhetoric of the Lost Cause helped to shape our perceptions and memory of that war. Certainly we can gain a deeper understanding of southern issues of race, states' rights, regional and local heritage, and the transmission and perpetuation of Confederate memories. Reading and thinking about these Lost Cause orations and rituals should help southern whites and blacks alike better understand their collective southern culture and its past, stretching back to the Civil War era at least, but, more important, the more recent past—the past of the civil rights movement and the debates continuing from the 1990s over the Confederate flag and other Confederate symbols. These issues have been at least partly driven by the foundation of belief, attitudes, and perceptions that was laid so successfully by the Lost Cause rhetors of the 1870–1920 period. Knowing what they said might, just might, help to show how our differences and our similarities can be cherished and appreciated more easily today.

Contemporary debates occasionally seem as bitter as those a century and more ago. For many black southerners, memory and perception of the Confederacy envisions a racist attitude, slavery, treason toward the nation, and an overall negative perception and attitude. For many white southerners the view is considerably different. Their attitude is a positive reflection of Confederate memories: the bravery and honor of their ancestors who fought for their beliefs, their property rights, their states' rights, and what they saw as the proper interpretation of the United States Constitution. If this view was the totality of white southern perspectives on the Confederacy, perhaps the issues could be settled a little easier. There can be no denying, however, that many extremist, racist, white supremacy groups and individuals have appropriated the Confederate symbols as their own and have distorted and misrepresented the views of southerners who simply want to honor their tradition and do it in an honorable, non-racist manner. This outlook was summed up well in an April 24, 2005, letter to the *New York Times Book Review* by Lewis Regenstein. Responding to a review of John Coski's *The Confederate Battle Flag,* Regenstein wrote: "My more than two dozen maternal ancestors who fought for the South made it clear, in their letters, memoirs and books, what that Lost Cause was: they were fighting for their homeland—not for slavery, but for their families, homes, and country. . . . The Confederate soldiers, often exhausted and hungry, sick and shoeless, wet and cold, outnumbered and outsupplied but rarely outfought, showed amazing courage, honor and valor. . . . That is why so many decent Southerners are proud of their ancestors, and their symbols." A bumper sticker seen occasionally around the region succinctly serves up this point of view: "Heritage, not Hate."

My purpose in this study is to illustrate the role played by public speaking in determining how southerners remembered the Old South, the Confederacy, the Civil War, the Reconstruction, and the Redemption. We will see how those recollections have lived on for well over a century and affected southern behavior and culture, especially as it relates to racial relationships and the use of the symbols of the Confederacy. There have been other influences as well, of course, such as the role of the United Daughters of the Confederacy (UDC) in demanding textbooks for public schools that told the story of the war and the Confederacy from a definite southern point of view. The work of the UDC in raising countless thousands of dollars for building Confederate monuments, and their care and persistence in creating and sustaining Confederate Memorial Day into the twenty-first century are all essential elements perpetuating Confederate mythology, as Karen Cox clearly shows in *Dixie's Daughters*. Thomas Dixon's books such as *The Clansman* and the movie made from it, Margaret Mitchell's *Gone With the Wind,* pro-South articles in popular magazines such as *Scribners'* and *Century,* and many other articles, books, and films did their share to reinforce the ideas of the Lost Cause. I am focusing, however, on the public oratory at the various events held across the South to commemorate the fallen Confederacy and heroic Confederates, as I have a deep respect for the role and power of the spoken word in American life—especially in the South.[5]

Confederate reunions are over, Confederate Memorial Day has lost most of its power, and heritage groups no longer wield the influence they once did, but debates over Confederate monuments and Confederate flags give people and groups who may think about their memories and understandings of the Civil War and its aftermath in very different ways a focal point around which to debate, discuss, and perhaps understand each other better. Understanding more fully the Confederate heritage in the South today can give disparate groups a better perspective on what divides—and unifies—them.

Nearly a century and a half after Lee and Grant rode away from Appomattox Courthouse, considerable energy, time, and money is being spent across the South and the nation at large remembering the Civil War. Four contemporary examples will demonstrate this continuing interest in the Civil War and the culture of the Confederacy. Every year, close to one million visitors tour the battlefield at Chickamauga, Georgia, and the Chattanooga National Military Park. The city of Chickamauga is developing a tourist trail to various battlefield locations in the area. City Manager John Culpepper remarked to the local newspaper, "It's just something that is born and bred in you. I'm proud of being a Southerner and proud of my Confederate ancestors." Dalton, Georgia, hosted the 2004 reunion of the Sons of Confederate Veterans, which attracted about three thousand visitors and generated an estimated one million dollars for the Dalton economy. The "last Confederate funeral" saw thousands of Civil War reenactors gather in Charleston, South Carolina, to honor and participate in the burial of the recently discovered crew of a Confederate submarine, the *H. L. Hunley.* The state of Georgia is anticipating the millions of dollars tourists are expected to spend in the state during the 150th anniversary celebration and is planning to spend five million dollars to refurbish Civil War sites and promote them as a comprehensive heritage package to attract visitors. Tony Horwitz, in *Confederates in the*

Attic, reminds us that Americans—not just southerners—remain "obsessed with the Civil War."[6] Much of this effort and obsession is due to the enduring legacy of Lost Cause rhetoric.

In chapter 1 we take a quick survey of the vital place of oratory in the life of the oral tradition in the American South. We see the role of ceremonial speaking and ritual in the defining of the southern tradition of the Civil War and Reconstruction and the importance of rhetoric in the shaping of collective memory, which has lasted into the twenty-first century.

Chapter 2 examines the three leading Confederate ceremonial events that contributed so much to creating and sustaining the Lost Cause. Confederate Memorial Day honored at first the war dead, but gradually it came to demonstrate love, respect, honor, and memory for all the warriors of the Confederacy, including the women back home. Reunions of Confederate veterans provided a focal point for recollection by those who wore the gray, and later for their sons and grandsons. Finally, dedication of the hundreds of Confederate monuments throughout the South serves as reminders of the Lost Cause not just for the postwar generation, but for observers 145 years after Appomattox.

The oratorical defense of the Confederacy and the Old South is described in chapter 3, as we examine the speeches that defended the right of secession and the constitutional basis in southern minds for the war. In spite of modern-day protestations of innocence by some southerners, the defense of slavery by Lost Cause orators is spelled out in this chapter, as well as the defining of the southern scapegoat for the war: the Republican Party, and the feelings about the inevitability of the war. We see in these speeches the "true believers" in the southern interpretation of the Constitution, the meaning of the Civil War, the distinctions between the races, and the belief in the idea of the superiority of the white race.

In chapter 4 we see the Lost Cause orators creating the mythology of the brave martyrs of the Confederacy: the foot soldier, the sailor, the leadership, and the women on the home front. The southern perception of why the Confederacy lost is an important part of this mythology of the war, and again, southern orators were quick to find a scapegoat for many of the South's postwar ills: General William T. Sherman.

The Lost Cause did not focus exclusively on the war. It also spent thousands of words condemning the evils of Reconstruction, the glories of Redemption, the strength of Reconciliation, and the New and Future South, as we see in chapter 5.

The final chapter brings us to the enduring legacy of the Lost Cause: its remnants in the last half of the twentieth century and the first decade of the twenty-first. The Lost Cause is far from dead in the minds of many white southerners—and other Americans—and debates still rage over the meaning of the residues of the Confederacy.

Although much of the research for this volume was carried out while working on my volumes of rhetoric and oratory of the nineteenth century, the twentieth century, and the civil rights movement, I want to thank Appalachian State University for a research grant in the summer of 2001 that enabled me to complete my research for primary sources—speech texts—in several university and public libraries across the South, including the University of North Carolina, the University of Georgia, the University of South Carolina, the University of Arkansas, the Tennessee State Library and Archives, the Mississippi Department of Archives and History, the University of Southern Mississippi Library, the University of Mississippi Library, Tougaloo College Library, the University of Virginia, the Virginia Historical Society, the Museum of the Confederacy, Emory University Library, the University of Texas Library, the Memphis Public Library, and the Library of Congress. Earlier research was supported by the University of West Florida while I was on sabbatical leave in 1997. The speeches surveyed had a life far beyond their enthusiastic, attentive audiences, and this popularity made them relatively easy to locate. Fortunately, these speeches were often printed in full or thoroughly described in local newspapers and printed as pamphlets for wider distribution. My searches for these primary source materials through many libraries over the years has yielded much fruit.

In sum, rhetoric and ritual commemorating and remembering war has been a part of human culture for ages and is likely to continue to be so. Remembering the American Civil War was a means of reaffirming the continuity of the past, the unity of white southerners, and their loyalty to the reunited nation. The American South has lived a dream and in a dream for generations. The civil rights movement of the 1950s and 1960s and the Sun Belt expansion of the late twentieth century awoke many southerners from that dream, but a fair number are still living in that world. I have focused on how the rhetoric and ritual of the Lost Cause has influenced southern thought and behavior for over a century and are likely to do so for decades to come.

1
Rhetoric, Celebration, and Ritual

Building a Collective Memory in the Postwar South

"That southern art": Oratory in the South

Perhaps in no other Western nation of modern times has the practice of public speaking played such a predominant role in the life of a nation as in the United States. Beginning with the earliest Puritan sermons and continuing into the twenty-first century, much of the history of America can be read through a study of political oratory and legislative speeches, religious sermons, public lectures, courtroom pleadings, ceremonial addresses, and biographies of the men and women who left their mark from the public platform. Ephemeral though they may be, and targeted to a specific audience at a specific time and event for a specific purpose, they provide a snapshot of that moment that captures the essence of that event and place. Many of them live on past that moment, whether it be a religious revival, a critical vote in the legislature or at the ballot box, a spectacular trial, or an annual Fourth of July celebration. Those who heard the speech later discussed it with their friends, family, and associates; or, as many times happened, the speech was printed and circulated widely. Today they appear in their entirety in major newspapers, or newsworthy extracts are repeated over and over on the news channels, blogs, and social media outlets. Scores have become classics of American literature and icons of American culture: Patrick Henry's "Give Me Liberty," George Washington's "Farewell Address," Abraham Lincoln's "Gettysburg Address," Franklin Roosevelt's "Four Freedoms" speech, John Kennedy's "Inaugural," Martin Luther King Jr.'s "I Have a Dream," and Ronald Reagan's eulogy on the *Challenger* disaster all come quickly to mind. There are thousands more that have shaped our history as a nation and a culture. Hugh Legaré, a leading nineteenth-century South Carolina orator and political leader, touched on the literary and enduring qualities of the art when he called oratory "poetry subdued to the business of civic life."[1]

Many historians have commented on the role of public address in the life of the new nation. Daniel Boorstin writes about "the exuberant development of oratory in the United States" and believes that "the most distinctive, most influential, and most successful forms of the new American literature were expressions in print of spoken American. . . . [I]t was aware of its *sound*, of its *audience*, of its effect as a stirrer primarily of common sentiments between a speaker (rather than a writer) and a listener (rather than a reader). It was a declamatory literature." In another place he proposes: "It would not be difficult to compile a complete American history . . . through the most dramatic and effective public speeches. . . . We can find few nations whose oratory can bring the student so close to their history." For Boorstin, the orator "acquired a mythic role," and oratory became "the main form of American public ritual."[2] Barnett Baskerville, a leading historian of American public address, believes that "throughout the greater part of our history as a nation the orator was chief among American folk heroes." Charles S. Sydnor points out that as early as the colonial period "a premium was put on oratory" in the Virginia House of Burgesses.[3] Public speaking is the lifeblood of decision making and community formation in the American culture as it has been since the colonial era and will continue to be as long as the Constitution endures, the Declaration of Independence is known, Lincoln's speeches are understood, and people recall Kennedy's "Ask not what your country can do for you . . ."

Probably nowhere in America (with the possible exception of New England) was oratory more vital, more "exuberant," and more honored than in the nineteenth-century South. A leading scholar of southern oratory, Waldo Braden, points out that "orality was at the center of antebellum southern life" beginning with the storytelling rituals around the fire and the African legends transported to America and passed down in the slave quarters and continued through the "many southern politicians [who] built their speaking around their storytelling."[4]

In his study of William Yancey, the "orator of secession," William G. Brown comments on the role and place of oratory in the deep South prior to the Civil War. According to Brown, "it was the spoken word, not the printed page, that guided thought, aroused enthusiasm, made history." Calling the various occasions for public speaking that flourished in the region the "true universities of the Lower South," Brown points out that "the man who wished to lead or to teach must be able to speak . . . he must charm them with voice and gesture." Brown concludes: "It is doubtful if there ever has been a society in which the orator counted for more than he did in the Cotton Kingdom."[5] Although Brown was writing about the antebellum years, this passion for speechmaking was evident until well into the twentieth century.

Southern leadership was quick to recognize the role of public address in a democratic republic. William C. Preston, noted by one historian as South Carolina's Cicero, and perhaps the leading South Carolina example of a "southern orator," expressed the relationship of rhetoric and democracy when he said, "Liberty and eloquence are united in all ages. When the sovereign power is found in the public mind and the public heart, eloquence is the obvious approach to it. Power and honor and all that can attract ardent and aspiring natures attend it. The noblest instinct is to propagate the spirit, to 'make our minds, the minds of other men.'"[6]

In the antebellum era and well into the twentieth century, oratory flourished in the southern United States as the expression and reflection of the values of the white male population of the region. Orators described and defended those values in a way that was appreciated by their audiences; as a result, they were respected and revered, and many historians and commentators have reflected on southern public address. Wilbur Cash describes "the Southern fondness for rhetoric" and claims that in the South, "rhetoric flourished here far beyond even its American average; it early became a passion.... The greatest man would be the man who could best wield it." Throughout the South, oratory was the focus of southern life for rural and small-town audiences who had few opportunities for entertainment and little connection to the larger world; it was called "that southern art" by a leading historian of the Civil War era. The impact of oratory ranged from frequent joint debates held in most political campaigns, which brought "together a great concourse of people," to Sunday sermonizing and summer camp meeting revivals, to courtroom lawyers arguing before their juries and large audiences of spectators, and to ceremonial occasions such as the Fourth of July. In the South, writes Francis P. Gaines, "oratory had peculiar dominance in the admiration, the aspiration . . . of that section. . . . The influence of the spoken word represents a unique quality of that civilization. . . . [It] responded more immediately and more eagerly to the oration than to any other mode of communication."[7]

A Mississippian reminiscing about the days before the Civil War wrote that "one of the most remarkable characteristics of the Southern people . . . was their universal enjoyment of public speaking and their intense appreciation of good popular oratory." James H. Thornwell, president of South Carolina College, pointed out that "among none is the facility of public speaking so indispensable to success in every walk of life." This point of view was confirmed by a historian of Thornwell's college, who averred: "No accomplishment was more highly respected in the Old South than oratory." Francis P. Gaines wrote about the "elaborate feasts of oratory, almost orgies of oratory" in the antebellum years.[8]

Southern colleges and schools all offered classes in oratory, and societies such as the Clariosophic and the Euphradian at South Carolina College provided additional training and opportunity to hone one's skills; for years, every student at the college belonged to one or the other of these organizations. In his history of the University of South Carolina, Edwin L. Green wrote that "speaking was the great road to success . . . so that the students became members of the societies as a matter of course." At the University of Georgia, "disputation" was a required course, and in the decade before the Civil War, literary societies were the main extracurricular activity in southern colleges. No graduation exercise was complete without several student-delivered original orations and declamations on the program. E. Merton Coulter summed it up in his survey of college life in the Old South: "There was no end to oratory in the antebellum South."[9]

Cash captured the quest and the passion for eloquence instilled in the young students of the antebellum era when he asserted: "To be a captain in the struggle against the Yankee, to be a Calhoun or a Brooks in Congress, or, better still, to be a Yancey or a Rhett ramping through the land with a demand for the sword—this was to be at the very heart of one's time and place, was, for the plantation youth, full of hot blood, the only desirable career." Richard Weaver believed the literature of the Old South was the "literature of the forum," that is, the public speech. In South Carolina, "society placed the lawyer-orator-politician in high esteem," according to Daniel Hollis. Virginius Dabney took this point of view as well, as he believed that the "cherished ambition of almost any young Southerner was for a public rather than a literary career." Referring to skills in public speaking, Bertram Wyatt-Brown asserted that a southern man's "reputation arose in large part from skill in its exercise at gatherings large or small."[10] In sum, oratory was the prime means of public education in the issues of the day, of religious instruction and inspiration, and of public commemoration; large amounts of entertainment were thrown in for good measure.

Not only was oratory a staple of college curricula and activities around the South, but it also was taught around the region's firesides. Katharine Du Pre Lumpkin of Charleston wrote about her early twentieth-century southern family ritual of the "Saturday Night Debating Club." With her Confederate veteran father presiding, "we argued topics of Southern problems and Southern history"; the "plaster walls of our parlor rang with tales of the South's sufferings, exhortations to uphold her honor, recitals of her humanitarian slave regime, denunciations of those who dared to doubt the black man's inferiority, and, ever and always, persuasive logic for her position of 'States Rights,' and how we must at all times stand solidly together if we would preserve all that the South 'stood for.'" When the debates and orations were complete, Katharine's father would "assume the role of teacher . . . pointing up delivery, commenting on gestures . . . taking pains to analyze each child's argument, to show its weak points, and wherein it could have been made stronger."[11] Her autobiography not only illustrates the importance of the spoken word even in the post–Civil War South but also helps to explain the long-lasting nature of the Lost Cause; southerners heard the message and were drilled and coached in the message and its delivery well into the twentieth century.

The public speech, regardless of the time, the place, and the goal of the speaker, is a public statement about the shared values of speaker and audience. It provides a bridge between what the speaker sees as reality and what he or she wants the audience to see and feel and do, on the one hand, with the audience's perception of reality on the other side of the podium. It deals with current, timely problems, issues, and concerns and attempts to provide answers to questions the audience may have about these pressing concerns; it seeks, as Preston put it, to "make our minds, the minds of other men." The speaker intends to influence his or her audience's behaviors, beliefs, perceptions, or attitudes and to gain respect for his or her values and ideas in the minds and emotions of the audience. Speeches are events in the history of a community: real people speaking to other real people about real issues and ideas that concern the community. Especially in an oral society, as the nineteenth-century South clearly was, "the opportunity to exchange ritual words or hear them eloquently pronounced was deeply cherished."[12]

In the postwar South, the defeated region's leadership had many tasks to perform, but chief among them was the need to help the mass of southern whites see and understand a meaning behind the defeat of war, to see a reason for the sacrifice and the struggle. For a region whose education, inspiration, and politics for generations past had come largely from the public orator, it was natural for the public speaker to mount the platform over and over again and remind his audiences how he (and it was virtually always a "he" in the male-dominated public culture of the late-nineteenth- and early twentieth-century South) saw the situation. Repeatedly, in hundreds of ceremonial gatherings on Decoration or Memorial Day, at Confederate veterans' reunions, and at monument dedications, a consistent story was told. This mythology of the Lost Cause was developed fairly quickly after Appomattox and was reinforced time and again for decades to come.

As the South and nation move into the twenty-first century, remnants of the myth still resound around the region in debates over the Confederate flag and the playing of "Dixie," the reenactments of Civil War battles and campgrounds, the celebration of Confederate Memorial Day, the building of new Confederate monuments and the repair of old, Internet websites devoted to elements of the Confederacy and the Lost Cause, and, yes, even in the meetings of, not Confederate veterans, but the Sons of Confederate Veterans and the Daughters of the Confederacy (and several additional generations long removed from the Civil War). These ceremonial speakers constructed for their audiences a useful past, showed how it could shape and guide future conduct, and created a memory of the war and the prewar South that was accepted as the "gospel truth" for several generations of southerners. To some degree it is an active construct in 2012. My belief in the importance and role of oratory in the United States and the South undergirds the assumption made in this book that ceremonial oratory created, shaped, and sustained the memories of the Lost Cause so powerfully that they are still alive today and will remain so well into the future.

Confirming Community: Ceremonial Speaking and Ritual

Ceremonial speaking, or epideictic oratory, has been recognized for over two thousand years as one of the major forms of public address, and it was perhaps the primary vehicle for creating and disseminating the Lost Cause to the South's oral culture. For Aristotle, who was among the first to define the genre, the epideictic speech was presented to audiences on special memorial and celebration days. It was designed for the praise or blame of a man or an institution and was one of the three types of oratory identified by the Greek scholar.[13] In America, the Boston Massacre and Fourth of July orations, Memorial Day addresses, funeral sermons, graduation and baccalaureate addresses, building dedications, Thanksgiving and Election Day sermons, after-dinner speeches, convention keynote speeches, and presidential or gubernatorial inaugural address are examples of this major speaking genre—the ceremonial or epideictic—which became early-on a part of our oral tradition. In the postwar South, three essential epideictic events were focused on the late Confederacy: veterans' reunions, monument dedications, and Confederate Memorial Day festivities.

Epideictic oratory is often thought of as "mere rhetoric" or oratory of "display" and considered less important and more superficial, more entertainment than substance. Its counterparts, judicial and legislative speaking, are evaluated as more important and the ceremonial speech as more ephemeral. It is, however, a viable, dynamic form of communication which, in the case of the Lost Cause, for example, can create, define, reinforce, and pass on the values and traditions of a culture. Celeste Condit calls it "this most important genre,"[14] and after studying these speeches carefully and seeing the long-term impact on the region, I would have to agree.

The basic function of speeches presented at ceremonial events is to confirm, support, reinforce, and affirm shared community values. Community solidarity, identification, and cohesiveness are all major goals of the ceremonial orator, and their purpose is generally to help establish and reinforce the nature of a community. That community may be as broad as an entire nation or region, as these speeches were in the South. These speeches are not controversial or argumentative, as they seek to reinforce existing audience values. John D. Groppe points out that "social ritual is employed on rather specialized social occasions, such as a group's formal, public occasions, as a means of manifesting and achieving solidarity." On these occasions, the speeches presented "are analogues of the creeds that are recited by congregations in Christian churches . . . to manifest the unity of the group." In writing about Memorial Day and rites such as Armistice or Veterans Day, Lloyd Warner says they are "rituals of a sacred symbol system which functions periodically to unify the whole community, with its conflicting symbols and its opposing, autonomous churches and associations." Samuel R. Johnson asserts that "American epideictic speaking is most often confirmational." He argues that the speaker's purpose may not be to praise or blame at all—Aristotle's description of the genre—but rather to "speak for maintenance value." William J. Brandt observes that ceremonial address reaffirms the "traditional values" of a community and is thus an affirmation of community solidarity. Far from simply "praise and blame," Jeffrey Walker describes the epideictic as "argument directed toward the establishment, reconfirmation, or revision of general values and beliefs."[15]

Several scholars have shown the important role of the epideictic in creating and sustaining a community's traditions and values. Condit describes a "three-fold set of paired functions for audience and speakers" in these ceremonial occasions: "understanding and definition, sharing and creation of community, and entertainment and display." The first is used "when some event, person, group or object is confusing, or troubling. The speaker will explain the troubling issue in terms of the audience's key values and beliefs." The second function gives opportunity to express and reformulate shared community traditions and heritage. Finally, the ceremonial event "offers speakers the opportunity for creativity by releasing them from concern with specific issues and charging them to take on broader vistas. The audience is 'entertained' by such speech in a most humane manner." These functions are carried out to the letter in this body of speeches that described, defined, and explained the troubling loss of the war they thought they would—and should—win. White southern values and traditions were stressed and reinforced over and over again by speaker after speaker. As they sketched out the past, current, and future South, their audiences could envision more clearly who and what they were, and the more they were entertained by this oratory, the more these issues were ingrained and, thus, were enduring. As Condit says, the most complete epideictic creates a "communal definition."[16] These Lost Cause ceremonial speakers did exactly that.

Perhaps one reason why Lost Cause values have endured so long in the region lies in Chaim Perelman and Lucie Olbrechts-Tyteca's observation that epideictic oratory "strengthens the disposition toward action by increasing adherence to the values it lauds." It "sets out to increase the intensity of adherence to certain values." Elsewhere, Perelman wrote that the "goal is always to strengthen a consensus around certain values which one wants to see prevail and which should orient action in the future."[17] The values of white southerners that prevailed through years of Jim Crow segregation and through the civil rights struggle in the 1950s and 1960s directly influenced the actions of segregationist leaders, as we will see in chapter 6. The monuments, reunions, and Memorial Day celebrations provided concrete events to reinforce the collective memories and set aside specific and recurring times for the community to recall the traditions they wished to recall. The oratory combined them all in an oral presentation that linked and gave strength and power to the experience of war and remembering.

An important aspect of the ceremonial address is its emphasis on community values. The focus is not upon expediency or practicality, as in deliberative, political, policy-making oratory in the legislative chamber; nor is the emphasis on guilt or innocence, as in a court of law. Instead, the ceremonial address is value oriented; it functions to reinforce commonly held community values. It goes to the bedrock of society and employs as its subject matter values that society holds dear. Speakers in these situations know they enjoy the support and agreement of their listeners. Audiences do not expect, nor do they want to hear, views that conflict with their purpose for gathering, which is to celebrate, recall, and memorialize people and events that reinforce their values. As D. L. Sullivan asserts, "Insiders usually come to hear epideictic speakers with expectations that they will say what they want to hear"; the audience is "caught up in a celebration of their vision of reality."[18] They do not expect or want carefully reasoned, thoroughly supported deliberative or forensic addresses, but rather a speech that helps them know more about who they are and where their community fits in the larger scheme of life.

Johnson suggests an additional purpose of ceremonial oratory in his discussion of ceremonial speaking as "oratory of display." He observes that sometimes the speaker may be addressing the audience "merely for the satisfaction of the audience and the speaker." Brandt also recognizes this characteristic, pointing out that "the orator who was not particularly awed by the ceremonial occasion could see in an epideictic oration a handsome opportunity for personal display." Edward P. J. Corbett, in discussing ceremonial address, describes it as the "oratory of display," in which the speaker is "not so much concerned with persuading an audience as with pleasing or inspiring it."[19]

J. Richard Chase, in his survey of "The Classic Conception of Epideictic," shows that Aristotle believed that in epideictic speaking the audience's "interest is centered upon the speaker's performance." Chase says this is the focus, for "in epideictic there is no burning issue that demands a decision. Thus the listener, not caught up in the conflict of ideas, can better appreciate the artistic efforts of the speaker." Brandt also makes this distinction, observing that "members of the audience were spectators, presumably because they shared the sentiments of the speaker even before he began."[20] James M. Mayo also concludes that ceremonial events have high expectations. They must be "performed flawlessly," and the special place set aside for the observance—a cemetery or a monument for fallen soldiers, for instance—is "enriched through written and artistic means with ceremonial performances to express desired human values."[21]

There are many examples how southern postwar audiences expected this "oratory of display" to be "performed flawlessly," and often commentators reflect this element of ceremonial speaking. Charles C. Jones Jr., the founder and longtime president of one of the major Confederate veterans' organizations and the group's annual reunion orator, "delivered . . . [a] chaste and eloquent address" at the dedication of the Augusta, Georgia, Confederate monument. After his 1878 speech, Jones was "approached by numbers of friends . . . who congratulated him upon his grand production. It was universally pronounced to be one of the finest addresses ever delivered in Augusta." Ellison Capers delivered a Memorial Day address in Greenville, South Carolina, that a reporter viewed as "worthy [of] the orator and his subject, eloquent, polished, graceful, pathetic and inspiring." Archer Anderson's address dedicating the Robert E. Lee Monument in Richmond was "chaste, eloquent, and . . .

worthy of its exalted subject and of the impressive occasion." Edwin P. Cox also addressed a Richmond audience of veterans, and as he was concluding he was "very loudly applauded. His address made an excellent impression, and its delivery was particularly facile," according to the reporter.[22] Many other examples of evaluative comment could be cited, but these sufficiently reflect the expectations of the audiences and how well the Lost Cause orators met them.

This study examines this ceremonial rhetoric of the late-nineteenth- and early twentieth-century white South in an effort to determine why and how it had such a lasting effect on the region and its mores. We will see how the values and ideas expressed in the 1880s and 1890s were driven home so sharply and deeply that they still were surfacing in the 1950s and 1960s in the battles over civil rights in the South, or the bellicose rhetoric of supporters of "Dixie" or the Confederate flag in the 1990s and on into the twenty-first century. Rabid segregationists were just as adamant in defending the "southern way of life" in the 1960s as a "fire-eater" was in 1860, or a Lost Cause orator was in 1890. In other words, the major issues of the Civil War—race, liberty, majority rule versus minority rights, federal versus local or state government as the locus of power, and even war itself—were not settled and put on the shelf by the peace that reigned after Appomattox. They are debated and discussed today in meetings of southern heritage groups, in Sons of Confederate Veterans conclaves, and around the campfires at Civil War battlefield reenactments. In short, there are no dead orators, as they live on in their audiences' memory.

What the South is, and what southerners are in 2012, is in part due to what these speakers said, how they dealt with their rhetorical situation, how they created the collective public memory of the Confederacy and the Lost Cause more than one hundred years ago. Targeted at a time-bound audience though it might be, the ideas, themes, and values of a speech, if repeated enough times and to enough people, can resound through history for generations. James Andrews identifies rhetoric as "an essential force in shaping our understanding of social reality." His contribution that rhetoric is "the substance of messages, the means whereby those messages are shaped and conveyed, the underlying assumptions on which those messages are built, and the root values and ideals that those messages depict"—in other words, "how events and ideas are talked about gives meaning to events and ideas"—is clearly demonstrated in these speeches.[23] A celebration or epideictic speech defines for the audience who they are collectively in the context of the event being celebrated and in the broader context of that local community, and in an ever-widening circle of ripples into that larger region called the South, or the "late Confederacy." This process is what happened to the mythology of the Lost Cause. We will take a look at the rhetoric and ritual that provided the setting and the rationale for the Lost Cause and trace the remnants of this mythology into the twenty-first century.

Waldo W. Braden identified four rhetorical myths that emerged from postwar southern oratory: the Old South, the Solid South, the New South, and the Lost Cause.[24] I am focusing on one, the Lost Cause, as it seems to give us the most understanding of the twentieth-century South and the crisis of race it passed through in the 1950s and 1960s, and the resurgence of interest in the trappings and the meanings of the Confederacy in the 1990s and into the twenty-first century. I also believe that the other three myths described by Braden can be seen as subsidiary, but reinforcing rhetorical elements of the overriding remembrance of the Lost Cause.

"That they may transmit it to posterity to come": Rhetoric and Collective Memory

It is safe to say that virtually all residents of the South in 1861–65 experienced the Civil War. The veterans had "been there, done that"; the women, the children, and the elderly may not have faced the dangers and rigors of battle, but they lived through the fears of wartime and the privations of home life. The veterans were in a position to tell of their experiences, what they saw and did, how it affected them and their comrades, and what they believed they had learned about living in the present while preparing for the future. Doubtless there were some, as in any war, who chose not to talk about it in later years, but many did, as the war was the major turning point in their lives and in the culture of their locality, their state, and their region. As James Mayo points out, "People are not obligated to have war memorials; they want them."[25] Probably nowhere has this desire been more prevalent than in the American South after the Confederacy's defeat as hundreds of monuments were raised in village and city squares and cemeteries, hundreds of reunions were held for the grizzled old veterans wearing the gray uniform, and the entire region celebrated Confederate Memorial Day in the balmy days of late spring across the South.

The narrator in Thomas Wolfe's story "Chickamauga" reflects years after the war: "Hit all turned out so different from the way we thought. And that was long ago, and I'll be ninety-five years old if I am living on the seventh day of August, of this present year. Now that's goin' back a long ways, hain't hit? And yet hit all comes back to me as clear as if hit happened yesterday."[26] These Lost Cause speeches repeated the themes of the war and stoked the fires of memory for years, almost "as clear as if hit happened yesterday."

Another southern writer, James Dickey, describes something along these lines when he points out that the "South has a long tradition of slow-moving, of standing and watching, of having the time—of giving ourselves the time— to sit on country porches and courthouse Confederate Monuments and on green benches in public parks and tell each other stories, gossip and use words in something like the same way one might use what I like to call binocular vision: that personal encounter with a fragment of lived and living time." The Civil War, as recalled by these Lost Cause orators, was a fragment of "lived and living time," or, to use a more recent term, collective memory. Bruce Gronbeck writes that "through evocation of collective memories, past and present live in constant dialogue . . . neither can be comprehended without the other." While the past is a major component in the building of a collective memory, the present is always present. John Bodnar reminds us that the creating of public memory has "the major focus" not on the past but rather on "serious matters in the present such as the nature of power and the question of loyalty to both official and vernacular culture."[27] After the Civil War, the Lost Cause advocates had to deal with the present, the realities of the new order of life in the South and the nation at large; their chief resource was the memory of the glories of the Old South and the doomed Confederacy, and their main tool was their Lost Cause oratory.

As Richard Weaver asserted, war destroys patterns of society and culture, and persons who are familiar with the patterns of one order are faced with the new patterns that evolve after war; they are "likely to be seized with nostalgia when struggling with a new pattern."[28] Dealing with the new order of the present, Lost Cause speakers returned naturally and easily to the past for their stories and narrations about their memories. These Confederate rituals and orations allowed for a link to the older patterns and provided a sense of continuity and order in the daily reality of overwhelming change. David Blight observes that the war "remade America. . . . How people of both sections and races would come to define and commemorate that tragedy, where they would find heroism and villainy, and how they would decide what was lost and what was won, would have a great deal to do with determining the character of the new society that they were to build."[29] Unfortunately, the South would try its best to build, through these speeches, monuments, reunions, and celebrations of the Lost Cause, a new society that was as close as possible a mirror image of the old one.

Two of our Lost Cause speakers will serve at this point to illustrate this goal of helping the southerner deal with the present by using the memory of the past. Just after the turn of the twentieth century, S. A. Crump, speaking to a veterans' reunion in Greensboro, North Carolina, hoped that the reunion and his speech would "serve to demonstrate to you that your sons' sons have learned the lessons of history truly; that we shall teach our children, that they may transmit it to posterity to come" the memory of the Confederacy. Two years later, in Memphis, Congressman John Sharp Williams reminded his audience of veterans that "a people who forget the history, despise the traditions, ignore the ideals and fail to share the aspirations of their ancestry are a people not apt to conserve anything."[30] In short, these Lost Cause rituals and speeches helped the audiences remember the events, traditions, and values that the community wanted and needed to remember.

The Lost Cause became not just the collective memory of the South regarding the war but also the "national memory of the Civil War; it has been substituted for the *history* of the war." Lost Cause orators told over and over again their epic stories of the heroic soldiers and stoic women, and these tales were passed from audience to audience. They soon became American versions of the Icelandic sagas or the Homeric tales of ancient Greece. In Alan Nolan's words, the Lost Cause is "an American legend, an American version of great sagas like *Beowulf* and the *Song of Roland*." In his study of the Lost Cause, Rollin Osterweis wrote: "By 1890, the Myth of the Lost Cause had achieved acceptance and power throughout the country"; this rhetorical process was not just a southern phenomenon.[31] Examination of these important speeches will show us a great deal about the collective memory of the South regarding the Civil War and its aftermath. These often-reiterated themes of the Lost Cause must be taken seriously if one is to understand the twentieth-century South of segregation, conservatism, and tradition and the ongoing life of the Confederacy in the twenty-first. These speeches are the records and archives of this critical era in the cultural life of the South. What was this American legend, this saga that still shapes attitudes and perceptions and opinions in the region? These speeches will provide an open window to this part of America's collective memory and remembered history.

2
Remembering the Confederacy

Ceremony in the Postwar South, 1865–1920s

Since before the beginning of recorded history, the human race has acknowledged the need to celebrate and honor the important aspects of culture—its religion, its heroes, its victories, and its defeats; archaeological findings and anthropological research conclusively show this human trait. As Victor Turner writes: "People in all cultures recognize the need to set aside certain times and spaces for celebratory use." According to Bernard Lewis, a culture's "remembered history" is "preserved in commemorative ceremonies and monuments . . . and in the words associated with them." James Mayo observes that "rituals temporarily add definitions to place, and communities use them to reach beyond the experiences of daily life."[1] The postbellum American South was no exception. The "experiences of daily life" in the years after the Civil War were experiences of devastation, defeat, poverty, death, a changed social order, a new environment of increased industrialization and commercialization, and a drastic change in the patterns of life. These grand festivities of Confederate remembrances, if even for only one day a year, took white southerners out of their dreary, defensive, devastated environment. As the speakers of the day painted their verbal pictures, white southerners remembered the glorious past as they wanted to recall it: the days of mastery, the days of victory and honor on the battlefield and the dreams of victory. Few Lost Cause orators spoke of southern defeats, such as Gettysburg or Vicksburg; their subjects were First and Second Bull Run, Chancellorsville, and other victories over the Yankees.

There were hundreds of events, institutions, and organizations created from April 1865 through the late twentieth century (and more will probably be created with the 150th anniversary of the Civil War in 2011–15) to honor and recall the Confederacy. Gaines Foster writes in detail about many of them: the Ladies' Memorial Associations created to decorate and tend Confederate graves and establish cemeteries for the dead soldiers; the Southern Historical Society, which operated out of Richmond to preserve the southern point of view about the war; the United Confederate Veterans (UCV), formed in 1889; the United Daughters of the Confederacy (UDC), established in 1894; and the United Sons of the Confederacy, which was organized in 1896. Annual reunions of the UCV, myriad military unit reunions, and state and local reunions swept the South for decades until the old veterans could no longer participate. Confederate Memorial Day and Confederate monument cornerstone dedications and monument unveiling ceremonies occurred in virtually every southern city and town of any significant size. The campaigns to raise the needed thousands of dollars to build the monuments and the cemeteries all presented many opportunities to add to the collective memory of the Civil War and its aftermath.[2]

These rituals and rhetoric sought to reaffirm the common sentiments of the southern people, much like a Sunday church service reaffirms the congregation's beliefs in the sacred creeds and sacraments of their faith. These events provided for continuity with the traditions and history of the white South, strengthened community solidarity against outsiders such as the military occupation and the hated "carpetbaggers," and promoted the confidence of the audience in an era of low self-esteem for many white southerners. Ceremonial oratory was part and parcel of these rituals and events and played a major role, perhaps the most important role, in the shaping of the Lost Cause mythology by which many southerners have lived for generations. David Blight writes about one of these events: "The Decoration Day speech became an American genre that ministers, politicians, and countless former soldiers tried to master."[3] I contend that all three types of events—Confederate Memorial (or "Decoration") Day, Confederate veterans' reunions, and the dedication of Confederate monuments—reached that same level of importance. Before we examine the rhetoric of these events, I will provide an overview of these occasions as they developed.

"In the gentle light of Spring": Confederate Memorial Day

As the Civil War ground to a halt in the spring of 1865, southern women began to clean and beautify the graves of their beloved Confederate friends and relatives.[4] Throughout the South, springtime flowers were brought to the graves as the survivors attempted to honor the tombs of the fallen soldiers. A long-running debate developed over the region regarding the origin of Confederate Memorial Day. A number of cities and groups claimed the distinction, including Warrenton, Petersburg, and Winchester, Virginia; Jackson and Columbus, Mississippi; and Columbus, Georgia.

An anonymous writer in the *Richmond Times-Dispatch* makes the claim for Warrenton with an event held on July 21, 1861, when the dead from the nearby battle of First Manassas were buried in the local cemetery and "memorial day was observed by the women and children" of Warrenton. In Mississippi, Sue Landon Vaughan, called the "Lady with the Roses," was known for decorating the graves of Confederate and Union soldiers in Jackson's Greenwood Cemetery. She issued a plea in the local newspaper for women to meet her at the cemetery on April 26, 1865, for a ceremony, and the Confederate State Monument in Jackson declares her the founder of Decoration Day. Back in Virginia, Petersburg lays claim to a memorial event organized by Miss Nora Davidson on June 9, 1865, on the first anniversary of a successful Confederate defense of that city. David Blight describes in detail an event sponsored by African Americans in Charleston, South Carolina, with some ten thousand in attendance, which should merit some recognition as one of the first Decoration Days, as it occurred on May 1, 1865. Blight concludes that recently freed slaves "gave birth to an American tradition." It was conveniently forgotten, however, by white southerners, as the debate over the date of the first Memorial Day continued. The following year, Columbus, Mississippi, and Columbus, Georgia, joined the contest when memorial events were inaugurated in the Mississippi city on April 25 and in Georgia on the next day. The Mississippi celebration supposedly inspired Francis Miles Finch to write a popular poem, "The Blue and the Gray," which was published in 1867. A little over a month later, Winchester, Virginia, began a memorial program on June 6, the date of Confederate general Turner Ashby's death four years earlier.[5]

The story of the Columbus, Georgia, Memorial Day is perhaps the most instructive of all these early programs to honor the Confederate dead, as it is one of the most carefully documented. In 1898 the local chapter of the UDC published a thorough history of the origin of their event. Several sworn affidavits from women who were involved in the founding of the celebration are included, as well as a great deal of detail about the establishment of what soon became a regional holiday.

According to this story, in January 1866, Lizzie Rutherford and Jane Martin went to the Columbus cemetery to clean and decorate graves of Confederates who had died in local hospitals. Rutherford mentioned to Martin a European custom she had been reading about in which graves were decorated on All Saints' Day. She went on to say she felt the women of the old Confederacy should do the same for their dead soldiers. The idea was immediately taken to the local Soldiers' Aid Society, which quickly adopted it.

The secretary of that organization, Mrs. Charles J. Williams, was charged with writing a letter to newspapers and to other aid societies around the South to encourage them to promote this idea as a regionwide project. Williams wrote:

> The ladies are now and have been for several days engaged in the sad but pleasant duty of ornamenting and improving that portion of the city cemetery sacred to the memory of our gallant Confederate dead, but we feel it is an unfinished work unless a day be set apart annually for its special attention.... Therefore, we beg the assistance of the press and the ladies throughout the South to aid us in the effort to set apart a certain day to be observed, from the Potomac to the Rio Grande, and be handed down through time as a religious custom of the South, to wreathe the graves of our martyred dead with flowers; and we propose the 26th day of April as the day.[6]

The date suggested, April 26, was the anniversary of General Joseph E. Johnston's surrender. The first celebration was held at the St. Luke Methodist Church, with Colonel James M. Ramsey the first orator of the day. The program was a success, so much so that the official history of the event would proclaim in 1898 that "the North looked on, thought the custom good, took it to herself and has hallowed it as she does her Thanksgiving obligation. April was too early for her flowers, hence she set apart May 30th." Two years later, in 1868, General John A. Logan, the commander in chief of the Grand Army of the Republic, ordered a day set aside to beautify the graves of Union soldiers.[7]

The event did, however, become a major celebration in Columbus and across the South. In 1896, Lizzie Rutherford Ellis was recognized for her role in formalizing the celebration when the local UDC chapter was named for her. She and Mrs. Williams had also been honored earlier when the Columbus ladies put tombstones on their graves that read, for Ellis, "In her patriotic heart sprang the thought of our Memorial Day," and, for Williams, "In loving recognition of her memorial work by her co-workers."[8]

One of the cities to receive Mrs. Williams's letter was Raleigh, North Carolina. A Ladies' Memorial Association was formed there in May 1866, and it went right to work to create a new Confederate cemetery for several hundred soldiers buried in the area. Its goal was to "protect and care for the graves of our Confederate soldiers." Their first memorial ceremony was held on May 10, 1867. The group claimed later that its Confederate cemetery was the first established in the South, but it did not come easily. Fund-raising in the cash-strapped region was difficult, so the association went to the state legislature with a petition for an appropriation of fifteen hundred dollars to finish the cemetery. The ladies packed the legislative galleries when the bill was discussed, and it easily passed both houses without a dissenting vote.[9]

The Charleston, South Carolina, Ladies' Memorial Association was also formed in 1866, "to take care of the Graves of the Confederate Dead, who were buried in Magnolia Cemetery, and to erect a suitable Monument to their memory." More than eight hundred headstones were placed to mark Confederate graves, and on May 10, 1870, eighty-four bodies of South Carolinians were reburied in Magnolia Cemetery from graves at Gettysburg.[10]

By 1875 this custom had spread throughout the South, although there was never any uniformity of date for the event, as it varied from town to town. Certainly there was not the consistency there was in the North, where May 30 began to be legalized as Memorial Day in several states, starting in 1868 and celebrated as such throughout that victorious section under the direction of various local posts of the Grand Army of the Republic. By 1916, ten southern states had selected June 3, Jefferson Davis's birthday, as the southern version of Memorial Day. But many localities continued to observe April 26 as the date—and some still do in the early years of the twenty-first century. In Georgia, Alabama, Mississippi, and South Carolina, Confederate Memorial Day is a state-observed holiday (the fourth Monday of April in Alabama and Mississippi, April 26 in Georgia, and May 10 in South Carolina). May 10 is the anniversary of Thomas J. "Stonewall" Jackson's death at Chancellorsville and of Jefferson Davis's capture at the end of the Civil War.[11] Some might argue that the dates were selected to fit the blooming dates of southern flowers as spring marched northward, but the wide disparity of dates is, perhaps, symbolically indicative of the states' rights tenet so widely held and strongly proclaimed by the creators of the Lost Cause. Every city and town had the right to set its own memorial date, and no regional group could dictate those dates.

As an indication of the independence and individuality of the various groups and celebrations of Memorial Day around the South, Richmond, Virginia, held, not one, but three memorial rituals for a number of years. The first was held on May 10 at Oakwood Cemetery, where many soldiers who had died in Richmond hospitals during the war were buried. A second event was held at the graves of thirty-one Jewish Confederates at the Hebrew Cemetery, also in May, and the third, and largest, was at Hollywood Cemetery on May 30.[12]

The annual ritual, regardless of the date, was one of the key factors that created and perpetuated the Lost Cause myth. The *Raleigh News and Observer* clearly expressed the prevailing sentiment in an 1887 editorial: "Again the 10th of May rolls around and we repair to the last resting places of those who wore the gray and died in that patriotic service specially to recall once more the heroic value of the sleeping army and the virtues of those who gave up all that made life sweet to go cheerily to war because it was for home and country. It is a custom as appropriate as it is touching, and we trust it will always and without breach be observed in our southland."[13]

An editorial in the *Atlanta Constitution* on April 22, 1887, explained some of the history and impact of the Confederate memorial observance: "For the last twenty years the people of the South have been accustomed to gather about the graves of the heroes of the 'lost cause' on the 26th of April to pay their tribute. . . . The women of the South instituted it, and they have constantly maintained it with loving pride and heroic devotion."[14]

A running controversy in the *Constitution* over the next few days gives further insight into the nature and importance of the holiday in the mind of the white South. The suggestion had been made to bring the South's celebration into line with the North's observance of Memorial Day by changing the often-accepted southern date of April 25 to May 30, which was by the 1880s a national holiday. Among the several comments between April 22 and 26 that appeared in the newspaper, there was this notable one from C. H. Williams, the son of the secretary of the Soldiers' Aid Society who had written for support of the idea for a southern Memorial Day. Williams wrote: "I do not understand how such a change could be seriously considered for a moment by any one who comprehends the true tenderly mournful meaning of our 'Memorial Day.' . . . [I]t is now woven into the sweet and tender traditions of the south as one of mourning not of exultation. 'Decoration Day' at the north is celebrated as a day of triumphant exultation over the last expiring gasp of the cause we seek to mourn for and sanctify in the memory of the youth of the land." The editorial writer wrapped up the discussion with the comment that the origin of Confederate Memorial Day "is something worthy of being remembered with patriotic pride. We owe the day to a noble southern woman's devotion."[15]

The women who established Confederate Memorial Day across the South seemed to focus on two leading purposes for these events. One was to provide a public time and place to remember and honor the Confederate dead. Mrs. Williams's letter expressed it well: "Let the soldiers' graves, for that day at least, be the Southern Mecca to whose shrine her sorrowing women, like pilgrims, may annually bring their grateful hearts and floral offerings."

A second goal, powerful but often unspoken, was to inculcate the ideals of the southern woman in the younger generations of the community. Anne Caroline Benning wrote in her history of the event that the women of the Memorial Association "hope that every Southern woman will teach the young of the South, not only to reverence the memory of the soldiers who have died for us, but we specially beg the women of Columbus to instill in the hearts of their children reverence for the soldiers and reverence for the women of the Memorial Association who inaugurated this beautiful custom."[16]

While the southern ladies, and their men, believed strongly in their "beautiful custom," northerners were not so inclined. The Grand Army of the Republic denounced the ceremonies decorating Confederate graves in the early years, while feelings were still high across the nation and southerners were still perceived by many northerners as traitors to their country. In New Bern, North Carolina, the Union occupying forces prohibited the ladies from having a parade to the cemetery. In Raleigh, the Union commander, Colonel James V. Bomford, was more lenient, as he not only allowed the women to have their parade to the cemetery, but even came to the event with his family and placed flowers at the site himself. By 1883 bitter feelings had diminished to the point in Richmond that the Phil Kearny Post of the Grand Army of the Republic marched in the Confederate Memorial Day parade for several years.[17]

Victor Turner tells us that "each kind of ritual, ceremony, or festival comes to be coupled with special types of attire, music, dance, food and drink, 'properties,' modes of staging and presentation, physical and cultural environment." The three celebrations that are the focus of this study all confirm Turner's observation. Memorial Day was filled with the accouterments of Confederate memory. Flags of military units, Confederate uniforms, badges indicating various units, pictures of Confederate heroes, poetry about the Lost Cause, and music of the South, especially military tunes—and, of course, "Dixie"—all added to the ambiance that reinforced the rhetoric. As Waldo Braden says, these aspects of the events are, "an integral part of the persuasive effort." In short, the sum is greater than the parts in preparing listeners' minds and emotions to hear the Lost Cause message.[18]

Memorial Day ceremonies in the South were similar across the region, regardless of the city or town in which they were held or the date of the event. There was usually a procession of the local Confederate veterans and the women and schoolchildren from the center of town to the cemetery, where bands and choral groups presented several "appropriate" selections. If the event was held indoors, the organizers (always the local Ladies' Memorial Association) prepared and arranged elaborate trappings such as black sashes and drapes, evergreens and flowers, and pictures of famous Confederates such as Jefferson Davis, Robert E. Lee, or Stonewall Jackson. Often, a large Confederate battle flag hung conspicuously at the rear of the platform. The organization's leading ladies were accorded places of honor both in the procession and on the platform. Their role on the program, however, was generally limited to musical selections, poetry reading, or a recitation. Prayers were offered by various clergy members, and there was always an oration, generally followed by more prayers and musical selections.

After the formal ceremony, the group disbanded and families walked through the cemetery to trim the new spring grass around the family graves and to put fresh flowers by the tombstones. On June 4, 1891, in Norfolk, Virginia, there were 467 "most handsome flower emblems sent to the cemetery." Colonel B. H. Rutledge, in a speech in Magnolia Cemetery in Charleston, admonished his listeners to "deck their graves with flowers, crown them with garlands, encircle them with reverence, bedew them with tears. May these oblations be perpetual with each revolving year, that the world may know that the Southern heart is ever mindful of the patriotism and devotion of the Southern soldier." Mindful southerners were, and they attended in large numbers.

Richmond's first Memorial Day, on May 10, 1866, attracted five hundred women who brought flowers to the Oakwood Cemetery; three weeks later, according to the newspaper account, twenty thousand people took part in a procession to Hollywood Cemetery where flowers were placed on Confederate graves. The celebration in Atlanta in 1874 had "ten or twelve thousand people" with a procession "near a mile long." In Norfolk on June 4, 1891, three thousand people gathered "to do honor to the gallant heroes who had fallen fighting for what they deemed, and held inaffably [sic] sacred." In Columbus, Georgia, on April 26, 1898, "thousands of people were waiting" as the procession from the Opera House arrived at the "beautifully decorated" cemetery where the "graves of the dead soldiers [were] literally covered with lovely flowers."[19]

A representative example is the Memorial Day observed at New Bern, North Carolina, on May 9, 1879. There was a choir "composed of many of the best voices of the city" as well as a band. The first number was a "well known requiem" written by a North Carolinian, Mrs. Mary Bayard Clarke, "The Guard around the Tomb." This was followed by "an appropriate prayer" by Rev. L. C. Vass of the First Presbyterian Church and another hymn, "Cover Them Over with Flowers." After these preliminary events, the oration of the day was presented by Alfred Moore Waddell, a prominent North Carolina political figure and former U.S. congressman. His speech was considered "most scholarly, beautiful and appropriate," one that, "for good taste and ability, has been rarely equaled and never surpassed by any similar oration in this city."[20] Waddell's introduction sums up in a few words the essence of the role of southern Memorial Day observances and the role of the "orator of the day":

> Ladies of the Memorial Association: It is customary on these occasions for those who perform the duty assigned to me today, to paint, as best they may, that picture of the past on which Southern eyes will always gaze with admiration, and before which, Southern hearts will always throb with mingled pride and sorrow. They try to portray in vivid colors the heroism, the splendid courage, the patient toil and suffering, the unselfish patriotism and the sublime devotion of our countrymen who died in an unequal struggle for the preservation of what they believed to be the sacred inheritance of constitutional liberty bequeathed to them by their fathers. The tribute is just, the service is proper, though mortal tongue may vainly strive to form in fitting words the thoughts which such an occasion and such a theme inspire. The season too, is meet, for it is redolent of hope and promise. Not beneath withered branches swaying in the winter wind, and amidst dead leaves strewed upon the naked earth shall such services be held; but in the tender spring-time, when to the music of soft winds, odorous with the breath of flowers and gladdened by the songs of birds, transfigured nature makes manifest the miracle of the resurrection. Amidst such surroundings we meet today in this silent city to do honor to the memory of our dead.[21]

Memorial Day provided an opportunity for the women of the South to participate more fully in the public life of their communities. The limits placed on women in the South for generations has been well documented.[22] But after the Civil War, these Memorial Day celebrations provided an opportunity for southern women to take an active leadership role in their community, as it was they who, by and large, founded, organized, and sustained the occasion through their local memorial associations. David Goldfield concludes that "preserving the Lost Cause and Reconstruction in stone and memory offered white women the opportunity to live up to expectations of their virtue, support their men, and find outlets for their talents." They took full advantage of these opportunities, but they seldom took a major role in the program itself; that was left to the men. In keeping with southern custom, women "relinquished their leadership role at the ceremonies themselves."[23] The celebrations demonstrated the gendered, patriarchal order of the South.

The women did the organizing, but the men spoke and handled the public and business aspects of the event.

The white male leadership of the community fully supported the ceremonies, doubtless out of respect for the women of the South. The Confederate soldiers felt they owed southern women a great debt; Memorial Day gave them an opportunity to repay it in part. As one newspaper writer expressed it, Memorial Day services were to be respected because of women's place in them: "In the gentle light of Spring, with the deep blue heavens above, fair women gather around the graves on the anniversary of the death of the Confederacy and cover them with choicest flowers. . . . Monuments of stone or bronze are naught compared to the beautiful ceremony of decorating the mounds over the remains of the heroes who were buried in the gray. . . . Then let us gather in our quiet cemetery tomorrow, and aid the devoted women of our city and country in paying respect to the dead of the Lost Cause."[24]

In addition to providing moral support, men had certain other tasks to carry out, such as arranging for property acquisitions for sites of cemeteries and monuments, taking care of whatever labor was required to build the memorial, and, of course, the public speaking at the ceremonies. John W. Daniel of Lynchburg, Virginia, pointed out the addition of the orator to the ceremony: "Soon the custom of accompanying the floral offering with memorial speeches arose, and Memorial Day has now become an occasion alike instructive and exalting."[25]

Many of the orations given during the Memorial Day ceremonies across the South sang the praises of the women who had organized the event and who worked the hardest in the community to preserve the traditions and the memories of the dead and the Lost Cause for which they died. Journalist John Temple Graves, one of the favorite orators of the period, waxed eloquently on April 26, 1876, in West Point, Georgia: "Every marble shaft, pointing heavenward above Confederate graves, breathes to the evening and the morning sunbeams, this whispered tribute to woman: Twin angel of war and peace. In the one she comes white-robed and cheering, bringing balm as sweet as Gilead's to the wounded and the dying. In the other she stands a spirit sentinel amid the hearts of our people, sounding her pure alarum at the near approach of oblivion or neglect." In 1890, Rev. Ellison Capers remarked at a Greenville, South Carolina, Memorial Day celebration: "To the women of the South a debt of deepest gratitude is due from every patriotic heart—from every man who respects himself and honors our dead—for the faithful and true observance of our memorial day."[26]

It was so important to southerners for the women to continue the me-

morializing of the dead that even in the late 1890s when President McKinley suggested that the federal government take over the care of Confederate
graves, the United Confederate Veterans welcomed the idea for those Confederates who were buried in the North, but went on record as urging that in
the South the women should continue to conduct that honor for the dead.[27]

There was an overtly religious element to these celebrations, as the ritual
was often compared to Christian elements of worship. In discussing the history of Memorial Day in Columbus, Georgia, Benning wrote of the founding of the Soldiers' Aid Society, the precursor to the Ladies' Memorial Association: "The parent organization was born under the shadow of the altar in
the Baptist Church of Columbus." Later, she refers to Memorial Day as the
"Sabbath of the South," and in perhaps the clearest statement of the religious
overtones of the event, she tells about the devoted women of Columbus and
compares them to Christian heroines: "Where were Mary Magdalen and the
other Mary after the crucifixion? At the sepulcher with sweet spices. So these
women came to the soldiers' graves with choice plants and bright flowers."
Again, she emphasized the connection to Christ: "Like the hope that spread
over the earth on the morning of the Resurrection, so the soft light of this
sentiment shone over Dixie, and when April came, Love wreathed her roses
where the soldiers sleep." F. A. Porcher, the historian of the Charleston Ladies' Memorial Association, wrote of the "several distinguished *martyrs* of
the Lost Cause [emphasis in source]" to whom monuments had been raised
by the association. Often, speakers would refer to the soldiers of the Confederacy who "fell holy sacrifices upon their country's altar," as Mrs. Williams's letter had done in 1866.[28] In the deeply religious South, this connection to Christian faith was a strong and effective rhetorical stroke.

There is no doubt that the Memorial Day event was a vital part of community ritual across the South. For decades, orator after orator focused on the
role of the occasion. As John Temple Graves, a nationally known orator and
newspaperman, pointed out in 1888, "this whole people come trooping with
flowers and heartfelt eulogy, gathering in hundreds—nay, in thousands—once
a year to do universal honor and especial homage to the soldier dead." Two
years later, James C. C. Black urged his Atlanta listeners to "gather around
their graves to render just tribute to the memory of the dead, and renew
the friendships engendered by the sufferings, sacrifices and perils of war."
North Carolinian Julian S. Carr spoke for many white southerners when he
reminded his audience in 1894: "My friends, it is well for us to honor our heroes and to commune on each returning tenth of May over the sweet, sad,
inspiring memories of the past."[29]

Perhaps the most representative and descriptive statement is Mrs. B. A. C.
Emerson's sketch of the day in her book on Confederate monuments:

The best monument to the soldiers is Memorial Day. There is poetry in it . . . a whole people turned poet. The South enacts a poem each year, on Memorial Day. When the day in springtime comes and the flowers are blooming, see the people close their houses and places of business; see the procession moving along the streets. They are there from grandfather to babe. . . . It is the story of the defeat of a just cause. It is the simple, primitive way of telling by symbols what is too deep and tragic to be told in words. . . . What a drama! What a poem! What a motion picture! What a monument to the memory of the Boys in Gray! who lived and fought and faded away![30]

More than a hundred years later, many southern communities continue to celebrate Confederate Memorial Day. In Pensacola, Florida, the United Daughters of the Confederacy still gather at the grave of Stephen R. Mallory, Confederate secretary of the navy, in St. Michael's Cemetery and place a flag on his grave, as well as on the graves of the two Union and nineteen Confederate veterans in the cemetery.[31] Traditions die hard in the South.

"A fond recollection of the days that are past": Confederate Veterans' Reunions

In the early years after the war, the Confederate veteran was content to nurse his wounds, begin to rebuild his economy, and learn how to live in the new and significantly different order of things. His structure of racial relationships was different; his labor supply was no longer under his direct control; his ego was sharply deflated; his role in the nation's capital was dramatically curtailed; and his economy was in ruins. He had left home in the spring of 1861 expecting the easy and quick vanquishing of the Yankees; he came back home in the spring of 1865 defeated and discouraged. After having expected to win an easy war—indeed, after having staked all that he had on the outcome—it was difficult to face the bleak future of defeat and despair.

Soon after the war's end, veterans organizations began to meet informally to cooperate with the women's groups to care for the Confederate graves in the local cemetery and to improve the condition of those colleagues who were disabled or unable to work or to care for themselves. After the grief and pain had become a bit less vivid, the gray-clad soldiers began to gather together to share memories and to tell war stories as veterans have done since time immemorial. At first these "reunions" were informal and unstructured, but as the years passed, many of the former Confederate military units began to organize, elect officers, and hold regularly scheduled annual meetings. By the 1890s these reunions were "the dominant mode of Civil War memory."[32]

At each of these events, parades and ceremony were the order of the day. The veterans would gather from their homes and communities, and there would be business meetings, election of officers, campfires, barbecues, reminiscences, and the usual oration by a southern military figure—often the wartime commander of the unit.

The Charleston, South Carolina, Washington Light Infantry celebrated their reunion on George Washington's birthday, and their 1879 gala is a representative example of the genre. The festivities were initiated by a ball the night before, which, according to the newspaper account of the reunion, "promises to be one of the most brilliant affairs of the season." At 9:00 A.M. on February 22, a parade of fourteen military units marched from the Citadel to downtown Charleston along King Street, Calhoun Street, and Meeting Street to the Charleston Hotel, where they passed the reviewing stand, before disbanding on South Battery. At 1:00 P.M. there was an oration by Hugh Thompson at the Academy of Music, and the full day concluded with an 8:00 P.M. reception at the Washington Light Infantry Armory.[33]

While the Memorial Day rituals were generally under the leadership and direction of the women of the community, veterans' reunions were sponsored and led by the veterans themselves. The women's groups participated, but only as auxiliary supporters of the veterans organizations. In some cases, local groups were open to any veterans and were not specifically related to a unit or command. In June 1889 these reunions gained some regional organization with the founding of the United Confederate Veterans in New Orleans. Its last reunion was in 1950, but at its peak around 1903 the UCV boasted 1,555 camps or local chapters.[34] These assemblies gained national attention in the last two decades of the century, and their rituals and rhetoric became a major source for the creation and maintenance of Lost Cause mythology. There is ample evidence that the veterans organizations were responsible for major financial support of the numerous Ladies' Memorial Associations that played such an important role in the Memorial Day celebrations and the building of Confederate monuments across the South.

One of the strongest and best-known of the veterans groups was the Confederate Survivors' Association of Augusta, Georgia. The organization was formed by Charles C. Jones Jr., a historian and writer, who described his association:

> The Confederate Survivors' Association consists of Confederate veterans. Every man who served under the Southern colors is admissible on being vouched for by two comrades and giving in [sic] his rank and command. Quarterly meetings are held, and on the 26th of April

each year, Memorial Day, the Association has its annual meeting, and after the transaction of business drinks in silence and standing a toast to the Confederate dead. At the funeral of each member, a detail, and sometimes the whole association, attends with a war-worn, tattered, and smoke-grimed stand of Confederate colors. The maimed members, who have lost arm or leg, are the color guard.

On Memorial Day in 1887 the Augusta group met, and according to the newspaper account, the reunion was a smashing success: "The celebration of Memorial Day this year will certainly be on a grand scale, the Survivors' and Ladies' Associations having entered into the movement with great earnestness and in thorough accord. All the railroads have arranged reduced rates, and thousands of visitors will be in the city." A committee asked all of the town's stores to close for the day.[35]

At the July 1875 reunion of Orr's Rifles in Walhalla, South Carolina, General Samuel McGowan described his vision of the typical reunion: "Let us in peace and in quiet, without malice or hatred to any, hold sweet converse one with another, talk over the past with all its hopes and fears, joys and sorrows; recount the stories of the bivouac and the camp-fire, and as we pass, drop a silent tear over the sweet memory of some comrade whom we buried on the battlefield, and recall the long marches and bloody battles in which we suffered and struggled, hungered and toiled, and fought and bled together." Apparently the reunion was a success, as the newspaper remarked that "the reunion of the Survivors of Orr's Rifles was everything that the most ardent Confederate and patriotic citizen could wish—no bitterness, no discontent, only a loving pride in the soldiers who fell, a fond recollection of the days that are past, and a fixed determination to be as true to their new allegiance as these brave riflemen were to the cause of the South."[36]

Most of the early reunions focused on two goals. The Robert E. Lee Camp of the Confederate Veterans in Alexandria, Virginia, claimed that their purpose was "to perpetuate the memories of their fallen comrades, and to minister, as far as practicable, to the wants of those who were permanently disabled in the service, to preserve and maintain that sentiment of fraternity born of hardships and dangers shared in the march, the bivouac and the battlefield." A large order, but one these organizations filled in the decades after the war. These goals were expressed in 1878 by General W. H. Lee of the Virginia Brigade, Army of Northern Virginia, as "the pleasure of comradeship" and "perpetuat[ing] the heroic deeds of the mighty men who composed our grand old Army." That 1878 reunion also raised $4,260.96 to send to their comrades in the Louisiana Division, Army of Virginia, who were suffering

from a yellow fever epidemic sweeping the Gulf Coast.[37] By the beginning
of the twentieth century, death was claiming more members of these groups
than they were recruiting, and the membership figures began to drop. But
at their height, the veterans organizations in Dixie provided valuable platforms for the advocates of the Lost Cause.

Katharine Du Pre Lumpkin recalls her father's involvement in reunions
and describes the efforts of many other southern men of his era:

> Father was an inveterate reunion-goer and planner. So were literally hun-
> dreds of his kind, men who were also of the Old South's disinherited,
> who had lost so much and regained so little, materially speaking. . . .
> Theirs was certainly a tireless effort in behalf of the Lost Cause, and
> a labor of love if there ever was one. These men expected to get noth-
> ing from it save people's warm approbation, perhaps, and the personal
> satisfaction that comes with a performance of a welcome duty; and
> of course—indeed above everything—their sense that by this means
> they were serving the paramount aim of preserving the South's old
> foundations.[38]

One contemporary observer, writing about the 1895 UCV reunion in Houston, focused on the role of oratory in the event's activities on the second day
of the reunion. The commentator wrote that the day was "characterized by
such a display of the wonderfully eloquent oratory for which the South is
noted, as is seldom given men to enjoy." He went on to describe the "feast of
eloquent utterances that was thrilling in effect."[39]

Not only was there oratory and formal business meetings of the veterans
organizations, but there were full days of teas, receptions, luncheons, ban-
quets, and dances. The historical booklet compiled for the 1895 reunion in
Houston describes some of the soirees in detail. For example, Judge James
Masterson and his daughter gave a "very elegant card reception" at which
the "elegant toilettes of the ladies, the faultless dress suits of the civilians,
the glittering uniforms of officers, and the crush and jam everywhere, reminded one vividly of state receptions at Washington at the height of the
season." A "delightful informal reception" was held at Mr. and Mrs. Charles
Bein's home, and Mrs. Julius Kruttschmitt's buffet luncheon honoring Varina
Davis, Jefferson Davis's daughter, "was delicious . . . and conversation rippled
and sparkled as in the olden days, so that the hours from 1 to 3 in the afternoon were winged." The governor of Texas was honored at a party hosted
by Mr. and Mrs. Charles House, at which "superb roses, jasamines and ferns
made bits of gay color in the daintily tinted drawing room, and soft mando-

lin music floated down from an alcove at the head of the massive stairway."
An afternoon tea served to a "large concourse of people" at the "handsome
residence" of Mr. and Mrs. S. K. McIlhenny was "one of the pleasantest affairs of the week." "Iced tea, deliciously flavored with lemon, mint and other
nice things, was served with cake."[40]

The important role of women at these reunions was highlighted at the
1899 Charleston reunion of the UCV. In a publication issued by the headquarters of the South Carolina Division of the UCV, the camps, regiments,
and brigades were urged to "appoint a Sponsor and her Maid of Honor";
"they will be welcomed to Charleston and to the Reunion." The call went
on to reflect the importance of this concern: "Appoint the descendants of
some Veteran to these offices, and encourage the rising generation to revere
the cause we fought for and ennoble the memory of those who laid down
their lives for the Southern Confederacy. We want the dear girls with us at
all such gatherings, and they will always find a warm place in the hearts of
every true Veteran."[41]

The women coming to Charleston would be hosted "at the N.E. corner
George and Meeting Streets, where the ladies have established this handsome
office for the reception of lady visitors and their escorts, where they can obtain information and meet their friends." The ladies' headquarters would
have a reception room; registering office; writing room, "where ladies will
find all the conveniences for writing"; and a bedroom, "where ladies can rest
when sick or tired," and which would be attended by a servant. Attached to
the bedroom was the "dressing room, with hot and cold water," and upstairs
was the "bath room and ladies' toilet."[42]

Lumpkin provides a full description of the 1903 UCV reunion in her
hometown of Columbia, South Carolina, clearly showing the key role the reunions played in the life of the early twentieth-century South, and suggests
how the Lost Cause myth flourished for so many decades across the region:

> Besides businessmen, all the leading people, and some not so lead-
> ing, were drawn into the effort. No, not drawn; they had poured, all
> anxious to have a part on this paramount occasion—institutions, or-
> ganizations, whole families, including parents, young people, and chil-
> dren. Entertainment, housing, parades, decorations, meetings—these
> were men's tasks. Feeding the veterans, in particular manning two
> free lunch rooms down town, was the ladies'. Social events fell to the
> young people, the Sons of Veterans . . . and the young ladies; they must
> plan for balls and receptions, and for the good times of over two hun-
> dred sponsors and maids-of-honor. . . . Local bands must serve. Local

militia . . . students of South Carolina College and the two "female" colleges; school children, two hundred of them, to strew flowers, sing in a chorus, execute intricate marches which took hours and days for training; the Cotillon Club, select dancing society; the town's "riding set" for the parade; the Metropolitan Club; the local lodge of Elks; merchants and manufacturers and other businessmen to give their time and money and elaborately decorate their establishments. Everyone must decorate. . . . Everyone must go home loaded down with red and white bunting and Confederate flags.[43]

Similar descriptions could have been written about scores of southern communities preparing for veterans' reunions.

Reunions were still major events as late as 1911, forty-six years after Appomattox, even though the ranks were thinning as the old veterans passed away. Little Rock, Arkansas, was the site of the 1910 reunion, as the city of 45,000 expected more than 100,000 visitors. The three railroad companies that served the capital sold 118,000 tickets to Little Rock that reunion week. A reunion lodging committee scrambled to provide accommodations for the huge influx of veterans and families, placing them in hotels, private homes, public school buildings, and finally, 10,000 in tents at the city park. Three giant dining tents were set up with twenty-five cooks and sixty waiters who prepared and served 54,000 meals that week. Twenty dishwashers were required to keep up with the flow of diners. The grand parade on the last day drew 150,000 spectators along the course, and they watched 12,000 veterans and fourteen bands pass by. The *Arkansas Gazette* bragged that the city had "set herself the task of entertaining the old soldiers better than they have ever been entertained before." Apparently, the city felt it was a success, as the *Arkansas Democrat* editorialized that "the reunion is worth all its cost. It demonstrates that the spirit of Southern Chivalry still lives, that King Arthur and his Knights of the Table Round were no whit more brave and tender than are these old heroes of a conflict the likes of which has never before and will never again be seen."[44]

"Marble and bronze tell in chiseled words the glory of the men who wore the gray": Confederate Monuments in the New South

Seeking more permanence than flowers and parades on Memorial Day, and luncheons and teas during reunions, southern white women launched campaigns around the region to build monuments to honor the Lost Cause and the Confederates who died in its defense. Cheraw, South Carolina, saw the first Confederate monument erected in June 1867 in the local cemetery; the first monument in a town center was erected that same year in Bolivar, Tennessee. As a historian of the United Daughters of the Confederacy wrote: "They began working for monuments to tell of the glorious fight against the greatest odds a nation ever faced, that their hallowed memory should never die." These women's work in many ways could be seen as against great odds as well in the war-devastated and poverty-stricken South of the late nineteenth and early twentieth centuries. The cost of commissioning a monument to be carved from stone or cast from bronze, having it shipped to the location, preparing the grounds, and assembling the monument and landscaping ran into the thousands of dollars. For a region in which many persons seldom saw a piece of folding money during this era, the fund-raising work was daunting. Athens, Georgia, demonstrated how important it was to immortalize the Confederacy and its defenders, however, as a concert held less than a year after Appomattox raised over two hundred dollars for a monument to the "Hero Dead."[45] The women were undaunted by the difficulties, and over several decades more than a thousand monuments were dedicated with the obligatory parade, ceremony, and oration.

In Pensacola, the fund-raising was turned over to the Ladies' Monument Association (LMA) after the men of Florida had reached a dead end in their quest to raise five thousand dollars for a state monument to be placed in Tallahassee. Most of the money had been raised in northwest Florida, so the project shifted to Pensacola, and the women took it over in 1890. One of their sponsored events was a public lecture by the local Episcopal minister on "The Charleston Earthquake." He had been the rector of a parish near Charleston at the time of the 1886 earthquake and was able to present a nearly firsthand account, for which the LMA sold tickets at twenty-five cents each. There was a dinner immediately following the lecture, and different items of food were sold. One young man auctioned items handed to him; a dill pickle brought a dollar, and a glass of lemonade added twenty dollars to the monument fund.[46]

One imagines that the fund-raisers in Savannah, Georgia, had to auction a lot of pickles, as the final cost of their monument was estimated to be $26,250 when it was dedicated in 1875; that was an enormous sum only a decade after Appomattox. Historian Mary B. Poppenheim summed up well the process and its importance to the postwar South: "With homes ruined, and poverty-stricken, these women, by selling pies, by having bazaars and ice cream suppers, and little home talent plays, gathered together nickels and dimes for monuments to their heroes." Front Royal, Virginia, is a representative case study, as they raised the four thousand dollars required for a monument with a series of oyster suppers, tableaux, bazaars, ice cream festivals, strawberry festivals, a Fall Chrysanthemum Show, a Baby Show, cakewalks, and an "Old Folks" concert. Cities and towns all over the South responded to the calls and somehow put together the resources to honor the Confederacy. Even a small community like Fort Mill, South Carolina, could boast of not one, but four, monuments by the turn of the century. The first, to "Confederate Soldiers," was erected in 1891; four years later, "Southern Women" were honored and a marble obelisk was dedicated to the "Faithful Slaves of Wartime"; and in 1900, ceremonies were held to dedicate a monument to a local group of Catawba Indians that had contributed soldiers to the cause.[47]

Regardless of the cost, and the sacrifices needed to raise the cash, monuments sprang up all over the South and became key components in the ritual of the Lost Cause. Large crowds were attracted to the dedication ceremonies. The small town of Front Royal attracted five thousand witnesses on September 23, 1899, to the dedication of a monument to some of John Mosby's Rangers who had been captured in the area and hung by Federal forces. Lexington, another small community in Virginia, saw eight thousand in attendance at the unveiling of the recumbent statue of Robert E. Lee on the campus of Washington College, where the Confederate commander had served as president after the war. In South Carolina, a month or so before the dedication of the state's monument in Columbia, veterans were urged to "make it a matter of duty—of honor to the mighty dead—to save yourselves for Columbia. Do this for the blood of the martyrs! Do this for memory's bow of promise! Do this for your fathers and brothers who lie in their graves of glory!" The appeal must have had some impact, as fifteen thousand people arrived on excursion trains from all over the state to see the dedication ceremonies. Even as late as 1922, two to three thousand spectators were attracted to an out-of-the-way location south of Tallahassee for the dedication of a monument at the site of the battle of Natural Bridge, where a group of "heroes of the Confederacy" defeated a Federal force and prevented the capture of Tallahassee. Apparently the largest crowd ever to attend a Confederate monument dedication was at the impressive Jefferson Davis Monument in Richmond, which was unveiled in 1907 before an estimated two hundred thousand persons.[48]

While the monuments were popular beyond belief in the South, there was organized opposition to them by northern groups, especially the Grand Army of the Republic, the Union counterpart of the United Confederate Veterans. The 1887 national encampment of the Grand Army voted that no post or department should support "the erection of monuments in honor of men who distinguished themselves by their services in the cause of treason and

rebellion." Rev. Randolph H. McKim saw the need to comment on northern negative reactions to Confederate monuments as late as 1904. Referring
to Daniel Webster's oration at the Bunker Hill monument in Boston, which
Webster claimed "was not erected 'to perpetuate hostility to Great Britain,'
much more can we say that the monuments we have erected, and will yet
erect, in our Southland to the memory of our dead heroes, are not intended to
perpetuate the angry passions of the Civil War, or to foster or keep alive any
feeling of hostility to our brethren of other parts of the Union." Of course,
much of the rhetoric of Lost Cause oratory was aimed at obliterating these
charges of "treason and rebellion," as we will see. By the end of the century,
however, reconciliation had taken hold, as in Jacksonville, where "a thousand
young men, the flower of the Seventh Corps of the United States Army, escorted Confederate Veterans of thirty-five years ago through the streets of
the city to the dedication of a monument . . . to the memory of Florida heroes who fell in the war which estranged for four years those who had been
before and have since been brothers."[49]

Northern participation was not the only debate that often surrounded the
creation of a monument in a southern city or town; the placement of the
statue or obelisk often prompted much hot discussion. The debate was largely
over whether to place the monument in the local cemetery, away from common, frequent view, or to situate it on the courthouse lawn or city square
or at a prominent corner in obvious public sight. In the early years after the
Civil War, the most usual location was in a cemetery as part of the grieving
and mourning process.[50]

The historian of the Ladies' Memorial Association of Charleston summed
up the debate in that city in words that echoed around the region at various
times:

> The Monument has been appropriately placed in the midst of the graves
> of those whose death it commemorates. It is plain and unostentatious,
> but neat and appropriate. As it is a memorial of a lost cause, it should
> not be a triumphal memorial. Placed in the City of the Dead . . . the
> sight of it cannot fail to call back the memory of the sad history which
> it commemorates. A splendid monument in the city would be only an
> ornament to be gazed on with listless and indifferent eyes; and, instead
> of being a memorial of the dead, would be only the object of cold, art
> criticism. Its proper place, therefore, is just where it is, in the midst of
> the silent slumberers, whose deeds, and whose failures, it is designed
> to keep alive in the memories of the people.[51]

But as the South began to recover spiritually, physically, and economically, the focus shifted to the center of the city and monuments began to appear with increasing frequency on the courthouse lawn. As Charles Wilson put it, they were the "marble embodiment" of the Lost Cause.[52] Monuments began to serve, not just as symbols of grief and mourning, but also as defiant public symbols of the Lost Cause and the glorious "Old South."

Oratory was as much a part of the ritual of the Confederate monument as it was of Memorial Day and veterans' reunions. Almost all newspaper references to monument dedications or cornerstone-laying ceremonies include at least a brief statement of praise for the orator of the day and a description of some aspect of his rhetoric. Again, as in the Memorial Day events, the oratory was men's work—women's role in public address was limited to brief descriptions of the Ladies' Monument Association or similar short, relatively unimportant statements. In many cases, simply being present on the stage seemed to be the extent of the feminine participation.

An interesting indicator of the importance of the oration was its usual length. A contemporary observer timed the oration presented at the laying of the cornerstone for the Robert E. Lee Monument in Richmond. Colonel Charles Marshall was the orator of the day and presented a speech that took him one and a half hours to read to his audience. But he spoke for a shorter time than Senator William B. Bate at the dedication of the Knoxville monument on May 19, 1892; the senator was timed at about two hours in his oration. There was little doubt, however, that the various speakers were thoroughly respected and were paid close attention. The dedication address for the Marianna, Florida, monument was delivered by Governor Cary A. Hardee, a "distinguished orator," who had never spoken to "greater advantage than in this address which was one evidently close to his heart."[53]

One of the common themes of the dedication orations was that communities since the beginning of time had praised the deeds of their forefathers in earthworks, stone, song, and word. The South, fully aware of the past, profoundly steeped in tradition, and passionately devoted to family and locality, could hardly do less. Southern editors waxed eloquently regarding the role of the Confederate monuments and their place in remembering the past and vindicating the cause that was lost:

> But yesterday this sentiment of which we have spoken took appropriate and enduring shape in the beginning of the erection of a monument which will remain to future ages a witness to the valor of Southern men and the devotion of Southern women.... This memorial shaft bears testimony in their behalf—is a protest to God and man of the

righteousness of their cause and the purity of their motives. . . . It is a vindication as well as a remembrance. It is put in our most public thoroughfare that it may be a landmark in our city; that it may be seen by every eye; that it may speak to the world of a cause crushed but not disgraced, of a people vanquished, but not dishonored. It commemorates the courage, the chivalry, the devotion of the dead and it bears testimony to the justice of their cause. There will be no shame for the children of the conquered. They will point with pride to this lofty column and say "so honored the South her heroes." In years to come the proudest patent of nobility will lie in the words "my father fought for freedom in the ranks of the Confederate Army."[54]

The important role of southern women in sustaining the monument fervor was recognized not only by the men, but also by the women themselves. In the history of the United Daughters of the Confederacy there is a proud description of the process: "The chapters of the United Daughters of the Confederacy have built hundreds and hundreds of monuments, until now nearly every county seat in the South has its Confederate monument in its courthouse square, or on a prominent corner, or in a cemetery—a shrine, a great object lesson to our youth, telling the story of a glorious past, of heroic deeds and unfailing loyalty to a beloved cause."[55] With this abiding interest in the remembrance of things past, it is easy to understand why the public discourse at these monument dedications and the monuments themselves played a vital role in shaping southern attitudes and values and gave so much support to the creating of the Lost Cause mythology. The dedication of Confederate monuments across the South has to be seen as one of the most important ritual events in the celebration of the Lost Cause.

The great folk hero of the Civil War for southerners was Robert E. Lee. Although his armies were eventually crushed by the might of Yankee forces, the gray-clad veterans revered Lee. Many monuments in the defeated Confederacy were dedicated to him, and the college where he served as president changed its name to honor him and also furnished a mausoleum for his body. At the unveiling of this tomb in June 1883, John Warwick Daniel, the "Lame Lion of Lynchburg," delivered the oration of the day. For three hours, Daniel praised Lee and the Confederacy in the most effusive way and held the eight to ten thousand persons in the audience "by the spell of his eloquence, moving it now to applause, and now to tears." Daniel's entire speech could easily be characterized as a eulogy not just to Lee but to the Lost Cause itself: "Robert Edward Lee made fiercer and bloodier fight against greater odds, and at greater sacrifice, and lost—against the greatest nation of modern history, armed with steam and electricity, and all the appliances of modern science; a nation which mustered its hosts at the very threshold of his door. But his life teaches the grandest lesson how manhood can rise transcendent over Adversity."[56]

One of the first communities to sponsor a memorial monument was Augusta, Georgia, the headquarters city of the Confederate Survivors' Association. After a bitter campaign over the best location for the monument, the citizens of Augusta voted to place it at the corner of Broad and McIntosh Streets. Some had wanted to erect it in the city cemetery, but the center of the city was selected. As was the custom, the Ladies' Memorial Association raised funds for the project.

On April 13, 1875, the officers of the association met to lay the first bricks of the foundation:

> About half-past three o'clock the ladies met at the site of the proposed monument, and going down into the excavation made for the foundation—where the ground was prepared, with brick and mortar at hand—took off their gloves and prepared themselves for work. . . . It was indeed a novel sight to the large number of spectators to see the ladies, with delicate, ungloved hands, laying brick and handling the trowel, but it was a holy duty they performed—one most appropriate to the occasion and the object—that of rearing a shaft of marble in memory of the brave men who fought and died for a cause they considered just.

On April 26 the city dedicated the cornerstone of the monument as the key part of a day-long festival in Augusta. City stores were closed at one o'clock, and the streets "began to be thronged with volunteers in uniform, members of societies, with badges, and citizens generally. Everything wore a holiday appearance. . . . Never before in the history of Augusta was there such a universal outpouring of the people known." There was a parade to the site of the monument, one that an observer effusively described: "The procession and the music eclipsed anything ever witnessed in Georgia since the dawn of civilization upon its soil!" Once the crowd had gathered at the site, a prayer was offered, an anthem was sung by the choir, and a selection by Mozart was played by the Eighteenth United States Army Band stationed in Columbia, South Carolina. Following these festivities, the cornerstone was lowered into position. It was dedicated by a Masonic ceremony with Grand Master C. E. Lewis pouring wheat, wine, and oil upon it, "assisted by the grand dignitaries and members of the Masonic order." Part of the cornerstone ritual was the placing of certain memorial items, such as the rolls of city and county officials lists of local church memberships, rolls of local societies such as the Georgia Society for the Prevention of Cruelty to Animals and the Hebrew Benevolent Society, the rolls of local schools, and of course, Confederate memorabilia such as postage stamps, money, a Confederate flag, lists of Confederate dead, and rolls of various Georgia military units. After the conclusion of the oration and another prayer, the procession re-formed and marched to the cemetery for the annual decoration of the graves.[57]

Whether the event truly "eclipsed anything ever witnessed in Georgia since the dawn of civilization upon its soil!" will never be known, but the hundreds of similar Confederate monument rituals around the South played a major part in creating and sustaining the Lost Cause ideal. It provided opportunity for a community to do its part in recalling the sacrifices made by the men and women of the Confederacy and thus kept the memories of what might have been—and what never was—fresh in the minds and lives of the participants. While the orgy of monument-building reached its heyday in the early twentieth century, the practice continued throughout the century. During the centennial of the Civil War in 1961–65, a number of monuments were erected. At the Gettysburg battlefield, Florida and South Carolina dedicated monuments in 1964. In 1971, Louisiana followed suit, as did Mississippi in 1973. The huge stone figures of Robert E. Lee, Jefferson Davis, and Stonewall Jackson were finally completed, carved in relief from Stone Mountain, just outside Atlanta, in 1979. These massive renderings rival even Monument Avenue in Richmond as the leading enduring symbol of the old Confederacy.[58]

Of the three ceremonial events we are considering, the Confederate monument is the most important. After all, the reunions are held no more (even though the Sons of Confederate Veterans and the United Daughters of the Confederacy still meet regularly throughout the South). Throughout the nation Memorial Day is not much more than just another holiday—it is too close to the end of school for it to be celebrated with a school holiday many places, and workers who do get the holiday off, generally spend it fishing or shopping or in some other non-commemorative fashion. There are some holdouts around the South who decorate the Confederate graves in the local cemeteries, and one can still hear the occasional oration from the past. But the monuments still stand in hundreds of town squares and in hundreds of southern cemeteries. They are perhaps beneath the consciousness of many of the southerners who see them, at least out of the corner of their eye as they drive past them or when they attend a funeral in the cemetery a few rows away from the statue of the "Confederate Dead." They are a constant, albeit subtle, reminder of defeat, humiliation, subjection, and loss at the hands of outsiders.

Confederate monuments served to remind white southerners that even though they lost the war, they were heroes in a heroic cause. They allowed the South to thumb its collective nose at the victors and to remind them as well of the heroes of the South. Additionally, the monuments were intended to be a guide for the future, to ensure that southerners never forgot their past. As we will see, this guide proved to be a harsh one, as the South fought the battles of the civil rights movement, and the white South defended the evils of segregation, using some of the same arguments and based on some of the same values of the rhetors of the Lost Cause a half century earlier. The UDC and UCV proved to be prophetic, however, as the values of the monument builders were carried along, even into the twenty-first century, in part, by the constant reminder staring with marble eyes at the southerner driving or walking past the courthouse lawn. The statue may have been at the edge of one's consciousness, but it is there, nevertheless, always as a reminder of the cause that was lost and of the outsiders who were the victors. James Mayo writes that "whether memorials are sacred or not, they subtly permeate our lives and affect us more than we realize."[59] A casual drive through any southern state will show these monuments still exhibited in places of honor and surrounded by well-kept grounds.

The tie to the past may be tenuous as we begin the twenty-first century, but for much of the last century these monuments were viable and visible symbols of the past that provided a sense of continuity and stability in an often confusing new world. The Confederate monument has faded from prominence and recedes in memory, but it still casts a long shadow across the courthouse lawns and quiet cemeteries of the South. William Faulkner caught the essence of this shadow as he wrote, "They approached the square, where the Confederate soldier gazed with empty eyes beneath his marble hand into wind and weather."[60]

Did these spring-day celebrations of Confederate Memorial Day, the wearying reunions of the old soldiers, and the Confederate monuments reflecting the "wind and weather" have an impact on the white southerners who participated in them? Listen to Sara Haardt, an Alabama native, southern writer, and wife of H. L. Mencken, who wrote in the *American Mercury* years after the heyday of these rituals and rhetoric: "I had lived too close to these dead and fading things to ever break away. The dying roses, the little mounds with their ghostly headstones, the hauntingly sad April evening, had brewed a philosophy of futility in my heart that is the curse of all Southerners, and their inescapable tradition. I might dream rebelliously of forsaking it, but it would never forsake me; my spirit was wholly entombed in loss and loneliness."[61] These events and the rhetoric inherent in them created a mythology of the South that white southerners lived "too close to . . . to ever break away." In the following chapters we will hear what the orators said at these events and how these words echo even into the twenty-first century. Maybe it is not a "curse of all Southerners," but it certainly is "their inescapable tradition."

3

The Road to Secession and War

The Oratorical Defense of the Confederacy and the Old South

There was never a Confederate Memorial Day celebration, a Confederate veterans' reunion, or a Confederate monument dedication without the program including at least one oration by a local dignitary, often a Confederate general or other high-ranking officer, or a local soldier who was always portrayed as a hero of the conflict. Occasionally, the orator of the day was a minister who had been a Confederate chaplain or who was well respected in the local area. Generally, there were several speeches: an introductory, welcoming address by the city's mayor or the president of the local monument association or veterans' group that was convening, followed by a speech introducing the "orator of the day." Especially at veterans' reunions, there were frequently several toasts presented to the soldiers; each was typically followed by a brief but heartfelt response that captured in capsule form some of the same topics and ideals of the major address. Over the next three chapters we will be examining some representative samples of this extensive body of speech-making to determine the pervasive themes of these special events.

An important goal of this oratory was clear: to establish and defend the legitimacy of the Confederacy and to vindicate the route southern leadership took in 1860–61. James C. C. Black, speaking on Confederate Memorial Day in 1890 in Atlanta, asserted that his role was to "proclaim to our countrymen and mankind that we were not traitors."[1] Many of the orators sought to rebut the charge of treason levied at southerners and the Confederacy. A related goal was to ensure that accurate knowledge of the war was passed on to future generations from a well-defended southern perspective. That same year, Confederate brigadier general and later Episcopal bishop Ellison Capers of South Carolinian, the "Orator Laureate of the Lost Cause,"[2] told his audience that southerners are required to uphold the "high duty of maintaining the character and the spirit and the courage and the patriotism of the men who carried us through the contest with honor, and sustained it to the bitter end."[3] Two years earlier, Colonel Peter Turney, a future governor of Tennessee, had been more blunt and to the point as he concluded his speech with a description of his purpose for a veterans organization in Nashville: "In this effort my purpose and desire have been to awake the Southern man and woman to the importance of having their children study our lost cause from constitutional, legal, and historical standpoints, that they be not misled."[4]

Another central purpose of their rhetoric was to explain to their listeners what the South had fought for. As Charles C. Jones Jr., a colonel of artillery in the Confederate army, put it in the 1881 version of the address he gave annually to the Augusta, Georgia, Confederate Survivors' Association, his listeners were "survivors of one of the most gigantic defensive wars ever conducted in maintenance of national independence and vested rights, for the preservation of property, and to perpetuate the privileges of home rule."[5] In short, the orators believed the South fought for the sovereignty of states and the role of local government as contrasted with the powers of the federal government, and for the perpetuation of property in slaves, as rights guaranteed by the Constitution. White southerners clearly understood and believed in these ideals, as Alfred M. Waddell reminded his audience in 1878: "They understood thoroughly what they were about, they knew exactly what they were fighting for." James McPherson's examination of hundreds of letters and diaries of Union and Confederate soldiers, *What They Fought For, 1861–1865,* shows clearly that "a large number of these men in blue and gray were intensely aware of the issues at stake and passionately concerned about them." These speeches clearly reflect this awareness and passion. Speaking to a survivors' association in 1881, William Boggs reflected on the "keen zest, and shrewdness too, with which around the camp-fire, you entered into discussions upon the issues of the war, the policies of the rival governments, and the conduct of public men."[6] We will examine in some detail these major themes, and others gleaned from hundreds of speeches presented throughout the South in the decades after Appomattox.

"The right of secession was clear": The Legality of Their Cause

Lost Cause orators often felt compelled to defend the legality of secession as a basis for their justification of the Confederacy. "Although the view of separate state sovereignty was warmly questioned by some in some parts of the land, it was never questioned in the South. On the contrary, it was held as sacred, vital and inviolable," Rev. Charles Vedder reminded his Charleston audience thirty-four years after Appomattox. Peter Turney believed that "under the principles of the Union as it then existed, the right of secession was clear."[7]

Why was this right so unmistakable in the minds of the southern orators? Mainly, it evolved as a logical result of the idea of state sovereignty, dating back to the end of the Revolutionary War, when Great Britain acknowledged the thirteen colonies as free and independent states. That sovereignty, according to Lost Cause spokesmen, was never surrendered when the states adopted the Constitution and formed the Union. William Boggs argued at a reunion in Chester, South Carolina, that each colony had its own government, customs, and religious establishment, and were, thus, "diverse in origins, in customs, and in their interests." He cited the Articles of Confederation, which held that "Each State retains its sovereignty, freedom, and independence." In one of the fullest and most complete inventories of why the states were believed to be free to withdraw from the Union, Boggs refers to many of the leading figures in the southern and American pantheon of heroes, starting with the delegates to the Constitutional Convention, who "derived all authority from their respective states." Boggs cites James Madison's voice of authority when he wrote in the *Federalist* that states are considered "a sovereign body, independent of all others." In the New York ratification convention, Alexander Hamilton asserted that "the States can never lose their powers," and Boggs reminded his audience of that. Madison's "Report" to Virginia in 1799–1800, Jefferson's Kentucky Resolutions of 1798, Massachusetts's threat to secede over the Louisiana Purchase in 1803, the debates over the annexation of Texas in 1844, during which some northern states threatened to withdraw their support of the Union, and, of course, John C. Calhoun's argument that the Constitution is merely a compact "between the states" all served to bolster Boggs's argument. Another example often used to defend secession was the move by the western section of Virginia to form the state of West Virginia during the Civil War—if western Virginia could secede from its mother state, why could not the entire southern region withdraw from its mother nation?[8]

Turney uses latter-day constitutional analysts to support the argument for secession. Judge Joseph Story's *Commentaries on the Constitution* claimed that "each [state] retains the powers to withdraw from the confederacy and dissolve the connections, when such shall be its choice," and Judge St. George Tucker, a law professor at William and Mary College, argued that even after ratifying the Constitution, "each [state] is still a perfect state, still sovereign, still independent, and still capable . . . to resume the exercise of its functions as such in the most unlimited extent." Fitzhugh Lee averred as he dedicated the Stonewall Jackson statue in New Orleans that his state of Virginia "declared in the convention that ratified the Federal Constitution that she had a right to resume her independent condition whenever she might desire to do so." Stonewall Jackson fought, Lee claimed, "for what he held to be the principles of free government," and "conscientiously" believed that his state of Virginia had this right of secession "guaranteed to his State by the Constitution of the United States."[9]

Rev. Vedder turned to a northern source, Yale law lecturer Roger Foster, "to show that the southern belief in the legality of secession was justified; that the south was warranted in fighting for its rights, and that it is an act of injustice to brand their secession as treason." Vedder quotes at length Bostonian Josiah Quincy's congressional speech on the admission of Louisiana as a state in 1811: "I am compelled to decide . . . that if this bill passes, the bonds of this Union are virtually dissolved; that the states which compose it are free from their moral obligations; and that, as it will be the right of all, so it will be the duty of some, to prepare definitely for a separation— peaceably if they can, forcibly if they must." He turned to the Declaration of Independence for support of the legal basis for separation: "when a government becomes subversive of the end to secure life, liberty and the pursuit of happiness to the governed, it was the right of a people to alter or abolish it." Another minister, Randolph McKim, pointed out to the Nashville reunion of the United Confederate Veterans that it should be remembered when the United States itself was formed in 1788, it was only after nine states seceded from the confederacy "which had existed for eleven years. . . . *Thus the Union itself was the child of Secession!*"[10]

In his Nashville speech, Turney uses the words of northern politicians to defend the right of secession. He quotes Abraham Lincoln's House of Representatives speech in 1848 which asserted that a people had the right to "shake off the existing government and form a new one that suits them better." Then he turns to the "eminent jurist," Mr. Rawle of Pennsylvania, who wrote that "the people have in all cases to determine how they will be governed." Turney cites Senator Wade of Ohio on the Senate floor in February 1855, when he remarked in reference to the unconstitutionality of a law, "a State must not only be the judge of that but of the remedy in each case." Finally, the Tennessean goes to the leader of the abolition faction in the House, John Quincy Adams, who held in an 1839 speech that "the people of each State in the Union [have] a right to secede from the confederate union itself." A final example of many is W. M. Hammond's 1903 speech in which he quotes Cabot Lodge of Massachusetts, who believed a state could secede from the "experiment entered upon by the States; and from which each and every State had the right peaceably to withdraw."[11]

Another major point made by several speakers was summed up the most clearly by William Boggs, using the patriotic argument that the Confederate secession was analogous to the American Revolution: "Secession was morally justifiable upon the same grounds as justified our fathers in separating from the British Empire." In the first place, the South had a similar "long-standing grievance of an unjust and burdensome system of taxation" in the protective tariffs that unfairly placed a burden on the agricultural states— the South—and allowed the "great bulk of wealth . . . [to be] accumulated around the manufacturing centers"—the North. Boggs asserted that "South Carolina and the agricultural States were as truly taxed without their own consent as ever the colonies had been." His second contention is that the South had a "great grievance" due to the legislation that prevented southerners from taking their property (slaves) into the common territories of the nation. Boggs remarks upon the "great grievance of persistent attacks by our associates upon that species of property, for the protection of which special guarantees had been given in the Constitution—guarantees without which, it is well known, the Union would never have existed at all." Further, northerners "repeatedly sought to incite servile insurrection" through supporting abolition agitators like John Brown. Not only that, but the "Personal Liberty Bills" passed by thirteen northern states "avowedly intended to render null and void the constitutional stipulations which guaranteed the rendition of fugitive slaves!" And finally, the last straw was the election of Abraham Lincoln, "a sectional candidate, on a sectional issue, and by a strictly sectional vote," which demonstrated to the South that "all these evils, crying aloud for relief, assumed a hopeless and remediless aspect." After reviewing "all these wrongs and provocations," Boggs concludes that "upon the ground of the inalienable 'right of revolution,' we had the same justification as the Boston patriots had when they threw the tea into the sea."[12]

The argument over the right and legality of secession was still being presented as late as 1910, as J. H. Martin declared at a Columbus, Georgia, reunion: "That secession was a Constitutional right was recognized and publicly declared in conventions and otherwise for over seventy years before the Civil War, not only by the Southern States, but by those of the North, East, and West." Among the examples Martin cited, such as the Hartford Convention in 1814, was the abolitionist convention in May 1851, held in Syracuse, New York, which declared that any state had the right to secede.[13]

Basing their beliefs in the legality of the cause, many southerners could easily agree with former Confederate president Jefferson Davis when he proclaimed to the Army of Tennessee's 1878 reunion: "My faith in that right [secession] as an inherent attribute of State sovereignty, was adopted early in life, was confirmed by the study and observation of later years, and has passed, unchanged and unshaken, through the severe ordeal to which it has been subjected. Without desire for a political future, only anxious for the supremacy of the truths on which the Union was founded, and which I believe to be essential to the prosperity and the liberties of the people, it is little to assume that I shall die, as I have lived, firm in the State rights faith."[14]

"The inheritance their fathers had bequeathed to them": The Constitutional Legacy

Closely related to the defense of secession's legality was the defense of the specifics of the constitutional legacy as southerners interpreted it. The right for states to secede from the Union was the starting point, but there were other elements that Lost Cause orators wanted the world to understand and accept, and all white southerners to defend. Many southerners echoed the prewar refrain that the North misinterpreted the Constitution and that only the South's interpretation was valid; only southerners were following the hallowed intentions of the founding fathers. Moses D. Hoge, the venerated Richmond minister, reminded his audience at the dedication of Stonewall Jackson's statue: "The people of the South maintained, as their fathers maintained before them, that certain principles were essential to the perpetuation of the Union, according to the original Constitution." They defended these principles with arms, and lost; since the war, they have "sworn to maintain the government as it is now constituted." But Hoge makes it clear that "it is idle to shut our eyes to the fact that this consolidated empire of states is not the Union established by our fathers." Jefferson Davis, in an address to a reunion of the Army of Northern Virginia, reinforced this same idea when he explained why southerners fought: "She [Louisiana] sent her sons to Virginia not to battle for Virginia—not to battle for the Confederacy merely, but to battle for something which was higher and brighter than these and all else, to battle for truth and political rights, liberty of her sons and the inheritance their fathers had bequeathed to them."[15]

   Just what was this inheritance as seen from the perspective of the Lost Cause orators? For Ellison Capers it was "the great right of a free people, of Anglo-Saxon blood and history, to choose for themselves the government which would but promote their prosperity and happiness." Capers not only accused the federal government of interfering with the prosperity and happiness of the people but asserted that the South "solemnly rejected" the government as "*unfriendly, inimical,* and *injurious to our interests.*" Charles Jones was more specific, pointing out that the war was "for the conservation of home, the maintenance of Constitutional government and the supremacy of law, and the vindication of the natural rights of man." These "natural rights of man" were "sacred rights" to the orators. William H. H. Cowles asserted they "were menaced and infringed in all, and it was for this we fought."[16]

Two favorite phrases of Lost Cause oratory were "constitutional liberty" and "constitutional rights." In a speech introducing Daniel H. Hill in Richmond in 1885, William H. F. Lee reminded his listeners that Hill "comes from our sister State of North Carolina, whose gallant sons poured out their blood so freely on Virginia's soil in defence of constitutional liberty." James A. Hoyt, speaking that year in Greenville, South Carolina, defended "the principles of constitutional right and individual liberty, coupled with local self-government, for which the men of the Confederacy fought and bled and died." Stephen D. Lee asserted that the South "believed a separate confederacy with their constitutional rights retained" would be better than a "union with these rights trampled upon and ignored or held together by force." A former governor of Virginia and Confederate soldier, William E. Cameron, claimed that the "god of battle was involved against usurpation and armed invasion; and when all the blossom of youth and flower of manhood in that fair land, rallied to a flag which stood for constitutional liberty as the fathers of the republic had asserted and defined—and against despotic rule and coercion by the bayonet as George the Third had exercised."[17]

The southern apologists at every turn linked "constitutional government," "constitutional principles," "constitutional rights," "constitutional liberty," and similar phrases to the founding fathers' interpretation of the Constitution. Their argument was that southerners simply wanted the Constitution to be interpreted and followed as they and the founding fathers interpreted it, which in plain English meant that state sovereignty was more important than the federal government, that local home rule was more sacred than centralizing powers in Washington, and, above all else, that property (slaves) would be protected. Boggs spoke of the "invaluable right of local self-government" and of the "sovereignty and independence of the States, as contrasted with and opposed to the centralization of extra-constitutional powers at the Federal Capital—this was the great end at which we aimed in seeking to separate from the Union." Landon C. Bell, as late as 1929, put it this way: "The crux of the matter was the forcing by a certain group of states . . . an unconstitutional government upon other states, which did not want the change, and did not desire to surrender their constitutional rights." For Bell, the "real issue of the war was the Constitutional rights of the states"; in other words, "Was the General Government the master of the states; did it possess the lawful right to coerce a state?" Jefferson Davis used biblical images to describe the issue: "The constitution of the United States, *interpreted as it was by those who made it*, is the prophet's rod to sweeten the bitter waters from which flowed the strife, the carnage, the misery and the shame of the past, as well as the foils of the present [emphasis added]." John Sharp Williams in 1904 also made a religious crusade of the southern stand when he called the battle over "the right of local self-government" a "sacred . . . [and] ancient!" conflict. Addressing an audience of veterans in Nashville, McKim took it back to the dim past and linked the southern cause to religion as well: the southern battle "was the sacred heritage of Anglo-Saxon freedom, of local self-government won by Runnymeade, that they believed in peril when they flew to arms as one man from the Potomac to the Rio Grande."[18]

Not only did the North try to force the South to accept a "new interpretation" of the traditional Constitution, but "in some of the States the Constitution was no longer supreme," James Black informed his 1890 audience in Atlanta. "Officers in high station who were sworn to support it, 'denounced it as a covenant with death and a league with hell.' A higher law was proclaimed, and this law bounds its willing subjects to cherish an implacable hatred of a domestic institution of some of the States that was recognized by the organic law of the Union and protected by legislative enactment." Black summed up the South's charge against the North: "In brief, the equality of the Southern States in the Union was denied, the property of their citizens endangered, their domestic tranquility and order disturbed by actual invasion, their social system abused, not only their political, but their moral and religious character defamed to the world, their self-respect insulted, their liberty imperiled; and for these wrongs there was no peaceful redress in the Union, for the Constitution was not observed, the acts of Congress nullified, the process of the Federal courts obstructed and their solemn judgments denounced." Landon Bell claimed that "a fanatical group" had "made an alliance with a considerable element of self-seeking politicians, and it was this unholy group who publicly burned copies of the Constitution and who avowedly sought the destruction of the Constitutional Union—it was this group who were responsible for the wicked and unjustified war which is known by the misnomer of the 'Civil War.'" Bell assured his listeners that "it was the South, not the North which fought for Constitutional principles."[19] For southern rhetors, the bottom line regarding the constitutional issue was whether the power of the government resided in the states or at the federal level. Of course, their answer was that it resided with the states. For generations that point had been argued and defended throughout the region, and it would continue to be supported throughout the twentieth century; we will see examples of it in chapter 6 when we examine the link to the opponents of the southern civil rights movement of the 1950s and 1960s.

"The right of property in slaves was co-existent with all other rights of property": The Defense of Slavery

At the core of the debate over the interpretation of the Constitution was the issue of slavery. Although James Black asserted that "we were not inspired in that struggle by the love of slavery any more than our forefathers were in-spired in the Revolutionary struggle by the love of tea," he was one of only a few who made that case. Regardless of how some argued, as William Cowles did, that it was "false" to believe that "the war was waged on the part of the South solely for the purpose of maintaining slavery," or as Landon Bell put it more than half a century after Appomattox, that "the war was not a war to free the slaves" and that "slavery was a wholly subordinate issue, and if a cause at all of the war, a minor and indirect one," most of the Lost Cause speakers surveyed (if they discussed it at all) acknowledged slavery's cen-tral role in the conflict. General John B. Hood, for example, speaking to a reunion in Charleston, said seven years after the war that "regardless of all other causes of differences, slavery, for which we were not accountable, was the secret motor, the mainspring of the war." For Hood, the issue was simple: the North was fighting for the "freedom of the negro, and the in-dependence of the Southern Confederacy was the only means to avoid the immediate abolition of slavery." Cowles argued later in his speech that "the right of property in slaves was co-existent with all other rights of property." Patrick Calhoun believed that if slavery "could be interfered with so could other rights," and the Confederates "saw themselves at the feet of a remorse-less majority compelled to yield to whatever their more powerful neighbors might dictate." "Safety seemed not to be in the Union," according to Chief Justice Josiah A. P. Campbell of the Mississippi Supreme Court, as he re-minded his audience about the "fanatical majority hostile to the great in-stitution of the South and intent on its final destruction." Peter Turney as-serted that "the agitation of the slavery question in its several aspects, with centralization for its great purpose, was a main cause of trouble and sepa-ration." He referred specifically to the refusal of the North to honor the fu-gitive slave clause of the Constitution, and claimed the North not only ig-nored the clause but aided slaves in their escape attempts. He also attacked the North for not allowing new territories to adopt or allow slavery and not honoring the arrest and return to the southern states of persons accused of stealing slaves and taking them to free states.[20]

Almost fifty years after the guns had cooled, a speech by W. Calvin Wells at the Twenty-Fourth Annual Reunion of the United Confederate Veterans in Jacksonville was entirely devoted to defending slavery and the South's right to hold slaves as property. Wells, a prominent lawyer in Jackson, Mississippi, and a young soldier in the Confederate forces, asserted that the "true cause of the war *was Slavery.*" From his point of view, "there was practically no other contention between the North and the South but slavery. The North contended that slavery was wrong and should be obliterated, and the South contended that it was right and should be perpetuated." Late in his speech, Wells acknowledged, "I have had no regrets that I believed in slavery and fought to maintain it." He was justified, he said, because, "the law alike, of both God and man, each of which we serve to maintain, tells us in no uncertain words, that we were right."[21]

One of the arguments repeated most often relating to slavery was to blame the institution on the North and to point out that abolition sentiment took hold in the northern mind only after slavery was proved to be unprofitable in that region. Addressing a reunion in Richmond in 1907, Robert E. Lee Jr., a grandson of the Confederate general, put the burden on the North for the slave trade, a common southern argument, and quoted Thomas Jefferson, who had written that northerners "have been pretty considerable carriers of them [slaves] to others." Lee then argues that the South had tried on several occasions to stop the trading in slaves, citing petitions from both the colonies of South Carolina and Virginia to the king of England asking that the importation of slaves be ended, and the acts passed by Virginia in 1778 and by Georgia in 1798 prohibiting the importation of slaves to their respective states. Lee went on to point out that the New England states voted in favor of extending the slave trade from 1800 to 1808 during the constitutional debates. He then claims that during the Missouri Compromise debates in 1820–21 it was shown that Virginia, Kentucky, and Tennessee were "earnestly engaged in practical movements for gradual emancipation of their slaves," a "good work" that continued until the abolitionist campaign brought an end to it by their demands for the "uncompensated freeing of the slaves." For Lee, such a "wholesale attack on private property by the State has no parallel in history."[22]

General William Ruffin Cox told a Richmond audience four years later that "the institution of American slavery, which, if not the cause, was the occasion of the War Between the States, and which so long vexed the patience of the pseudo-philanthropists of Old and New England, was introduced by those governments into the Colonies against the protest of Virginia. . . . From climate and production New England found the institution unprofitable, and by prospective legislation shifted the onerous burden upon her Southern sisters."[23]

In 1917, Chief Justice Eugene B. Gary of the South Carolina Supreme Court claimed to the United Daughters of the Confederacy that "the North is responsible for the odium of slavery" and that "history shows that the South recognized the immorality of slavery long before it seemed to prick the conscience of the North." His evidence was, first, that Virginia had ceded her territory northwest of the Ohio River to the United States in 1784 and allowed the Northwest Ordinance to ban slavery in that territory. Second, a Virginian, Thomas Jefferson, had introduced the first bill to allow a slaveholder to free his slaves and wanted to introduce a provision into the Declaration of Independence to forbid slave trading, but was rebuffed by John Adams, a Massachusetts man, who was opposed to the idea. Third, Gary asserted that five Virginians (Jefferson, Edmund Pendleton, George Wythe, George Mason, and Thomas Lee) were appointed to a committee to revise the laws of Virginia and "prepare all slave-holders in the State, for the gradual emancipation of their slaves." He then claimed that Jefferson, George Washington, Henry Clay, General Lee and his mother, and Jefferson Davis were all supporters of gradual emancipation, and that John Randolph had "freed his slaves and bought territory in Ohio, where they might live." Finally, Gary pointed out that "there were in the United States at one time 130 abolition societies—106 were in the South—and 5/6 of the members were Southern slave holders." What went awry? According to the jurist, "The Abolition Crusade which began at the time of the Missouri Compromise in 1820, and which reached an intense pitch in 1839, caused Southern men to withdraw their membership in abolition societies." He goes on to assert: "The South for years had been preparing for the emancipation of the slaves. If the South had been victorious, there is no doubt that slavery would have been abolished. The emancipation would have been gradual, and as said by President Lincoln, that would have been the best for them."[24]

The orators occasionally went to great lengths to defend slavery, especially the nineteenth-century speakers. By the twentieth century, this strategy was not as popular. William Boggs sounded in 1881 much like an antebellum defender of the institution as he went to the Old and New Testaments to illustrate the biblical support for and authorization of slavery. Boggs asserted that anybody "with half an eye can see" that opposition to slavery is "totally inconsistent" with the "moral standard of the Old Testament, or of the New."

He goes on to state that it is "unquestionably recognised as a lawful institution not only in the political regulations of the Jewish State, but in the Decalogue itself." He then turns to the New Testament and shows that not only did the Apostles admit "slaveholders into the Christian Church, as all who read the New Testament know, but they freely treat of the reciprocal duties of masters and slaves, without so much as a suspicion in their minds that the relation was an evil in itself." Even Paul "went so far as to send Onesimus, a runaway slave whom he found in Rome, back to his master, Philemon." Later in that same speech Boggs returned to the theme of slavery and defended it with the same arguments used by many antebellum orators, that the slaves were infinitely better off under slavery, as they were brought under the banner of Christianity. As Boggs describes it: "They came to us debased savages, the naked worshippers of *fetiches,* the dupes of Obi-men, and of Gre-gre women, some of them being eaters of human flesh. Under our tuition they were taught the habits of order, decency, and industry. Under us they forsook their bestial idolatry. Hundreds of thousands of them, more, indeed, than have been won to Christ on heathen ground by all the devoted missionaries of Christendom, have become sincere worshippers of the God of heaven."[25]

John Brown Gordon, known as "Gallant Gordon" and the "Hero of Appomattox," was a heroic icon of the white, postwar South. In 1887 he delivered what was perhaps the fullest defense of slavery in the postwar years in "The Old South," which he presented to the Augusta, Georgia, Confederate Survivors' Association. Two years away from his election as commander in chief of the United Confederate Veterans, Gordon had for ten years been recognized as "one of the foremost southern spokesmen." Only Lee was more important in the hearts and minds of Confederate veterans. When the "living embodiment of the Lost Cause" defended slavery, it was about as close to an official pronouncement as could be made.[26] In a passage reminiscent of James Henry Hammond's famous 1858 Senate proclamation that "Cotton *is* king,"[27] Gordon developed his defense of slavery: "The agricultural development in certain sections of the South was almost wholly dependent upon this southern institution. . . . Let it, therefore, be placed to the credit of that institution that through its agency this section has . . . wrought a mighty change in the world's products, achieved an immense increase in the world's commerce, and a vast augmentation of the world's wealth and comforts."

Gordon echoes Boggs's argument about the positive influence on the slave and God's role in creating the institution for the slaves' benefit: "This institution was the instrumentality selected by Providence, for the civilization and religious training of four millions of the African race." Gordon claims that "the native African was vastly benefitted by his transfer to America and by his southern service" and that the "patriarchal care and kind government of the southern masters, and . . . the holy teachings of southern Christian women" were far superior to his "native barbaric rule." For Gordon, "the southern home was the schoolhouse in which he was instructed in the methods of civilized life, fitted in God's own time for freedom, and taught to aspire to usefulness, holiness and Heaven." Gordon believed, with many other white southerners, that "however great were the evils (and there were many) of negro slavery, it was far, very far, from being an unmitigated evil."[28]

Alfred M. Waddell argued in 1878 that "not one man in one hundred living there at that time, and perhaps not one in a thousand, would have shed one drop of his blood simply to save that institution." The next year, however, he admitted that the "destruction of slavery" by the war "was resisted to the last by us" but agreed there was a "threefold advantage" to its demise. The South was "relieved of what was an incubus upon us . . . and what was esteemed a reproach in the eyes of other nations; we have secured the inestimable benefits of free labor; and we have returned to our position in the Union . . . there to remain."[29]

"Loving honor more than life and believing in their utmost souls that their cause was just": The True Believers

Constitutional principles, states' rights, property rights, slavery, liberty—whatever issue reverberated the most in the hearts and minds of individual Confederates, there is no question that they believed it totally, committed everything to it, and held it dear for four years of bitter, bloody conflict, and for decades thereafter. There could be no doubt that they all felt they had a duty to defend their beliefs. The orators of the Lost Cause made certain their audiences were aware of the intensity of the Confederate soldiers' attitudes. Charles H. Olmstead, for example, praised the "intelligent, high spirited, daring" southern soldiers, who, "loving honor more than life and believing in their utmost souls that their cause was just," would be remembered "so long as courage, faithfulness and devotion are recognized and valued on this earth." J. Q. Marshall defended the Confederates and boldly asserted that "we have a right to feel proud of the fight we made for the principles we believed to be true." James A. Hoyt exaggerated a bit, but he praised the "grand inspiring sight to behold an entire people rise up to defend their hearthstones and as one man resist what they deemed to be aggression."[30]

Many Confederates were never willing to admit that secession and their passionate stand for their principles was wrong or unreasonable in any way.

Peter Turney was not alone when he boldly asserted: "We retract nothing, and believe the cause for which our comrades fell was just; that they and we were not traitors or rebels against the authorized action of that government from which we seceded." Many examples can be cited of this refusal to admit they were wrong or to apologize for the Confederacy. Jefferson Davis, as might be expected, stated his commitment to the cause of the South on many occasions, such as this one at the dedication of the Stonewall Jackson statue in New Orleans: "Jackson died confident of the righteousness of his country's cause. . . . [W]ith the same conviction I live today, and reverently bowing to the wisdom of Him whose decrees I may not understand, I still feel that the Confederacy ought to have succeeded because it was founded in truth and justice."[31]

Southerners believed the war clearly demonstrated two virtues: the *honor* of the South and individual southerners was at stake, and it was the *duty* of the white southerner to defend that honor. Kent Gramm, in his book *Somebody's Darling: Essays on the Civil War,* demonstrated clearly that "among the many things the Civil War was fought for, honor must be placed near the forefront"; these speeches clearly support that. Charles Olmstead believed they refused to "yield when they believed themselves to be right. . . . [Hence] honor was preserved, self-respect was preserved, the right to say to the world, 'we did our best for what we thought was just,' was still ours." The former Confederate president defined the defensive nature of Confederate strategy and submitted that "it is questionable whether war is ever justifiable except for defense, and then it is surely a duty. No calling or condition in life exempts the citizen from service when his countrymen think he can be useful." Davis never lost his belief that "the independence and sovereignty of the State carried with it the obligation of the allegiance of the citizen to his State. To refuse to defend it when invaded would be treason. To respond to its call and go forth with those who 'hung the banner on the outer wall,' was a legal duty and obligation to his home and all it held dear—alike binding on the father, the brother, the son and the citizen." In a speech during his 1878 tour of the South, Davis spoke again of duty—the duty to pass on the memories of the Confederacy "to your children as a memory which teaches the highest lessons of manhood, of truth, and of adherence to duty—duty to your State, duty to your principles, duty to the truth, duty to your buried parents, and duty to your coming children."[32]

While references to duty can probably be found in virtually every speech surveyed in this study, three more examples will illustrate this point. Rev. John Kershaw proclaimed to his Charleston audience that Confederate virtues should be the "very foundation and inspiration of our life" and that the "highest tribute we can possibly pay the memory of those who, when duty called, flung every weight and every incumbrance aside and stood forth steadfast even unto death, ready to do and to suffer" for that duty. The minister urged his audience to "be the servants of duty, not the slaves of error," and proclaim to the world, "we died for what we deemed our duty." D. B. Lucas took a unique approach in a speech in 1895 to the Virginia Division of the Army of Northern Virginia, as he calculated that for the "last two years of the war, they served, practically without pay. . . . I find that the average pay of the Confederate soldier, reduced to gold, was less that thirty-five cents per month." What could drive men to risk death for that paltry amount of pay? The "sense of duty," as they were "rewarded only by the gratitude of their countrymen."[33]

One of the frequent stories repeated by Lost Cause orators was some variation on the last words of some unknown Confederate soldier; these dying expressions always reflected this cultural foundation of duty or honor. Rev. Randolph McKim perhaps captured this appeal best: "'Tell my father I tried to do my duty,' was the last message of many a dying soldier boy to his comrades on the field of battle. . . . They were not soldiers of fortune, but soldiers of duty, who dared all that men can dare, and endured all that men can endure, in obedience to what they believed the sacred call of country. . . . But one thing they knew—armed legions were marching upon their homes, and it was their duty to hurl them back at any cost."[34]

Several orators referred to a letter Robert E. Lee wrote to his sister on the day he resigned from the United States Army, which showed clearly the appeal to duty and commitment to the southern—in this case, specifically Virginian—cause. Wade Hampton quoted Lee: "With all my devotion to the Union and the feelings of loyalty and duty of an American citizen, I have not been able to make up my mind to raise my hand against my relatives, my children, my home. I have therefore resigned my commission in the army, and save in defence of my native State, with the sincere hope that my poor services may never be needed, I hope I may never be called on to draw my sword. Think as kindly of me as you can, and believe that I have endeavored to do what I thought right."[35]

The sense of commitment to their cause and their overwhelming sense of duty to defend that cause was assured to be Truth in the eyes of the white South. With a strong sense of self-confidence in his Lost Cause, James Black reinforced this belief when he told an audience in Atlanta that in order to "justify our effort to dissolve the union as it then existed and establish for ourselves a separate nationality," he would simply "appeal to the undisputed facts of history."[36]

"All died in the performance of their duty to the political, social and religious principles held sacred by us all!": The Holy Cause

There was more to the story than the "undisputed facts of history." Lost Cause orators often dwelled on the high-minded, moral, and even sacred aspects of their failed campaign for independence. Time and time again, these speakers referred in some way to Confederates who "died in a righteous and holy cause." South Carolinian Ellison Capers reminded his Memorial Day audience in 1890 that the Confederate dead "all died in the performance of their duty to the political, social and religious principles held sacred by us all!" In a monument unveiling address in Memphis, William Y. C. Humes reaffirmed to his audience that "there is no holier spot of ground than this, strewn with the sepulchres of dead heroes of the South." The Memphis attorney and former Confederate brigadier general asserted that the monument to the Confederate dead is a "Mecca to which the youth of our country may resort in all coming time, and receive loftier aspirations, a firmer courage and renewed strength for the duties and battle of life."[37]

Jefferson Davis compared the death of bishop and general Leonidas Polk to the biblical story of Cain and Abel when referring to Polk's death in 1864: "When he fell on the field of battle, slain, like pious Abel, by his brother, the earth never drank nobler blood than his, and no purer spirit ever ascended to the Father." After the war, the mission of the South to raise monuments to the Confederate dead became a "holy mission," as Kentucky lawyer, historian, and former Confederate colonel Bennett Young told the crowd at the dedication of the Jefferson Davis Monument in New Orleans.[38]

Martyrdom and self-sacrifice appeared often as characteristics of the Confederate dead. William Boggs's remarks in 1881 were typical of this approach: "I declare, impugn it who will, that they died, true men, valiant warriors, and devoted patriots, martyrs in the defence of truth and right!" In referring to "dark stains" on the Sixth Regiment's battle flag, Boggs pointed out that these were "the sacred drops of patriot blood, which hallow, but cannot defile."[39]

Elizabeth Lumpkin, "a daughter of a Confederate" and the older sister of Katharine Du Pre Lumpkin, spoke to the veterans at a 1903 reunion in Columbia, South Carolina, reminding them that "the land in which you live is holy, hallowed by the blood of your fathers, purified by the tears of your mothers."[40] Given the cultural significance of Protestantism in the post-bellum South, such sentiments are not surprising.

"It was a sectional war . . . and the Republican Party of that day was the agency and instrumentality of a sectional and factional group": Creating a Rhetorical Scapegoat

A major rhetorical task of Lost Cause speakers was to define who was to blame for the war. Obviously, the North was to blame in the eyes of the white southerner, and the scapegoat was easy to find, identify, and attack. The North was evil in intent, and the South was good personified. An "us versus them" mentality was the order of the day, and the defensive nature of southern rhetoric, so obvious in the antebellum period, came to the forefront once again. Landon Bell clearly described the North, and the northern sectional party, as the scapegoat: "It was a sectional war, for sectional economic domination, advantage and ascendancy, and the Republican Party of that day was the agency and instrumentality of a sectional and fanatical group." Perhaps one of the clearest statements of the southern point of view was recorded by J. W. Jones in a speech to the Houston convention of the United Confederate Veterans: "If there were any rebels in that war they did not live in the South, but north of the Potomac and the Ohio. They were the men who denounced the Constitution of our fathers as 'a league with death and a covenant with hell,' and who fought to overthrow the great principles of constitutional freedom, for which Jefferson Davis and Robert Lee drew their stainless swords."[41]

S. A. Crump told his Greensboro, North Carolina, audience in 1902 that the divisiveness engendered by the North began with the Missouri Compromise, which "divided the country on acute lines and exacted great conservatism from the South to weather the storm of vilification, abuse and downright lying which blew from the North with a chilly blast." Eight years later, J. H. Martin was even more definite in his attack on the North: "It was the North that trampled under foot, nullified and destroyed the Constitution which guaranteed our rights and protected our liberties." William Lloyd Garrison burned the Constitution, and Joshua Giddings "advised the insurrection of the slaves and the extermination by them of their masters." Charles Sumner "strenuously warred against the Constitution"; William Seward "declared there was a higher law than the Constitution"; Wendell Phillips said "it is the North arrayed against the South." Martin concluded his litany of grievances against the enemy by saying, "such were the feelings of bitterness and hate entertained towards us of the South, that the assassination of our citizens by negroes was strenuously urged; the diabolical murderer John Brown who dragged innocent men and helpless children from their beds at night and brutally massacred them . . . was declared the equal of our pure and holy Savior."[42]

South Carolinian Eugene B. Gary was one who made a clear distinction between the North and the South, dating to the beginning of the colonial era, when he asserted that "the colonists of Jamestown and Plymouth Rock, were of different types and different ideals." Perpetuating the stereotypical picture of the colonists, Gary saw the Virginia colonists as patriarchal agriculturalists from the landed gentry of England and those in Massachusetts as from Puritan stock who were against the king and the landed gentry. The Jamestown settlers "came from English blood born to rule, their very instincts of life, tended to develop political leaders and statesmen." In the other section, "settling in towns and cities, made a cohesive civilization and developed traders, manufacturers, and men fitted for commercial control of the country." The Plymouth colonists were "methodical, painstaking and exact in all business calculations," whereas the "Jamestown Colony thought little of the value of statistics. They were big-hearted, open-handed, free-livers, given to hospitality, and often lived far beyond their means." The "Plymouth Colony also produced gentlemen and gentlewomen, but they were of a different type . . . they lacked the social graces, and charming manners that the civilization of the Old South produced." So, for Gary and many other southerners, these ancient differences were deeply embedded in the spirit and culture of the two sections. He blamed the war on the differences between the cultures, which were really "two distinct civilizations." This difference, "in large measure, caused the Civil War."[43] Whether these distinctions were true or false is irrelevant. They were the stories the white South believed and by which they lived.

Alfred M. Waddell described the differences between the sections in the way they fought the war. The best of the northerners went to war to conquer "a land that most of them had never seen," while the "less sincere and honorable among them were influenced by mercenary motives or a spirit of revenge." On the southern side, in contrast, "How different was it with us! No man volunteered to fight for the Confederacy who was not prompted to do so by the most natural and the most powerful incentives that can influence human conduct. Each and every one of them felt that . . . he was defending not only his heritage of liberty, but his home and his property from the lawless hand of an invader, who sought to subject them to his will."[44]

Jefferson Davis had a slightly different take on this theme of how the sections fought the war. Again, the South was virtuous and good, the North evil and cruel. Davis made it clear that the South never practiced a policy of re-taliation against the North: "While your homes were laid waste and your families often left destitute, the peaceful home of an enemy suffered not at your hands; nor had the non-combatants cause to tremble at your coming, either in their body or estate . . . you preferred to share your canteen with the wounded enemy and your half-rations with a hungry prisoner." On the other side, however, Davis painted a verbal picture of "the instances of cruel and unmanly conduct of the enemy towards the aged men and helpless women and children of our land; if it were possible to forget, it were well such acts were forgotten."[45]

For William E. Boggs, the distinction between the sections lay in the dif-ferences in the manhood and womanhood of the two cultures. He admitted that the North "excel us far in all that pertains to material civilization. But there is one product in which we have never been surpassed by you, and that is the quality of our men and women." After lifting up the examples of George Washington, Robert E. Lee, Albert Sidney Johnston, and Stonewall Jackson, Boggs affirms that "such men are formed in God's school—*the Chris-tian home*," which, to Boggs, must not exist in the northern reaches of the country, as is demonstrated by the "fearful decline in the character and in-tellect of public men in other parts of the country."[46] Even the Gilded Age figured into the Lost Cause critique of postbellum America.

A frequent and important argument raised by Lost Cause orators was the South's leading role in the nation's history. They suggested clearly that the contributions of the South were superior in every way to the quality and quantity of anything the North had brought to the founding of the nation and the development of the Union. Echoing many antebellum speakers who bragged again and again about the national leadership provided by the South, postbellum speakers rode the same horse. James Black, Julian S. Carr, and William R. Cox led the parade extolling the contributions and the strengths of the Revolutionary and early national period southerners, but many speak-ers used this same theme.

Black started with Thomas Jefferson, the "Southern statesman [who] drew the Declaration of Independence, the greatest manifesto ever issued in the name of freemen." He followed this praise with the Revolutionary War sol-diers who were "led by a Southern general," and noted that the "final sur-render of the British army was made on Southern soil." Later, the "Constitu-tional convention was presided over by a Southern president," and the system of government was put into "successful practical operation" by a "Southern president, and a Southern Chief Justice."[47]

Julian Carr was even more detailed in his description of the early southern contribution to the nation's history, as he bragged: "The South loved the Union. Had she not cause to love it? Had she not done more than any other section of the country to create it? Had she not guided and protected the Republic for nearly a century prior to sixty one?" He then lists the sixty years of southern presidents compared to the twenty-four years of northern presidents; the eighteen southern U.S. Supreme Court justices compared to the eleven northern justices; the fourteen southern U.S. attorneys general versus only five from the northern region; and the eighty-six foreign ministers from the South as contrasted to only fifty-four from the North. He claims as well that the "vast majority of the officers of the Army and Navy were Southrons." Furthermore, "her sons had stood in defense of the Union, upon the historic fields of the Revolution. . . . [and] the immortal Southerners Jefferson, Henry, Madison, Marshall, and Washington were the fathers of American liberty, and the architects of her institutions."[48]

Orator after orator extolled the role of the South in the early history of the nation. These leading heroes were, of course, Washington, Jefferson, Henry, and Madison, all Virginians, with only slightly less respect paid to other Virginians George Mason, John Marshall, Richard Lee, and Nathaniel Bacon, among others. Randolph McKim included in his litany of praise an extended passage in which he glorified "the Old South" for the "planting and training of Anglo-Saxon civilization on these Western Shores." He developed as examples the founding of Jamestown in 1607, well before Plymouth Rock in 1620, and the first representative body on American soil: the Virginia House of Burgesses in 1619. John B. Gordon included in his discussion of the "remarkable contribution made by this section to the inauguration and support of republicanism in America" the North Carolina declaration of independence in 1775, the Virginia Resolves, Andrew Jackson's leadership in the War of 1812, and the role of southern troops and officers in the victory over Mexico. As a final example of many, General William Ruffin Cox praised the Old South, and especially Virginia, and discussed Washington, "one of the grandest men known in the tide of time"; Lee, "the pages of history will be scanned in vain to discover the equal of the peerless Lee in the hour of adversity"; Mason for his writing of the Bill of Rights; Jefferson for the Declaration of Independence; and Governor Patrick Henry for his "liberty or death" address.[49]

The imbalance in economic and manufacturing development between the regions was the prime difference for Colonel Edward McCrady Jr., who concluded that "the war was one of machinery against chivalry, in which the knight-errant was bound to be run over by the locomotive, if not overthrown by the windmill." McCrady was among the most realistic and honest of the Lost Cause orators, at least on this point. Few were willing to accept as he did the inevitability of Confederate defeat.[50]

"A war that was inevitable from the adoption of the Constitution": It Was God's Will

But the inevitability of the war was another thing. Many southern speakers referred to the inevitability of the crisis leading to war, especially given the differences in the two cultures or "civilizations" the orators described, and in which the South believed. Colonel McCrady told a reunion in Richmond that it was "our lot, my comrades, under God's providence to take part in a war that was inevitable from the adoption of the Constitution."[51] Bishop Capers also believed in Providence, as he explained in detail to a Memorial Day gathering in 1890:

> The war was *inevitable.* Aye—in the mystery of that good Providence that rules in the affairs of nations, as of individuals, the war was *necessary* to our distracted country. It was necessary to end the long, bitter, relentless debate between the sections—necessary to decide issues which touched the interests and consciences of men so deeply, so thoroughly, so absolutely, that the sword could be the only arbitrator—it was *necessary* to bring peace and prosperity to our country, and to ennoble our people through the firey trial of suffering and loss through which they passed—and *necessary* it was, because it was the last resort of millions of American freemen to maintain what they cherished of American freedom and independence.[52]

Robert E. Lee's grandson acknowledged that the problems between the sections were "not of recent origin . . . it was the result of the existence of antagonizing forces which had been operating in the country for a long time, the seed being first sown by the forefathers, some in the fertile valley of the James, and some on the rock-bound coast of New England. Sectional differences exhibited themselves before the adoption of the Federal Constitution." Lee cited an order from General Washington in 1785, as the colonial army was near Boston, in which he "promised exemplary punishment to any man who would say or do anything to aggravate what he calls 'the existing sectional feelings.'"[53]

James Black believed that the "seeds of dissolution had been sown long before; their roots were in the convention that framed the Constitution. . . . The country was thoroughly sectionalized . . . irreconcilable differences pervaded not only the politics of the country, but the schools, the press, the literature, the domestic, the social and the religious life of the people. Reason had failed, argument was exhausted, there was no resort but to the sword." Again, cultural differences between the sections made the war inevitable: "One section insisted on the Union without the Constitution, the other would not submit to the Union except under the Constitution." Francis Dawson summed up the South's point of view: "the 'conflict' which the North, not the South, had made 'irrepressible,' came at last."[54]

Lost Cause orators worked desperately hard to trace the Confederacy's legacy to the Revolutionary era's heroes and to the founding fathers, who apparently for them were all Virginians—at least southerners. Some even tracked the lineage back to Runnymeade, to ancient Greece, and even to Jesus himself. The overriding goal of their rhetoric was to build and enhance the legitimacy of the Confederacy and the Civil War. Richard Weaver wrote that the "central aim was to prove that the South formed the Constitutional Union Party." For Lost Cause orators, the Confederacy was all about defending what they believed to be "traditions bequeathed to them by the Fathers": the concepts of liberty, freedom, constitutionally based government which protected property and acknowledged that true power lay with the states, not the central government. As James McPherson found in his recent study of the letters and diaries of Confederate and Union soldiers, both sides "believed themselves the custodians of the legacy of 1776"; they just interpreted that legacy differently.[55] As we will see in chapter 6, that different interpretation did not end with the early years of the twentieth century, but was still alive and well in the mid to late century, and its heart is still beating as we work our way into the twenty-first century.

4
Creating the Myths of the War

Martyrs and Scapegoats of the Confederacy

Concurrently with their defense of the right of secession and the rights of states, Lost Cause orators defined, described, and defended the mythology of the Civil War. Southerners had not believed they could lose in their struggles with the North, as they believed God was on their side and that they were correct in their belief in secession, rights of states, and slavery—but they did lose the war, secession was forever laid to rest, and slavery was abolished. In short, the region that had for generations prided itself on its manhood, military heritage, and political leadership skills found itself humiliated in spirit and crushed politically, militarily, economically, and socially—in short, to use a southern colloquialism, "They had been whupped—and whupped good!" Therefore, in their effort to offset that total defeat, Lost Cause orators found a ready audience and many opportunities to glorify and magnify that heroic effort, and to make certain that everyone in current and future generations knew of that glory, as they recalled it and as they wanted it to be remembered.

The southern Civil War generation entered the conflict confident in who they were, how they had gotten there, and where they were going. In praising the Confederate soldier, Major General Daniel H. Hill described the stereotypical white southern elite: "The independence of a country life, hunting, fishing, and the mastery of slaves, gave him large individuality and immense trust in himself. Hence he was unsurpassed and unsurpassable as a scout and on the skirmish line." Wilbur J. Cash wrote about this characteristic years later, when he pointed out "the conviction of every farmer among what was essentially only a band of farmers, that nothing living could cross him and get away with it." Cash believed this conviction was "the thing that sent him swinging up the slope at Gettysburg on that celebrated, gallant afternoon";

many Lost Cause speakers shared the conviction of the "band of farmers" as well.[1]

This "immense trust in himself" is demonstrated by the many glowing and enthusiastic references in this body of speeches to the excitement and eagerness with which the Confederate soldier marched off to war in 1861. From the start, confident they would carry the day and gain independence, southerners looked on the coming war with a positive expectation. It is easy to hear this excitement in Alfred M. Waddell's description of the bombardment of Fort Sumter in April 1861. Waddell took a train into Charleston for the dramatic event, and, after hearing the first thunder of the artillery shelling the fort, "the excitement on the train at once became intense, and the engineer, sympathizing with it, opened his valves and giving free rein to the iron horse, rushed us with tremendous speed into the historic city." Once in Charleston, Waddell and his colleagues ran through the streets to their hotel and climbed quickly onto the cupola overlooking the harbor. As he watched the puffs of smoke from James Island and saw the Stars and Stripes "float[ing] proudly and defiantly" above the besieged fort, Waddell "realized with emotions indescribable that I was looking upon a civil war among my countrymen."[2]

That excitement felt by the observers in Charleston lasted for months. John Q. Marshall reminded his veteran audience about the continuous round of "pleasure and gaiety" as "old men, women, and children came from far and near, bringing with them the best the land afforded to gratify the capricious wants of their beloved." As the soldiers of Orr's Rifles trained and prepared for war, "the sun never shone on fairer women or on braver men than were here assembled." Writing years later, Thomas Wolfe described the grand send-off as his "Chickamauga" narrator's unit marched off to war: "People were hollerin' and shoutin' the whole way. All the women folk and childern were lined up along the road, bands a-playin', boys runnin' along beside us, good shoes, new uniforms, the finest lookin' set of fellers that you *ever* seed—Lord! you'd a-thought we was goin' to a picnic from the way hit looked."[3]

Charles H. Olmstead echoed even more specifically Daniel Hill's assessment of the southerners' individuality. For him, "the most striking peculiarity of the Confederate soldier . . . was his *individuality*. . . . The lawyer, the merchant, the mechanic, the farmer, carried into service the same habit of independent thought, the same readiness of resource, the same confidence in his ability to overcome all obstacles, that had marked him in private life." Each "consecrated" his personality to the cause, and "beneath the banners of the Confederacy," helped to "place the standard of Southern soldiership upon a plane as high as that of any people under the sun."[4]

The Confederate soldier, whether private or general, believed this stereotype—especially Hill's "unsurpassed and unsurpassable" part—for at least two and a half years. Their manhood, their Anglo-Saxon heritage, their invincibility, and the ultimate victory of their forces was always on their minds. Manhood was perhaps foremost in their priorities and interests. There was no question that issues, ideology, partisanship, and patriotism all played a role, as we have seen, but for many, the war was to be a test of their masculinity, an opportunity to test themselves in the crucible of war. Major General J. H. Martin claimed there were no differences between officers and privates in the Confederate forces, "for they were all of the same noble lineage and true nobility of soul . . . each one being that highest type of genuine manhood—a Southern gentleman." The orators echoed these sentiments over and over. "What spirit animated these heroes?" asked Julian S. Carr. His answer: "A splendid manhood reared in a land of chivalry and beauty, inspired by loftiest principles, and a sublime patriotism." Charles C. Jones asserted that the memories of the "brave and consecrated past . . . justly encourage expectation of present and future loyalty and manliness. From gallant loins should spring a race competent to cope with every difficulty—willing to respond to every emergency." John Warwick Daniel was very clear about the importance of manhood for the Confederacy. In speaking of the southern soldier, Daniel pointed out, "the odds against him in war were tremendous-odds of numbers, odds of resources, odds of science, odds of art, odds of organized government and public credit, odds of opportunity to draw upon the world for reinforcements in material and in men, odds of everything but manhood. In that the Confederates never found odds against them anywhere, whatever the numbers of men, sabres, batteries and bayonets." Even states were included in discussions about manhood and manliness. General William R. Cox explained that when Virginia withdrew from the United States, the state "acted as her honor, her manhood, and her self-respect dictated."[5]

The Civil War was to be the supreme test: to hold up the standards of classical Greek and Roman soldiers, of the heroes of the Round Table, the Wars of 1812 and Mexico, to see if they could match their ancestors' courage and attention to duty. For many Confederates, that is what the war was all about; that attitude was as much at the core of the struggle as was slavery or states' rights, or constitutional liberty—maybe even more for many soldiers. William Faulkner caught the essence of this concern for manhood when he wrote in "The Bear": "Who else could have declared a war against a power with ten times the area and a hundred times the men and a thousand times the resources, except men who could believe that all necessary to conduct a successful war was not acumen nor shrewdness nor politics nor diplomacy nor money nor even integrity and simple arithmetic but just love of land and courage."[6]

Texas governor Charles A. Culberson welcomed the United Confederate Veterans to Houston in 1895 and compared the southern soldier to the Spartans, the Cavaliers, and King Arthur: "Brave as Spartans and knightly as the old cavaliers, 'somewhere in eternity within some golden palace walls where old imperial banners float and Launcelots keep guard and Arthurs reign and all the patriot heroes dwell,' they will abide with brothers."[7] John W. Daniel also traced back centuries, and held up for review their history as many white southerners saw it and believed deeply in it; manhood and masculinity was at its heart:

The Anglo Saxon race is a fighting race. The standard of Harold, the last of the Saxon kings, bore on it the figure of a fighting man; and the fighting man will be until the millennium comes, the world's grand hero. Harold died under his standard borne down by the Norman onset— died fighting like a King. The Norman overran and conquered his kingdom, but the Anglo Saxon spirit in the blood would never die. It asserted itself in the long war—it assimilated all that came in contact with it, with the prepotency that belongs to strong blood, and England the conqueror is the child of England conquered. The Confederate soldier was the scion of that conquered and then conquering strain. No army more purely American, more purely Anglo Saxon than the army of the Confederate forces ever stood in battle array. And the exploits of that army contribute the greatest military achievements in the history of the most martial race of modern times.[8]

Suddenly, however, these "greatest military achievements" were for naught. On April 12, 1865, Lee surrendered to Grant at Appomattox Court House and the deep South city of Mobile was turned over to Union forces. Six days later, General Joseph E. Johnston negotiated terms with General William T. Sherman, and all Confederate armies east of the Mississippi River were surrendered. By the end of May virtually all scattered units of the Confederacy, mostly in the West, had laid down their arms and started the long trek home. The Confederate world was turned upside down, much like the world had been inverted in 1783 at Yorktown, or as it would become different in 1964 and 1965 at the peak of the successful culmination of the civil rights movement, or in 1989–90 at the fall of the Berlin Wall and the collapse of Communism in eastern Europe, or after the attacks on the World Trade towers in 2001. The South was a different world, and southerners—black and white—were different people.

Mark Twain wrote about the importance of the Civil War in the minds and hearts of southerners in *Life on the Mississippi:* "In the South the war is what A.D. is elsewhere: they date from it. All day long you hear things 'placed' as having happened since the waw; or du'in' the waw; or befo' the waw; or right aftah the waw; or 'bout two yeahs or five yeahs, or ten yeahs befo' the waw or aftah the waw. It shows how intimately every individual was visited, in his own person by that tremendous episode." Twain understood this phenomenon well, and postwar orators likewise knew and often discussed the overall lasting impact of the war. John Temple Graves, speaking on Confederate Memorial Day in 1877, reminded his La Grange, Georgia, audience: "The memories of the war have thronged the Southern air for years, like ghostly spectres pointing with mournful fingers to the gaping wounds and mouldering ruins that rose around them." Alfred Moore Waddell, speaking in Richmond ten years later, talked about the lasting impact of the war on the participants as he described the nightmares and dreams that have haunted soldiers since the beginning of human warfare: "The pictures it [the past] has painted on our memories it has also engraved upon our hearts. In the years that have passed since the close of our bloody drama, how often in the silent watches of the night, and even in the pursuit of our ordinary avocations, has each of us found himself contemplating those pictures with all the varying emotions which they awaken!"[9] The Lost Cause orators were able to paint a glorified picture of the horrors and agonies, the violence and reality of war. They typically drew a more friendly description of the reality of the dusty, hot, wet, cold bivouacs, the grimy, exhausting marches, the trash- and flea-ridden campgrounds, and the limited food and other supplies endured by soldiers everywhere, but especially by the Confederates.

John Warwick Daniel, who bore the scars of war for the rest of his life and earned the nickname "Lame Lion of Lynchburg," painted a glowing and romantic view of the war to an audience in 1891. Daniel talked about how the memories of war were more meaningful to the veterans he was addressing than to the others in his audience, then portrayed what those reminiscences meant to the aging veterans: "It means a time as fresh in mind as though it were but yesterday, when the big guns thundered over the noble waters of Hampton Roads or when a cheer resounded like a bugle call rolled up through the battery smoke of Gettysburg, and names that signifies [*sic*] but places to those who read, sends the blood singing yet through the veins of men who were there when the Merrimac sailed forth to challenge a navy, and when Pickett's men charged an army entrenched on lofty heights." Even after the turn of the century, the memory was strong and vivid. William E. Cameron told his Richmond audience of veterans that others, even other southerners, would not understand "that the four years we spent as soldiers of the Confederacy, despite the trials and losses that attended and the unspeakable disaster that crowned them, are treasured in and sanctified to our heart of hearts as the best and proudest and dearest experiences of our life."[10]

A twentieth-century student of the war and its aftermath, Robert Penn Warren, wrote perceptively: "We may say that only at the moment when Lee handed Grant his sword was the Confederacy born; or to state matters another way, in the moment of death the Confederacy entered upon its immortality." One of the major ways that immortality was created was through the rhetoric and ritual of the Lost Cause as these speakers personalized and glorified for their ready audiences what it meant to be a hero of the Confederacy. In their efforts to overcome the stigma and shame of defeat, they glorified war in a thread that runs through most of the Lost Cause speeches: the honor, the excitement, the majesty of war. Seldom does one find depictions of the horrors of war, except in the descriptions of the southern soldier facing overwhelming odds, or the verbal pictures of his dejected and humiliated return to a desolate and destroyed home and family after the surrender. On the contrary, as James Mayo points out, "Southern defeat is given dignity by portraying the Confederate soldier as a brave and heroic figure." One of those brave and heroic figures was described in a story told by John Temple Graves: "A gallant officer of the war fell in a charge with Stuart's Cavalry, and as the shadows of death gathered dark around him and the life-blood ebbed away, he raised his head one eloquent moment and with the old warrior light in his eye, his life went out with the thrilling words: 'I will die with my face to the foe.'" A typical depiction is Rev. John Kershaw's portrayal on Confederate Memorial Day in Charleston in 1893, as he speaks of the southerner at the end of the war: "We loved to hear and tell of the sunken road at Fredericksburg, Jackson's great flank movement at Chancellorsville, Longstreet's magnificent charge at Second Manassas, the bloody angle at Spottsylvania, and the sublime but ineffectual rush of the embattled host against the foe in the three days' agony at Gettysburg. It was all we had to comfort us in those dark days." Living in "those dark days" of defeat, a destroyed social system, a crushed economy, a topsy-turvy labor system, orators of the South created a glorious antebellum era worthy of King Arthur and his knights and Walter Scott's tales of old Scotland, and a cause that was lost, but not forgotten; gone, but justified and vindicated. Southerners had to create a past that was worthy of pride, of honor, of duty. Lost Cause rhetoric and ritual urged white southerners to reflect on the Civil War as a noble, just, honorable struggle fought by true heroes for all the right, and righteous, reasons. James C. C. Black summed it up when he asserted to an 1890 Confederate Memorial Day audience in Atlanta, "We have come to celebrate the events of war."[11]

The defeated South needed a new regional identity: What did it mean to be a white southerner in the postwar years and on into the twentieth century? These speakers were trying to define, describe, and defend "what" and "who" southerners were in the context of Civil War, Reconstruction, Redemption, and Reconciliation. In order to define that southern identity on a positive note in opposition to a defeated image of themselves, these speakers painted grand word pictures of heroic Confederate soldiers and their almost Christ-like leaders. At the same time, they sought to make clear why the Confederacy failed and to identify the scapegoats of defeat, as these became an integral part of the myth of the Lost Cause.

"They fought like lions; they endured like martyrs": Honoring the Confederate Soldiers and Sailors

Many of the orators of the Lost Cause devoted their speeches not to the Lees and the Jacksons but to the private soldier, whose praise they lifted to the heavens. Always, the soldiers fought against overwhelming odds and their heroism would live forever in the hearts and minds of liberty-loving people everywhere. "They did gallant deeds," claimed John Temple Graves; "they reflected the lustre of Southern heroism, through all ages and into all lands; they illustrated her chivalry and courage in the blood drops of her sons that have empurpled every field from Austin to Appomattox. They fought like lions; they endured like martyrs, and they bore the tattered flag of the sovereign States through gloom and joy, through sunshine and through storm, with an heroic faith, a matchless patience, a splendid patriotism that will live as long as the fame of Jackson and the name of Lee." A typical tribute to the Confederate soldier is found in this speech by James A. Hoyt to the Palmetto Riflemen of Greenville, South Carolina: "They are a part of the history of our country, and when the marble shafts erected by loving hearts in honor of the Confederate dead shall have crumbled into dust, the deeds and memories of such as these will be blossoming afresh, as future generations look upon their great sacrifices, their heroic struggles for the maintenance of the right as they viewed it, and the sublime calmness with which they met final defeat."[12] This generalized song of praise was typical of many speakers, the orators apparently feeling that all within reach of their voice would personalize it with their own experiences of valor; doubtless they did.

Some events of the war forced themselves to the chamber in the oratorical canon and lent themselves well to the ritual settings primed for praise of the Confederate soldier. Gettysburg, of course, was one of these. Just seven years after the war, General John B. Hood reminded the Charleston Survivors that "if we search the annals of history we shall not find more fearless and self-reliant troops than those which formed the grand old army that stood in front of the heights of Gettysburg." Julian Carr described it vividly: "And when the charging column of Longstreet at Gettysburg, advanced slowly across that valley, in perfect order, with their red battle flags flying, and a forest of glittering steel above their heads, closing up as the shells tore great gaps in their ranks, and then rushing like a whirlwind of flame upon the Federal guns, the enemy felt a respect for the South and the Confederate soldier." Earlier in that speech, Carr had favorably compared the charge of the Light Brigade at Balaklava to the charge of the Twenty-Sixth North Carolina Regiment at Gettysburg, which "surpassed that of the Light Brigade," as it was "a tide of living valor, that Regiment eight hundred and twenty strong, [which] went into the fire of the batteries, and came out with eighty men." Carr sums up his perception of the southern soldier: as he looks "down the centuries, I see no figure comparable with the soldier of the South, clad in the simple uniform of the Confederate private, with the old slouch hat and glistening bayonet."[13]

Vicksburg was another iconic place for Confederates. Jefferson Davis praised the defenders of Vicksburg: "The heroic deeds of the defenders and the long bombardment and frequent assaults on their hastily constructed entrenchments will, when better understood, shed imperishable lustre on General Pemberton and his gallant army." Suggested in this passage is a theme reflected often by the Lost Cause orators, namely, that Confederate soldiers were superior to those of the North. John B. Hood lists and discusses sixteen major battles in which he claimed that, although southern troop numbers were significantly smaller than the Union forces, the South was the victor due to superior courage, commitment, or bravery.[14] Gettysburg and Vicksburg are never mentioned as major defeats for the Confederacy, but always in these heroic terms describing the valor of the southern soldier and the Confederate cause.

Even Union generals were called upon for testimony regarding the southern soldier. Eugene B. Gary, a chief justice of the South Carolina Supreme Court, told a Confederate Memorial Day audience in 1917 that William Sherman called the Confederate cavalry the best on earth, because "they rode around his army whenever they felt like it." Gary also told of Fighting Joe Hooker's assessment of the Confederate soldier at Chancellorsville, who, "for steadiness in action and discipline . . . had no equal."[15]

Most of the oratory celebrated the soldier in general, glowing terms, like John Kershaw's claim that what would "call forth our deepest emotions of reverence and admiration" was "their dauntless devotion to duty, their heroic self-sacrifice, their grand unselfishness in laying down their life so freely and willingly upon the altars of their country's need."[16] Some of the speakers were more to the point regarding the rigors of war. Slightly over a decade after the end of the war, John T. Graves described in detail how war worked:

> As we gaze we see again the gory glow of war—the fierce flame that leaped from cannon-mouths and flashed from musket pans—signaling the dread work of courage, blood and death. Now we see the glittering sabre gleam in the bouyant [*sic*] hand and then dash onward to the foe; the grand leaders calm, serene and dauntless in the jaws of death, breathe their own enthusiasm in the serried ranks and sound the furious charge that leads to death or victory. Then the roar and the rush, the shout, the groan, the sabre stroke, and death shots falling thick and fast, like lightening from the mountain's cloud. Then the red field, lost or won, with victor and vanquished mingled undistinguishably amid the thick volumes of sulphurous smoke that sweeps like clouds of stormy sorrow over the blood-stained field. Then the slow ambulance and the heated hospital, and the mangled, bleeding loved ones coming home to linger or to die.[17]

Another graphic picture was drawn by Daniel H. Hill in 1885, when he recalled the early days of the war, the "brimless slouch hat, the fragment of a coat, the ragged breeches, the raw-hide shoes" of the new Confederate soldier. He was "self-reliant always, obedient when he chose to be, impatient of drill and discipline." But in spite of his independence, "he was proud of his regiment, scornful of odds, uncomplaining of fatigue, ungrumbling at short rations, full of strong drollery and mockery at suffering." The abstraction of that unnamed soldier, "proud of his regiment," took on a name, when Julian S. Carr delivered a Memorial Day address on Henry Lunsford Wyatt, the first Confederate soldier to die. While "few facts" are known about the "first hero who fell in defense of Southern homes and Constitutional liberty," Wyatt will "live in the hearts of his countrymen as long as those of the great Commanders whose deeds illuminate the pages of history."[18]

John Q. Marshall touched on the horrors of war when he referred to "the armless sleeves, the scars and wounds you bear upon your persons," which "testify in language stronger than could be uttered by human tongue." S. A. Crump, speaking after the turn of the century, praised the southern soldier, who, "without arms or ordinance, without commissary or quartermaster," faced the "best armed, best equipped, and best drilled soldiers money and power could command," yet "you killed and wounded more than three times as many of your enemies as you had enlisted men on your rolls!" Bennett H. Young praised the determination that produced those scars and wounds in his speech dedicating the monument to Jefferson Davis in New Orleans. "The men of the South fought for more than a political dogma," Young asserted; "they fought for their homes and firesides, and they fought with a grim determination and unfaltering courage that made them, wherever there was equality in number and position, practically invincible." He points out the Atlanta campaign and the Wilderness battles as those in "which every Confederate soldier killed or wounded an average of more than one man on the other side." Young was especially concerned for the South always to recall the valor of the Confederate soldier as he enumerated four points that he believed exemplified the courage and righteousness of the southern cause. First, said Young, "No nation of equal numbers . . . enlisted proportionately so vast a number of men under its standards." According to him, the Confederate forces had a higher percentage of enlisted men out of the total free population of the South than "any people similarly situated who ever engaged in war." In the second place, "No nation of equal numbers ever undertook to defend so vast a territory." And third, "No great army ever fought so many battles in so brief a period or suffered such tremendous losses. . . . Proportionately, the Confederate armies had more men to die under its standards than any army that ever aligned under a flag." Finally, "No nation or country has ever shown such universal regard for the memory of its soldiers, nor builded [sic] proportionately so many monuments to voice their heroism and their valor. . . . This alone demonstrates the power of Confederate conviction, its persistence and the splendid spirit and courage of those who constituted the hosts who stood for what it held to be right."[19]

Alfred M. Waddell also praised the commitment of southerners to the Confederate cause. Like Young, he took pride in the numbers of enlistments. "The Confederate Soldier and the male citizens of the Confederate States were nearly absolutely synonymous terms," he said. "In no other country, with such a population and territory, was there ever such an approximation to universal soldierhood as was exhibited there. No other government was ever charged with 'robbing the cradle and the grave' to recruit its melting armies." He brags on his own state of North Carolina, "which was so averse to the conflict before it was begun." In spite of this opposition, there were six thousand more soldiers than there were voters, "a fact which, I believe, is without parallel."[20]

J. H. Martin summed up the feelings of many veterans as he concluded his speech to Georgia veterans in 1910; he hoped that "when your epitaph is engraved upon the marble slab that will mark your last earthly resting place there shall be inscribed thereon the grandly suggestive and impressive words, than which none import more exalted honor: 'He was a Confederate soldier.'"[21]

"There was none . . . who faltered in the hour of peril": Portraying the Glories of Confederate Leadership

Lost Cause orators consistently lifted high the reputations of Confederate military leaders. Charles C. Jones Jr., when talking about Georgia's Confederate generals, made it clear they had done their best for their homeland: "Among them all there was none, so far as I know, who proved recreant to the trust reposed, who faltered in the hour of peril, who failed in the exhibition of unselfish love of country, or who neglected to manifest those traits which should characterize a military leader contending in a defensive war for the conservation of all the heart holds most dear."[22] Similar statements of loyalty and support for their former leaders echoed through Lost Cause speeches for decades. Generals Robert E. Lee and Thomas J. "Stonewall" Jackson and President Jefferson Davis were the favorites of the Lost Cause orators.

"The greatest soldier whom the English-speaking people had produced": Robert E. Lee

Robert E. Lee was the most revered southern hero, and orators made tremendous efforts to strengthen his reputation and his status as a role model throughout the region. In a tactic designed to widen his appeal from simply a military hero, an anonymous article about the Lee monument in Richmond averred that the mourning for Lee "was for the loss of a father rather than of a leader." One of the major speeches focusing on Lee shortly after his death was General Wade Hampton's address on October 12, 1871, to the Society of Confederate Soldiers and Sailors in Baltimore. Hampton, a Confederate hero in his own right and later the Redeemer governor of South Carolina and senator from his home state, employed a common tactic used in almost all Lee eulogies: the commander was linked closely and carefully to the father of his country, another Virginian, George Washington. After spotlighting Gustavus Adolphus of Sweden, the "hero of Sweden" and "champion of religious liberty" in his victory at Lutzen in 1632, Hampton asserts that "the world has seen but twice the glorious spectacle of such an army, led by Chiefs who were his equal in virtue. Once, when Washington fought for liberty, and again, when Lee struck in the same great cause. . . . Few indeed, and far between, are the names written on the page of history, which will live as long in the esteem, the admiration, and the affection of mankind, as that of the great Virginians." Regardless of the audience, this linkage of Washington with Lee (soon to be made official with the renaming of Washington College, where Lee served as president after the war, to Washington and Lee College) was a favorite line of argument. When Archer Anderson spoke at the dedication of Lee's monument in Richmond, he bragged on the state of Virginia, remarking that "it is the singular felicity of this Commonwealth of Virginia to have produced two such stainless captains. . . . [We] will this day confirm our solemn declaration that the monument to George Washington has found its only fitting complement and companion in a monument to Robert Lee."[23]

Another common tactic was to compare Lee favorably with other generals and wartime leaders of Europe. John Warwick Daniel flatly asserted that Lee was the "greatest General ever sprung from the English-speaking race." Rev. Charles S. Vedder, in a 1901 message in Charleston before a local camp of the United Confederate Veterans, took that praise further. He first quoted Theodore Roosevelt, who called Lee " 'the greatest soldier whom the English-speaking people had produced,' " and another northern source, Dr. E. Benjamin Andrews, president of Brown University, who believed Lee " 'was a warrior worthy to rank with the greatest of all history.' " Then, using another southern source, Vedder quoted at length an Atlanta speech on Lee by Senator Benjamin H. Hill in 1874: " 'Gen. Lee was possessed of all the virtues of other great commanders without their defects. He was a foe without hate; a friend without treachery; a soldier without cruelty; . . . a victim without murmuring. He was a public officer without vices; a private citizen without wrong; a neighbor without reproach; a Christian without hypocrisy; and a man without guile.' " Not content, Vedder went on quoting Hill, " 'He was Caesar, without his ambition; Frederick, without his tyranny; Napoleon without his selfishness; . . . submissive to law as Socrates, and grand in battle as Achilles!' "[24] How could one argue with this range of comparisons—Caesar to Achilles!

The terms of surrender sought and won by Lee at Appomattox were often a source of pride and yet another example frequently used to illustrate Lee's greatness. James A. Hoyt celebrated Lee's "great concern . . . for the men of the Confederacy . . . that they were to remain free and undisturbed so long as they obeyed the laws. To this determination on the part of Lee, and not to the magnanimity of another, was due the terms of surrender . . . and the lesson taught even a conquering enemy that the 'men who wore the gray' were part and parcel of this great country."[25]

The most impressive events honoring General Lee were the various rituals relating to the monument raised to him in the capital of the Confederacy. Beginning within days of his 1870 death in Lexington, Virginia, the effort to memorialize the hero continued for almost two decades before it was completed. Organizations were quickly formed and competed to raise the money needed, competitions were held for the design of the statue, and the entire South was enlisted to participate in the fund-raising and the events in Richmond. There was a large ceremony when the cornerstone was dedicated in 1887, and another, even larger commemoration when the monument was dedicated in 1890. Naturally, speechmaking was at the core of the rituals.

Lieutenant General Jubal A. Early, the senior surviving officer of the Army of Northern Virginia, published a letter on October 25, 1870, calling for a meeting in Richmond on November 3 of "all survivors," officers, soldiers, sailors, marines, regardless of where they lived. Despite such short notice, the First Presbyterian Church was filled with "the grandest gathering of Confederate soldiers which had met since the war," including twenty-eight generals, eleven colonels, "scores of others of our leading officers, and hosts of the 'ragged veterans' of the rank and file." In his welcoming address, General Early mentioned Lee's loss of citizenship and disfranchisement by Congress and urged his listeners to "vindicate our manhood and purge ourselves of the foul stain by erecting an enduring monument to him that will be a standing protest, for all time to come, against the judgment pronounced against him."[26]

The group elected Jefferson Davis the permanent chairman of the Lee Monument Association, and Davis made a speech that "enchained the attention and thrilled every heart from the beginning to the end." Naturally, he praised Lee effusively: "It was not his to make a record, it was not his to shift blame to other shoulders; but it was his, with an eye fixed on the welfare of his country, never faltering, to follow the line of duty to the end." Davis, who had fought with distinction alongside Lee in the Mexican War, praised his efforts in that conflict and asserted that when Lee returned he was recognized "as one of the ablest of his country's soldiers."[27]

The Lee Monument Association formed an executive committee operating in Virginia and established a chairman in each southern state. General

Early was elected president, and the group urged the "co-operation of the ladies of the Hollywood Memorial Association," the Richmond ladies' group.
In a competitive situation, the ladies' organization and the larger southern
association for the Lee monument, run by the veterans, were at odds at first
and for several years over how to raise the money and what to do with it.
The women appealed quickly to "all the churches in the South to take up
a collection on the fourth Sunday in November" to go toward the monument. Several thousand dollars were raised, but this was only a small part
of the total needed. The poverty of the postwar South prevented for several
years the meeting of the budget for the monument builders—even for Lee's
monument.[28]

In 1884 the two groups were combined by an act of the Virginia Assembly,
and genuine progress began to be made. Noted artists from the United States
and Europe were sought to prepare models, from which the sculptor would
be chosen. Antonin Mercié, a French artist, was selected, and Otway S. Allen
donated the lot for the site. The cornerstone was laid on October 27, 1887. "All
of Richmond turned out," even though the "day was most disagreeably wet,
being a continuation of a three day's rain," but the "procession was imposing." Rev. Dr. Mose D. Hoge, a longtime Richmond pastor and "the intimate
personal friend of General R. E. Lee," was "most appropriately selected to
make the prayer." The cornerstone was laid with a Masonic ritual employed
by the Grand Lodge of Virginia "in due and ancient form and with the imposing rites of the order." Heavy rain hit at that moment and the rest of the
exercises were suspended until that evening at the House of Delegates, where
the ceremonies continued with the hall "packed to its utmost capacity," while
"hundreds, if not thousands," were turned away.

A poem by James Barron Hope, read by Gordon McCabe, continued the
tradition of linking Lee with Washington:

The Father of His Country
Stands above that shut-in sea
A glorious symbol to the world
Of all that's great and free;
And to-day Virginia matches him—
And matches him with Lee.

After comparing Lee to Peter the Great, Arthur and his knights, the Nor-
mans, the Goths, and the Romans, the poet returns to his theme of Lee and
Washington:

And here to-day, my Countrymen,
I tell you Lee shall ride
With that great "rebel" down the years—
Twin "rebels" side by side—
And confronting such a vision
All our grief gives place to pride.

These two shall ride immortal
And shall ride abreast of Time;
Shall light up stately history
And blaze in Epic Rhyme—
Both patriots, both Virginians true,
Both "rebels," both sublime.

Colonel Charles Marshall, Lee's military secretary, delivered the corner-stone dedication address, in which he said the purpose of the event was to "lay the corner-stone of a monument to one who is generally regarded as the most formidable enemy that the Federal Government ever encountered, and to make known to all men our veneration for his exalted character, our admiration for his great deeds, and our gratitude for his great services and sacrifices in the cause of the Southern people."[29]

Finally, two and a half years later, the monument was ready, and was moved to Richmond by train. On May 7, 1890, "a simple announcement of the press that the statue of the beloved commander would be removed from the cars . . . to its destined site, convoked . . . a dense throng. . . . It was a mass of both sexes, representing every age and condition. . . . by 4:30 o'clock it was a mass more than a half mile in extent. The street was packed, windows and balconies were thronged, housetops were covered."

The published account of the transporting of the statue to the site tied Lee again to Washington as it told the story of the moving of Washington's statue from the train to its site in 1858. The horses and mules originally hitched to pull the wagon did not pull well together, so ropes were pulled by men and boys who "easily, gracefully, and expeditiously" hauled it to the site. With that precedent before it, the Lee Monument organizers made no attempt to use mules or horses, but immediately men, women, boys, and girls seized the ropes and pulled the wagons hauling the several pieces of the statue to its location. The account claimed that "the heaviest wagon was drawn with ease. Only the slightest touch of the ropes were required, so great was the number of people pulling." Not only were many of the population of Richmond enlisted in the transporting of the statue, but most of the white population seemed to be involved in some way. The written account pointed out that "on all the porches and at the windows the fair women of the city were to be seen. Confederate flags were waved. . . . To the groups of matronly ladies the picture brought back recollections of the terrific conflict. . . . To the fair girls the view stirred in their hearts the thoughts of war. . . . To the young men it fired their hearts with patriotism, and impressed more indelibly on their minds the facts that are recorded in the 'Lost Cause.'" After the wagons reached their destination, there was a frenzy of rope-cutting, so that everyone could have a souvenir. "Many of those who tugged at the rope, male and female, wore bits of rope on the breast on their return as badges of honor."

The celebration continued into the night, as the band of the First Virginia Regiment gave a concert judged as an "excellent rendition of southern airs." The last piece played was "Dixie," and as "the first notes of this delightful old southern melody floated out on the evening air cheer after cheer arose from thousands of throats. Some of the old veterans were especially demonstrative, and the populace generously joined in the cheering, which was genuine and vociferous."[30]

The impromptu celebration while moving the statue into place was just the beginning of the great event. May 29 was the grand day for the dedication of the monument, and according to the report, it dawned clear and balmy, "with all nature in its gayest garb." Celebrants began to gather on the twenty-eighth, and at 6:00 A.M. the first of many special trains arrived from around the region. By 9:00 A.M. the crowds began to line the streets along the parade route. There were an estimated fifty thousand visitors, which was said to be the largest crowd ever gathered in the Virginia capital. Militia units and veterans from across the South and from as far north as New York attended. It was an exciting day in Richmond, and "it was asserted on all sides that the parade, decorations, and everything connected with the jubilee exceeded anything ever witnessed in the South."

As early as 10:00 A.M., many people had gathered at the monument site, where veterans with muskets were stationed as guards around the statue. A grandstand for two thousand people had been built near the monument, and a dais was arranged for about one hundred people. At 2:15 P.M. the procession reached the site and the dignitaries began to take their seats. It took more than another hour for all the marchers to reach the scene. At 3:45, Governor McKinney called the ceremony to order and began the introductions.

According to the historical account of the event, one hundred thousand persons attended the unveiling ritual. Archer Anderson was the orator of the day and delivered a lengthy memorized address, which was noteworthy for the reporter, as he claimed that he never referred to his manuscript while speaking. Although "it was a matter of profound surprise to many that Colonel Anderson could deliver his speech without reference to manuscript," he had a reputation for memorizing his orations; the account mentioned an earlier address he had delivered from memory at the reunion of the Association of the Army of Northern Virginia.

After Anderson finished his speech, General Joseph E. Johnston unveiled the statue of Lee and his horse Traveller to the "cheers of 100,000 people, the roar of the cannons and the thunder of the muskets. . . . Hats and handkerchiefs were thrown into the air. . . . [T]he smoke from the guns become so thick the Exposition buildings were invisible from the monument." Some troops then fought a sham battle, "which stirred the hearts of the old soldiers."

That night, a two-and-a-half-hour fireworks display offered a "fitting close to the ceremonies of the day." One of the pyrotechnic displays was a picture of Washington with the legend "The First Rebel," which "elicited much applause," but the "picture of the night was a very correct representation of the Lee monument. When this piece was set off the applause of the crowd was tremendous."[31]

The statue that generated all this attention is an equestrian statue with Lee riding Traveller. The total height of the work is almost sixty-two feet, and an early historian of the monuments of the Confederacy described it as a "classical composition, Grecian and modern. . . . The lion's head upon the pedestal denotes courage, the oak, endurance, the laurel Lee's right to be crowned as one of the world's great heroes." The total cost of the monument was about sixty-five thousand dollars.[32]

Two other monuments to Lee were erected before the Richmond statue; both provided ample opportunity for Lost Cause oratory. One was the recumbent figure of the general on his mausoleum at Washington and Lee College in Lexington, and the other was a towering column topped with a bronze statue of Lee in New Orleans, dedicated on Washington's birthday, February 22, 1884. The story of the New Orleans monument is similar in some respects to the Richmond campaign. As the historian of the monument writes: "Those were dark days with every citizen of Louisiana, and poverty and anxiety sat by every honest hearthstone." After the founding of a memorial association in 1870, just after Lee's death, the fund-raising campaign struggled, and by 1876 it was being debated whether it should continue. When the directors of the association "stood face to face with the proposition to abandon the work, their patriotic impulses refused to accept it, and inspired them with the determination at all hazards to complete it." So they did, with New York sculptor Alexander C. Doyle creating the bronze figure of Lee and local architect and Confederate veteran John Roy preparing the foundation and the granite shaft on which it would rest. The entire project cost more than thirty thousand dollars. At the ceremony, President Jefferson Davis was an honored guest, along with Davis's daughters and Lee's daughters, Mary and Mildred. The organizers of the event prepared seats for thousands around the monument. The seats were filled with ladies, and the surrounding streets were packed with New Orleans citizens "eager to do honor to the memory of Lee." Charles E. Fenner was scheduled to be the orator of the day, but just as the ceremony was to begin, a storm "burst in torrents of rain which lasted for hours, dispersing the immense audience and rendering it impossible to proceed." Fenner's oration was later published for wide dissemination.[33]

Another early monument to the Confederate commander was a recumbent statue of Lee in Lexington, Virginia, dedicated by John W. Daniel on June 28, 1883. The story of the creation of this monument is typical of so many of these memorial efforts. On the day of Lee's funeral in Lexington, a group of former Confederates met in the courthouse and "resolved to take steps to erect a monument in honor of their great leader." The Lee Memorial Association was formed and began the difficult task of raising the money. Edward V. Valentine, a "distinguished Virginia sculptor," was selected to carve the statue, and Mrs. Lee suggested a recumbent figure of white marble to be placed over Lee's body in the chapel at Washington College. Donations came in slowly from around the South. On April 1, 1875, Valentine completed his work, and the monument was brought to Lexington and stored in a room at the now-renamed Washington and Lee College. Later commentators called it "one of the most noted works of art in this country." The association turned to the work of building the mausoleum to house it, and again, money slowly drifted in from the region. In May 1877, architect J. Crawford Neilson of Baltimore offered to design the mausoleum at no expense, and his offer was accepted. The cornerstone was laid on November 29, 1878, but funds ran out again in 1880 before the building was completed. The association, feeling that they had raised their limit, offered to transfer the building and the monument to the trustees of Washington and Lee if they would agree to fund the five-thousand-dollar balance needed to finish the structure. The trustees agreed, and the project was finally completed twelve years after it began. June 28, 1883, was selected for the dedication, and Daniel was chosen as the orator of the day.

The citizens of Lexington and Rockbridge County spared nothing to highlight the event and welcome the thousands of visitors who flocked to the small community. Special trains on the Richmond and Allegheny and the Shenandoah Valley Railroads were run to Lexington, and an estimated eight to ten thousand people attended the event. On the morning of the twenty-eighth, General Wade Hampton led a procession to the grave of Stonewall Jackson in the Lexington Cemetery. Later, Daniel "for three hours held his audience by the spell of his eloquence, moving it now to applause, and now to tears." A salute was fired from two guns used by Jackson at the Battle of First Manassas, where he earned his nickname, Stonewall, and the recumbent figure was unveiled by Jackson's daughter. Immediately after the ceremony, and until dark, the throngs of visitors filed through the building to view the statue. That night, "houses of citizens of the town were everywhere thrown open, and handsome entertainments were provided at many of them."[34]

Daniel's oration was well received. The reporter for the *Baltimore Day* said the "Lame Lion of Lynchburg" was "listened to with breathless attention, the audience at times being fairly carried away by some of his highest flights of eloquence." The *Washington Post* devoted its entire front page to the speech, and reprints of it were in "constant demand." L. Q. C. Lamar, a famed orator in his own right, wrote that the speech would "be one of the great enduring orations of the 19th century."[35]

"A Natural Genius for the Art of War": Stonewall Jackson

The little town of Lexington, Virginia, was the final resting place for the two major heroes of the southern Confederacy, Robert E. Lee and Thomas J. "Stonewall" Jackson. The latter had made a career as a professor at the Virginia Military Institute, and after his death at Chancellorsville he was buried in Lexington. Lee became the president of Washington College and was buried on its campus, not far from Jackson's grave. Both men were effusively praised by orator after orator in the postwar South. General Daniel H. Hill said in Richmond in 1885, "Every one with Southern blood in his veins places in the front rank of the world's great commanders, the two modest men who sleep so quietly and so unostentatiously at Lexington, Virginia. Every one with Southern blood in his veins cherishes in his inmost soul the memory of their great deeds as a precious legacy to the land they loved so well." General John B. Hood told the Survivors' Association of South Carolina that "in time of battle our Confederate soldier was equal from two to three of the foe. Our Generals likewise as a body were superior, and two of them must rank with the most illustrious of the world." After listing Greek and Roman soldiers of antiquity, Charlemagne and Napoleon, Frederick the Great, Von Moltke, Marlborough, Wellington, and Washington, Hood contends that "in no instance do we find surpassed the military genius nor its rare combination with Christian virtue, which distinguished Robert E. Lee." Hood then calls attention to Jackson: "It is almost as difficult to adduce a parallel when I contemplate the exalted character and the heroic deeds of Stonewall Jackson." He then links the two: "Lee and Jackson were farther removed from doubt, in time of fiercest conflict, than any generals with whom I have had the honor to serve. They possessed that intuition of the true warrior, which makes him bold in strategy and determined in battle." Eugene B. Gary extolled their virtues in 1917: "The verdict of the world is that Robert E. Lee and Stonewall Jackson are beyond question, the greatest Generals the United States has ever produced."[36]

With this high praise, it can be expected that Jackson would have his share of monuments built in his memory. Two major statues were erected for Jackson, one in New Orleans and one in Richmond, the latter on what became Monument Avenue, fittingly near to Lee's statue. The Richmond memorial was erected first, in 1875. Moses Drury Hoge, a leading Presbyterian pastor in Richmond, was the orator of the day. A biographical sketch of Hoge expresses the belief that this speech was "perhaps the noblest oration of his later life." According to the Charleston, South Carolina, newspaper accounts of the ceremonies, the event was the "most imposing pageant ever seen" in Richmond. A history of Virginia in the postwar years asserts there were forty thousand persons watching the two- to three-mile-long procession to the statue. The speaker's stand was crowded with a "'who's who' of Virginia Confederate and political leadership." David Blight sums up the importance of the event: "As a public ritual and a mass statement of the meaning of Confederate defeat and Southern revival, the event had enormous political significance."[37]

Hoge was perfectly suited to deliver the oration of the day. Currently serving as the moderator of the Presbyterian General Assembly, he was well known for his devotion to the Confederate cause and for a blockade-running trip to England during the war to obtain Bibles for southern soldiers. Hoge "was not only an orator but a teacher.... He never for a moment relinquished or lowered his conception of the teaching function of the ministry," and this strategy is apparent in this oration. Hoge sounds more like a professor than a minister, as he answers the rhetorical question, "How has he, the most unromantic of great men, become the hero of a living romance, the ideal of an inflamed fancy, even before his life has been invested with the mystery of distance?"

Hoge has three explanations for Jackson's fame. In the first place, "he was the incarnation of those heroic qualities which fit their possessor to lead and command men, and which therefore always attract the admiration, kindle the imagination, and arouse the enthusiasm of the people." Then follows a lengthy list of Jackson's "distinctive characteristics as a soldier and commander": "a natural genius for the art of war . . . ; a power of abstraction and self-concentration which enabled him to determine every proper combination and disposition of his forces . . . a conviction of the moral superiority of aggressive over defensive warfare . . . ; an almost intuitive insight into the plans of the enemy, and an immediate perception of the time to strike the most stunning blow, from the most unlooked for quarter; a conviction of the necessity of following every such blow with another, and more terrible, so as to make every success a victory."

The second trait was more subtle and sublime. "His was the greatness which comes without being sought for its own sake—the unconscious greatness which results from self-sacrifice and supreme devotion to duty"—that foremost southern cultural icon: duty. The third characteristic that endeared Jackson to the people was, for the minister, the most important: "the sincerity, the purity, and the elevation of his character as a servant of the Most High God." His renown as a soldier of his country placed him in a position to be known as "a soldier of the cross." People cannot think of Jackson without "associating the prowess of the soldier with the piety of the man . . . his great military renown is the golden candlestick, holding high the celestial light which is seen from afar and cannot be hid." While one would expect a minister to focus on his subject's Christian faith, a hard-charging general—the only person to earn a star in both the Confederate service and later in the uniform of the United States—was almost as laudatory in his dedication of the statue to Jackson in New Orleans six years later.[38]

On May 10, 1881, the tomb for the Army of Northern Virginia Association and the statue to Jackson were unveiled and dedicated in the Crescent City. General Fitzhugh Lee, a nephew of the Confederate commander, was the orator of the day, but there were several other noteworthy speeches. The memorial to Jackson was fifty feet tall, capped by a larger-than-life statue of Stonewall. According to the anonymous report of the proceedings, the "likeness is excellent, the form and posture well nigh perfect, while the old cadet cap, tilted on the nose, the cavalry boots, the uniform coat, the spurs, the sabre . . . combine to give not an ideal Jackson of the artist's fancy, but the veritable 'old Stonewall,' whom we used to see standing on some roadside, along which his veterans were hurrying into line of battle." In front of a crowd estimated at twelve to fifteen thousand observers, Stonewall's daughter, Julia, pulled the cord that revealed the statue, while a military band played "Hail to the Chief."

In a passage depicting the setting in old New Orleans, John B. Richardson, the president of the Army of Northern Virginia Association, painted a verbal picture of the spirits of Jackson and the southern martyrs: "The first rays of the morning sunlight, and the last gleam of evening will linger around yon silent, solitary sentinel, and in the still, quiet watches of the night, when the pale moon's beams fall upon the dreamless sleepers here, the spirit of the great Stonewall, loosened for a while from the prison-house of the faithful departed, will wander forth to guard the noble band of martyrs who are slumbering here in peace."

After this mystical and ghostly depiction of the tomb and statue, Fitzhugh Lee delivered the oration of the day. The Virginian was "received with enthusiastic cheers, was frequently interrupted with applause and delivered in admirable style, an eloquent and most appropriate address."[39] Lee told the story of Jackson's early years, when he was orphaned and sent to live with a relative. That relationship did not prove successful, and the youngster walked eighteen miles at age eight to his father's half brother. A year later, he left that home with an older brother, and they took a Mississippi River flatboat to an island in the river where they cut timber and sold it to passing steamboats. Jackson soon became ill with malaria and returned home. Later, he was selected to attend West Point, graduated, fought in the Mexican War, and became a professor at Virginia Military Institute. Lee praised Jackson's service to the "Southern cause" and said the monument would "serve as a beacon light to show the coming generations how to march with steady step in imitating his virtues," which he identified as "self-denial," "moderation and justice," "wisdom and courage," "purity and piety," and "simplicity and grandeur," all traits that devoted southern youth should try to emulate.[40]

As soon as Lee finished his oration, there "were loud and persistent calls for President Davis. When he arose, the scene was inspiring. Men flung their hats around their head and cheered wildly, the women waved their handkerchiefs, and as with clear, ringing voice and graceful gesture he delivered his gem of a little speech, he was again and again interrupted with an enthusiastic applause. Which showed that he is not only still 'a Master of assemblies,' but has a warm place in the affections of the people." Davis added his praise of Jackson, stressing his character as did Hoge and Lee: " 'Jackson's character and conduct so filled the measure of his glory that no encomium could increase or adorn it. When he came from the academic shades of the Virginia Military Institute, who could have foreseen the height of military fame to which the quiet professor would reach. He rose with the brilliancy of a meteor over the blood stained fields of the Potomac, but shone with the steady light of the orb of day, a light around which no evening shadows gathered, but grew brighter and brighter the longer it shown.'"[41] Quite clearly, Thomas J. Jackson was one of the major heroes for southerners, and the dedications of these monuments served as strong focal points for enhancing and spreading his reputation around the region. There is considerable evidence of the central position he held in the Confederate pantheon, and a recent biographer points out that Jackson's death by "friendly fire" at Chancellorsville "began the defeat of the Confederacy" in the minds of many southerners. A Lexington citizen, among many others, wrote that Jackson's death was "the first time it had dawned on us that God would let us be defeated."[42]

Alfred M. Waddell perhaps summed up the essence of the region's love and veneration of Jackson when he painted a vivid verbal command for the ex-Confederates listening to him: "Just sixteen years ago, God's courier, mounted on the pale horse, beckoned Stonewall Jackson to the shores of immortality, and the great warrior, ere he robed himself in his garb of glory for the final march, gave his last command, 'Let us cross over the river.' The advance column has obeyed, and now rest with him on their eternal camping ground, beneath the shade, amid the green pastures, and by the still waters. We follow."[43] Doubtless, many in the audience looked forward to crossing over the river and seeing in heaven the hero of First Manassas.

"The Sublime Endurance of a Martyr": Jefferson Davis

Jefferson Davis was a third vitally important figure for southern rhetoric and ritual. Often maligned during and after the war for micromanaging so much of the Confederacy's war effort, he was still loved and revered by many former Confederates, and his luster grew as the years moved on and the various contentious issues of the war years dimmed in the memory. Wade Hampton, perhaps only slightly less iconic than the trio of Lee, Jackson, and Davis in the eyes of white southerners, spoke of Davis in almost Christ-like terms as early as 1871. For Hampton, Davis "lived to bear vicariously for us in his own person, with the sublime endurance of a martyr, the sufferings, the humiliations, the wrongs of the whole South." In his 1872 oration to the South Carolina Survivors' Association, General John B. Hood proclaimed, "Thanks, a thousand times thanks, that we were saved from the disgrace and humiliation by the ability, firmness and patriotism of Jefferson Davis."[44]

In late April and early May 1886, Davis took a highly successful public tour from his home at Beauvoir on the Mississippi Gulf Coast to Montgomery, Atlanta, and Savannah. John B. Gordon talked about that outpouring of southern pride in Davis when he spoke to Confederate veterans in Augusta, Georgia, one year later. Gordon had just discussed the funeral that had been held for

General Ulysses S. Grant, and he moved on to a description of Davis's tour: "So on the other hand the almost equally great demonstration in the South one year ago, over the living President of the dead Confederacy, was potential in the formation of southern character. Every bonfire that blazed on the streets of Montgomery; every cannon shot that shook its hills; every rocket that flew on fiery wing through the midnight air; every teardrop that stole down the checks of patriotic southern women, was a contribution to the self-respect, the character, and the manhood of southern youth."[45] In sum, southern young men should emulate the character of Jefferson Davis, and it was the duty of the South to hold him up to the youth as a viable role model.

James C. C. Black fully supported this appeal to the valor and devotion of President Davis, and his suffering for the South, as shortly after Davis's death he called for a monument in his memory and honor: "As President of the Confederacy, he never swerved in his devotion to the Cause for which you imperilled your lives, and when it fell, through no fault of his, but overcome by numbers, he suffered for you in chains and dungeon. By what he was, and did, and suffered, I charge you this day with the patriotic and sacred duty of honoring and venerating his name and memory and planting somewhere on this Southern soil a monument that shall forever perpetuate the purity and strength of his character—stand as a worthy expression of your love and devotion, and be an inspiration to your descendants in all the ages to come."[46]

Naturally, southerners did not have to be persuaded to fund one or more monuments to Davis. Richmond took the lead with its addition to what became known as Monument Avenue. On July 2, 1896, under balmy air and clear skies, the cornerstone was laid for the monument to the Confederate president. The Masonic ceremony of dedication for the cornerstone began at 4:20 P.M. in front of the large crowd. After the ritual was complete, the president of the Davis Monument Association, J. Taylor Ellyson, introduced the orator of the day, Stephen D. Lee, a renowned Confederate general. Lee early on built a case for how Davis had gone from "the rugged surroundings of a frontier State. . . . [won] the triple glory of the soldier, the orator, and the statesman. . . . became the ruler of 7,000,000 people." But his "government was overwhelmed, his fortune swept away. He was bound as a criminal and prosecuted for his life. He became an exile . . . denied the rights of citizenship . . . defamed, denounced, insulted, ridiculed to the hour of his death. . . . [A]nd yet he died by millions more sincerely mourned and deeply beloved than any other man in the history of the nation." Lee believed that if Davis had been executed after the war, "he would have been the most conspicuous figure in American history." In spite of all his troubles, the South loved Davis and the orator discussed at length many reasons why, summing up: "He was the accomplished soldier, a great statesman, and a consummate orator. He was the typical Southerner of his day and of all times."[47]

William Boggs praised Davis's postwar apologia, *The Rise and Fall of the Confederate Government,* as a "protest against hasty and harsh judgment of us." Boggs urged his audience to ensure that "your children become familiar with that able discussion, and they will be in no danger of growing ashamed of the cause for which you contended, or of the manner in which you acquitted yourself."[48]

Citizens of New Orleans, a short distance from Davis's postwar home on the Mississippi Gulf Coast, dedicated a monument to their hero on February 22, 1911. As usual, it was difficult in the impoverished South to raise the necessary funds. The local monument association was founded in 1898, but it did not get its first substantial contribution until 1905. At one point, the group considered simply establishing a chair of history at a local college or some other fitting memorial, but the association finally received enough state and local government aid to build the monument. On a "raw and chilly" day, as winter can be in New Orleans, several thousand southerners braved the weather and attended the ceremony at Canal Street and the newly named Jefferson Davis Parkway. A notable part of the ritual was the sight of five hundred New Orleans schoolchildren dressed in red, white, and blue sitting in a design depicting the Confederate battle flag. Louisiana governor Jared Y. Sanders echoed Stephen Lee's assessment of Davis, pointing out that Davis "is symbolic of all that is and has been good in Southern manhood. In every place, and under every condition, he proved himself a man; fighting for his country on bloody battlefields of the Mexican war . . . he typified the valor of Southern troops. . . . As a senator from the commonwealth of Mississippi, he upheld the best traditions of the South."

Bennett H. Young from Kentucky was the orator of the day. He and most of the speakers who extolled Davis's virtues developed a narrative of all the trials and adversity through which Davis had passed in his career, especially his suffering at the hands of his Union captors and his disfranchisement after the war. But, for Young and the others, Davis dealt with the issues "as to command the respect and confidence of those with and for whom he acted." As in many of the speeches that mentioned Davis, Young, while not specifically mentioning Jesus, referred to Davis's suffering in such a way that, for the overwhelmingly Christian audiences in the postwar South, the allusion was clear: "As sons and daughters of the South we are here to-day to declare this spot sacred, and ever to remain sacred, in the Southern hearts . . . to proclaim our love for him because of the sacrifices he made at the call of duty, and to bedeck with fresh laurels and with revered praise him who bore the deepest humiliation for the Southern people." It was especially in prison that Davis "bore incalculable suffering for the Southern people . . . [he] realized that he was enduring all this for the men and women of the South, and submitted himself to his surroundings with a dignity that touched the hearts of his countrymen."[49]

"How sublime their influence, their patience, their sufferings, their aspirations, and their example!": Reinforcing the Pedestal for Southern Women

The soldier and the general were not the only southern citizens praised and celebrated in Lost Cause rhetoric and ritual. Southern women were described as strong women making deep sacrifices for the southern cause; as angels on earth carrying out spiritual and inspired tasks for their families and the support of the Confederacy; and after the war, as holding the home place together in the face of defeat, destruction, and desolation. They were shown as having the character and qualities to inspire and lead the campaigns to honor the Confederacy and the veterans of the war, through monument building and Memorial Day celebrations. All the pictures of the southern woman came together in Julian S. Carr's speech on Memorial Day 1894. Harking back to classical stories, Carr reminds his audience: "We are thrilled by the splendid heroism of the Greek, Roman, and Carthaginian women, as they sustained the fainting spirits of the defenders of their countries, but history records nothing equal to the patience under unparalleled hardship, courage in the face of peril, and hope in the darkest hours of misfortune, shown by the women of the South since sixty-one."[50]

The first sacrifice, of course, was the male members of their families: their sons, brothers, and husbands who were sent off to war. Francis W. Dawson reminded his audience in a speech on "Our Women in the War," that every white southern family was touched, and many in a large way. According to the Charleston journalist's accounting, a family in Georgia had twelve members in the Confederate service; nine were killed. The Shuler family of Orangeburg, South Carolina, had fifty-one direct family representatives in the southern forces, and the Easterling family in the Palmetto State had sixty-three. John B. Gordon spoke of the "Spartan courage and self-sacrifice of Southern women. . . . sending their husbands and their fathers, their brothers and their sons to the front. . . . I had witnessed the Southern mother's anguish, as with breaking heart and streaming eyes she gave to her beloved boy her parting blessing: 'Go my son,' she said, 'go to the front. I perhaps will never see you again; but I freely commit you to God and to the defense of your people.' "[51]

Giving up family members was not the only sacrifice southern women made. They served in hospitals and homes for the wounded; as Rev. Charles S. Vedder pointed out, the "organized ministry of loving hands went out from our city to the soldiers in camp and on the march and in hospital." Dawson described in some detail two services established by Confederate women. In Columbia, South Carolina, women opened Wayside Hospital in March 1862, which remained open until February 1865. Supported entirely by voluntary contributions, the women cared for seventy-five thousand soldiers, and Dawson claimed the service was the "first of its kind, not only in this country, but in the whole world." Women in Charlottesville, Virginia, opened the "Ladies Kitchen" in 1862, and, "unused to labor as they were, these gentle women kneaded huge trays full of bread and withheld not their hands from any task, however irksome and laborious."[52]

Not only were they burdened with everyday household tasks, farms, plantations, and other family enterprises, but the women had to raise money for food, clothing, and medical supplies for the armies. Around Richmond, according to W. M. Hammond, some four hundred thousand dollars' worth of food and clothing was "put into the hands of the struggling armies" over one winter. Hammond challenged the men of the South to recognize what he called these "Spartan Mothers of the South" for their "matchless heroism [and their] unselfish devotion and the patriotic labors of these Cornelias of the Nineteenth Century."[53]

Dawson compared the situations of northern women and their southern counterparts; as one can imagine, Confederate women were found to be in a much more difficult condition. Not only did the South have a higher number of persons risking their "own flesh and blood than the North risked, family by family," but "Northern women had no special care or discomfort." Dawson believed "they were in no danger themselves," as they were not faced with southern generals who were like northern generals such as Butler, Sheridan, or Sherman, who would "taunt and upbraid them, to strip them of their most precious mementoes, to steal or scatter their scanty store of provisions and burn their homes over their head." In addition, the privations endured by the southern women became more and more difficult as the war worn on. "There was actual lack of meat and bread in many parts of the South. And, behind the black spectre [of slave revolt], there was the threat of rapine and revenge whenever a raiding party should come within reach." Once medicines were exhausted, women had to resort to homemade "remedies and devices" and had to "go to the woods for bark, and roots, and herbs."

They made quinine out of dogwood and poplar, used gourd and persimmon seeds for buttons, used sassafras for yellow dye, made tea from blackberry leaves, and made coffee from parched meal, rye, wheat, or corn until they discovered that "parched sweet potatoes was the best substitute for coffee." Dawson quoted from a number of women's reports of their struggles and deprivations. One of the most dramatic was that of Miss A. C. Clark of Atlanta, who claimed to know women "to walk twenty miles for a half bushel of coarse, musty meal with which to feed their starving little ones. . . . Yet these women did not complain, but wrote cheerful letters to their husbands and sons . . . bidding them to do their duty and hold the last trench."

Captain Dawson ended his psalm to the women with a tribute to the men and to the women of the Confederacy, but it is clear where his love lies: "The men, the soldiers, were the strong right arm, the mighty body of the Southern Confederacy, as with spirit undaunted they trod, with bleeding feet, the way of the Southern Cross. But as the men were the body, so the women were the soul. The men may forget the uniform they wore—it is faded and moth-eaten today. But the soul, the spirit in our women incarnate, cannot die. It is unchangeable, indestructible, and, under God's providence, for our vindication and justification, shall live always—forever!" Charles C. Jones Jr. echoed the words of countless Lost Cause orators in a speech to his Confederate veterans organization in Augusta twenty-four years after the close of the war: "Through the long and dark hours of that protracted struggle for independence how sublime their influence, their patience, their sufferings, their aspirations, and their example!"[54]

After detailing many of the contributions that southern women made in the war years and after, Julian Carr summed up: "Her influence inspired him in battle. Her hand soothed him in sickness. Her voice encouraged him in poverty. Her efforts rears [sic] monuments to perpetuate his memory. And the beautiful memorial custom of strewing Spring's sweetest, rarest treasures upon his grave, is an Institution sanctified by her love. God bless the women of the South."[55]

"The Southern army, half clad, half fed, half armed": Why the South Lost

So far we have seen part of the mythology of the Confederacy and how the orators praised the soldiers as well as the leaders, paid great tribute to the women, and, overall, glorified war. The rest of the mythology was not, of course, so glorious and wonderful; after all, the South had lost the war, and southerners have been dealing with that defeat since 1865. Defeat, destruction, devastation, and demoralization was the southern fate, and orators of the Lost Cause were determined to develop for their audiences a master narrative of why the Confederacy failed and their perceptions of just how extreme conditions in the South really had been in the following decades.

White southerners had been taken by surprise by the final arbitrament of the sword. For a good portion of the war, many believed that the South would prevail, and some thought that to the very end. But after Jackson's death at Chancellorsville in May 1863, the "high water mark of the Confederacy" on July 3, and the surrender of Vicksburg to Grant on the next day, some began to doubt. Southerners' belief in the invincibility of their soldiers and generals began to fade as the handwriting began to appear on the wall. Alfred M. Waddell spoke of that fateful July weekend: "That they would succeed was the universal conviction up to the 4th of July, 1863. Until that date I never saw a soldier who entertained the least doubt of it for a moment; but when the wires whispered simultaneously the disastrous news from Vicksburg and Gettysburg on that fatal day, a change was perceptible in the serious faces which met one at every turn, and it was evident that, for the first time since the war began, an uneasy suspicion as to the final result was beginning to force itself, both upon the army and the people." John B. Gordon, in his lecture on the "Last Days of the Confederacy," presented many times on the lecture circuit around the country, admitted that "the simultaneous fall of Vicksburg and the disaster at Gettysburg did set the Southern boys to thinking, and right seriously, about the future."[56]

Orators in the waning years of the nineteenth century and into the opening decade of the twentieth still spoke in glowing terms of their warriors and their spirit, but they made it clear why, in their mind, the South had lost. The defeat was not due to a failure of will or spirit or martial ability handed down through their Anglo-Saxon heritage, but because of the overwhelming superiority of the northern military and industrial might (not moral superiority), augmented by the flood of immigrants sweeping into Yankeedom from Europe.

Six years after Appomattox, General Wade Hampton, in his Baltimore eulogy on Robert E. Lee, spelled it out as he discussed the northern strategy of relying on superior numbers rather than on skillful military maneuvering. One can almost hear the disdain in his voice as Hampton describes the "system, looking as it does for success only to the employment of brute force, requires rather the strength that numbers give, than the genius of the soldier, but the bloody sacrifice of lives it involved was a matter of slight consequence to the Federal Government, so long as the mercenaries of Europe and the slaves of the South could be used as substitutes for the patriots of the North, who could thus fight safely for the Constitution and the Union." The Confederacy, in contrast, was "cut off from all foreign aid,—with the ear of the world closed against her by the misrepresentations of her enemies—surrounded on all sides by danger—subjected to treatment which violated every principle of civilized warfare—with thousands of her sons sleeping beneath the soil they died to defend, or by a worse fate, perishing in Northern prisons—had no resources save in those heroic armies which had so long upheld the cause of their country. Hardships, starvation and the bullets of the enemy were diminishing these daily, and she had no mercenaries to fight battles for her sons."[57]

Charles C. Jones Jr., the leader and annual orator for the Augusta Confederate Survivors, used the words of the "venerable historian, Mr. Gayarre, of Louisiana," to describe what the Confederacy was up against. Gayarre had written: "If Minerva, with wisdom, courage, justice, and right, was on the side of the Southern champion, yet it was Minerva not only without any armor, but even without necessary garments to protect her against the inclemencies of the weather; whilst on the other side there stood Mars in full panoply, Ceres with her inexhaustible cornucopia, Jupiter with his thunderbolts, Neptune with his trident, Mercury with his winged feet and his emblematic rod, Pluto with his hounds, Vulcan with his forge and hammer."[58] How could the South have expected to win against *those* odds?

Comparing northern and southern strength was a favorite strategy for Lost Cause orators. In 1878, Alfred M. Waddell, in words foreshadowing those of Henry Grady a few years later, and on an occasion similar to that faced by Grady in 1886, contrasted the returning soldiers of the Union and of the Confederacy. Speaking of the southern forces, Waddell said to his New York audience, "You overthrew him, and returned, amid the acclamations of rejoicing millions, to happy and prosperous homes." The Confederate soldier "went back through a wilderness, to find a solitary chimney where his cabin stood, and to kiss his ragged children, who cried for bread." The northerners' march home "was along a path strewed with garlands, and gladdened with songs of triumph; his was trod silently through a land of tears." The victor "found awaiting you a grateful nation, overflowing with riches, and proudly conscious of its power," while the defeated "returned, ragged and penniless, to a ruined country."[59]

Jabez L. M. Curry, speaking in Richmond in 1896, pointed out the obvious comparisons. On the one hand, the North had sufficient transportation and systems of distribution and supply, in addition to ports open to the world's trade, "plenty of money, greater population, and an inexhaustible and available European supply of men." On the other hand, "What a contrast to the

Southern army, half clad, half fed, half armed, without any adequate supply of the needed transport, of the needed medical staff, of the needed en-
gineers for bridging, for telegraph work and other engineer duties, with few
depots of supply, and a gradually constricting area of territory shut off from
the sea by a rigorous blockade."[60]

Daniel H. Hill simply summed it up in a phrase: "Their defeat was due
to overwhelming numbers." Ellison Capers put it more effectively as he told
about the spring of 1865, when "100,000 Confederate soldiers, half-clad, half-
shod, poorly fed, stood by their colors, scattered from Petersburg to the Mississippi, and beyond, confronting 1,000,000 Federal troops superbly armed,
perfectly equipped, well fed and clothed, with the resources of all the world
at their command." Carr expressed it in terms of numbers as well: "our armies
worn away, until divisions become brigades, brigades regiments, and regiments companies," and then, "like some mighty monarch of the forest that
has defied the storms of years, [was] forced at last to yield."[61]

A minister drove the nail into the Confederate coffin with his pronouncement in 1904 that the Confederacy failed "for no other reason but this—God
decreed otherwise. . . . [T]he military genius of our commanders was not at
fault, the valor of the Confederate armies was not at fault; but it was God's
will that this country should not be divided into two rival nations jealous of
each other; armed against each other."[62] After going into the war feeling that
God was on their side, the veterans must have found this admission shock-
ing, but it was an effective assertion that helped close the debate for God-
fearing southerners.

"For the malignity and brutality of Sherman, I can have nothing but indignation and resentment": Creating Another Rhetorical Scapegoat

God may have willed the defeat of the Confederacy, but the military power
of the Union contributed to that defeat as well. Southern leadership seemed
eventually, and sooner rather than later, to accept that the North's overwhelming superiority in resources, manpower, transportation, communication, and industrial power had enabled the North to preserve the Union. One
thing they did not accept, forgive, or forget was the "March to the Sea" and
back into the Carolinas carried out in the last months of the war by General William T. Sherman's forces. The mythology that developed around this
campaign was elaborated and strengthened by many Lost Cause orators. As
Edward McCrady said, the "malignity and brutality of Sherman" caused him
to "have nothing but indignation and resentment." McCrady explained fur-

ther. "When I come across . . . the pictures of the burning of Columbia and Winnsboro, and read the unpitying and exultant comments upon the misery they depict, I can feel it no part of Christian or patriotic duty to suppress the just indignation which fills my heart alike against the perpetrators and boastful recorders of such inhumanity."[63]

Francis Dawson used his oration on the women of the Confederacy to develop a tirade against Sherman as well. After discussing the various privations and problems southern women faced during the war, Dawson said the "worst of the agony of the wives and mothers of the South, the worst of their trials and sufferings, was yet to come." For the Charleston editor, the "culmination of insult and wrong was reached" by the "brutal and barbarous conduct of the invading armies. . . . [T]he raiders and bummers had no respect for age or sex, for young children, tender women, decrepit old men." Dawson then at length goes to accounts of various southern women in South Carolina, Virginia, and Georgia who were accosted by Sherman's men or other northern soldiers. He sums up his attack on Sherman's tactics by quoting at length from a report from a Select Committee of the Confederate Congress which stated: "Our invaders have been utterly regardless of every principle of lawful warfare, every precept of the Christian religion, and every sentiment of enlightened humanity."[64]

Several orators unfavorably compared Sherman's march to Lord Cornwallis's march through some of the same area on his way to defeat at Yorktown. North Carolina's wartime governor, Zebulon B. Vance, quoted at length from the British commander's original order book in which he repeatedly reminded his troops, for example, "It is needless to point out to the officers the necessity of preserving the strictest discipline, and of preventing the oppressed people from suffering violence by the hands from whom they are taught to look for protection!" Again, "It is expected that Captains will exert themselves to keep good order and prevent plundering." As opposed to these "civilized" orders and expectations, Vance went to a letter Sherman wrote on December 24, 1864: "The truth is, the whole army is burning with an insatiable desire to wreck vengeance upon South Carolina."[65]

Another frequent rhetorical tactic was to quote General Lee's order to the southern troops as they moved toward Gettysburg in 1863, then relate some of the contrasting stories from Sherman's foray into Georgia and the Carolinas. For example, Wade Hampton in his eulogy on Lee quotes at length from Lee's order:

The Commanding General considers that no greater disgrace could befall the army, and through it our whole people, than the perpetration of the barbarous outrages upon the innocent and defenseless, and the wanton destruction of private property that have marked the course of the enemy in our own country. . . . It must be remembered that we make war only upon armed men, and that we cannot take vengeance for the wrongs our people have suffered, without having ourselves in the eyes of all whose abhorrence has been excited by the atrocities of our enemy. . . . The Commanding General, therefore, earnestly exhorts the troops to abstain with most scrupulous care from unnecessary or wanton injury to private property.[66]

Judge D. Gardiner Tyler, addressing a reunion in Richmond in 1915, asserted that "this order was so implicitly obeyed by his soldiers that in the language of a distinguished Federal officer: 'I doubt if a hostile army of equal size ever advanced into an enemy's country or fell back from it in retreat leaving behind less cause of hate and bitterness than did the Army of Northern Virginia in that memorable campaign that culminated at Gettysburg.'"[67] Sherman was consistently held up as the antithesis of Lee's gentlemanly manner and approach.

Several speakers reinforced the unacceptability of the Union general's actions by using examples from the classical world for support of their condemnation of Sherman. For example, Charles C. Jones Jr. quoted from the Greek historian Polybius: "When men proceed to wreck their fury on senseless objects, whose destruction will neither be of advantage to themselves nor in the slightest degree disable their opponent . . . what else can we say of such proceedings except that they are the acts of men devoid of all feelings of propriety and infected by frenzy? For it is in no way the object of war, at least among men who have just notions of their duty, to annihilate and utterly subvert those from who they may have received provocation." Zebulon Vance also went back to antiquity, quoting the Persian general Cyrus in 400 B.C., who gave "an order directing that his army . . . should not disturb the cultivators of the soil," and Abubekr, Mohammed's successor, who wrote in 634: "Let not your victory be stained with the blood of women or children. Destroy not palm trees nor burn any fields of corn." The North Carolinian then cited several modern legal scholars, such as Union major general Henry W. Halleck (who had written the book on law of war used as a textbook at West Point), Frances Lieber's code for armies, and other "great writers on public law," each of whom "condemns in unmistakable terms the destruction and indiscriminate pillaging of private property of unarmed people in a time of war."[68]

Finally, so there could be no mistake about the nature of the ruin caused

by Sherman's soldiers, several speakers quoted this line from Sherman's official report: "I estimate the damage done to the State of Georgia at one hundred million dollars, at least twenty million of which inured to our benefit,
and the remainder was simply waste and destruction." Vance follows this
statement with a lengthy section in his speech detailing the path of Sherman's troops through Georgia.[69]

Regardless of the approach they took, Lost Cause orators attacked Sherman in great detail and in some cases with obvious bitterness and even hatred. These attitudes and the mythology about Sherman lasted throughout
the South for generations, and even today he is held in low regard by many
white southerners—the mythology is still rock-solid for some.

Sherman was not the only cause of southern defeat or the only target of
southern bitterness. The overwhelming nature of the defeat stung for generations. Orators were obsessed with describing the sad state of southern
affairs after the surrender. The most famous, of course, was the passage in
Henry Grady's New South speech, which countless southern youth memorized and declaimed for years. But many others included those terrible conditions in words similar to Grady's. "Reflect upon our conditions when Lee
and Johnston laid down their arms," Charles Olmstead asked his listeners in
Savannah: "the enormous aggregation of capital represented by the institution of slavery, swept out of existence as property; the entire system of banking, upon which all trade rests, absolutely gone; the railroads, with scarcely
an exception, wrecked and ruined, their rolling stock run down to worthless-
ness, the roadbeds torn up; bridges, factories, colleges and public buildings
of all kinds destroyed by hundreds; the stock of horses, cattle and sheep reduced to a minimum; the land without a circulating medium, so that in in-
terior places, the people were reduced to a system of barter; on every hand
ruin and desolation." But the worst losses were the spiritual ones of the soldiers. As William E. Cameron put it, "They had been first worshipers at the
birth, they were the last mourners at the grave of the vanished nation."[70]

5

Creating the Myths of Reconstruction, Redemption, Reconciliation, and the New and Future South

The Rest of the Story

Lost Cause rhetoric included not only defense, glorification, and justification of the Confederacy and the Old South and its war heroes, but also the clearly connected and relevant mythology of what happened to the region after Appomattox. The Civil War may have been the great epic event of southern history, but the decades that followed were almost its equal. The narrative of tradition, defeat, wartime glory, and inevitable disaster had to be rounded out with the additional stories of the black days of Reconstruction, the satisfaction of Redemption, the patriotic appeal of Reconciliation, and, based on all that, the New and Future South, which included segregation for black southerners as much as it included industrial growth. The rhetoric of the Lost Cause spread its net widely, capturing the culture of the white South in so many of its various manifestations. These speakers and their Lost Cause rhetoric about the postwar era fostered and reinforced the demagogues and racists of the mid-twentieth century as much as or more than did their oratory about the war itself. The breadth and depth of the Lost Cause formed and shaped the South for decades to come—many would say even into the twenty-first century.

"In the hands of carpet-baggers and brigands": The Story of Reconstruction

That old devil, General Sherman, was not the only scapegoat burned on the altars of the Lost Cause. Reconstruction, that "cruelest injustice and violence," "the Stygian darkness," "the blackest page of national history," the "high carnival of crime," compares well with the "habits of the revelry of a Caligula or a Nero" in the mythology created and reinforced over and over by southern speakers. For many Lost Cause orators, it was as if the North were taking unfair advantage of the defeated South, sort of a "kicking us while we are down" attitude. Landon Bell reflected this perception when he reminded his audience in 1929 that "for a long time after the end of the war . . . the South was prostrate, in the hands of carpet-baggers and brigands, commissioned and backed by the government, which was controlled by vindictive men." As historian James C. Cobb puts it, and as scores of Lost Cause orators confirmed, "the Reconstruction era was a time of shock and upheaval for Delta whites"—and, by extension, most whites across the region.[1]

There were many rhetorical pictures of Reconstruction, but a striking one was the verbal portrait painted by wartime governor of North Carolina, Zebulon B. Vance. He alluded to the original terms of surrender offered by General Sherman to General Johnston in North Carolina at the end of the war, terms that, if "ratified at Washington" rather than rejected, would have allowed the officials of every southern state to swear allegiance to the Constitution, "and the domination of the Union would have been complete at once." The result of these terms, according to Vance, would have been, "no such thing as *reconstruction;* no such thing as eleven States reduced to military districts, with all civil authority overthrown and the bayonet become due process of law. There would have been no such thing as eleven blood-stained, war-ridden and desolate States plundered of two hundred and sixty millions by the last and infinitely worse invasion of the army of carpet-baggers. . . . The terms would have saved the South the horrors of reconstruction."[2]

An even more belligerent and "unreconstructed" view of the decade following the Civil War was developed in a 1892 speech to a veterans' reunion in Jackson by Josiah A. P. Campbell, the chief justice of the Mississippi Supreme Court. Campbell's diatribe is close to the stereotype depicted in this part of the Lost Cause mythology through much of the twentieth century. Justice Campbell claimed that "the long, dark night of reconstruction," with its "hideous deformity," could truly be described by "neither tongue nor pen." Later, he asserted, "the long, dark, wearisome night of reconstruction, with its blighting, withering, devastating effect on the country . . . the extreme descent which civilization could endure . . . society trembling on the very brink of the awful abyss of anarchy and barbarism . . . borne down and repressed by the strong arm of federal power" could be summed up as the "terrible period of reconstruction . . . that hideous era." The period was so horrendous in the minds of defeated southerners that it seemed "unaccountable to us that the brave men of the North should have condescended to heap upon us such useless indignities and oppressions as the 'Reconstruction' period developed," said William E. Boggs in an 1881 South Carolina speech.[3]

But heap they did, and many white southerners believed the period was even worse than the war itself. J. C. C. Black was one of those, and he told his audience at the Benjamin Hill statue dedication in 1886 that "there are trials severer than war, and calamities worse than the defeat of arms." The South had to "pass through such trials and be threatened with such calamities" by the events of Reconstruction. His description of the era was typical: "Law no longer held its benign sway, but gave place to the mandate of petty dictators enforced by the bayonet. . . . ; the sanctity of home was invaded; vice triumphed over virtue; ignorance ruled in lordly and haughty dominion over intelligence; the weak were oppressed; the unoffending insulted; the fallen warred on; truth was silenced; falsehood . . . stalked abroad unchallenged; . . . . arrests made, trials had and sentences pronounced without evidence; madness, lust, hate, and crime of every hue, defiant, wicked, and diabolical, ruled the hour."[4]

The evils of Reconstruction seemed to grow larger and blacker as the years went by. Seventeen years after Black delivered his speech, W. M. Hammond, speaking to a veterans' reunion in Wadesboro, North Carolina, recounted the "blackest page in the long history of oppression and wrong . . . reconstruction, with its unspeakable horrors, its infamous defiance of every principle of humanity. . . . Suffice it to say, that whatever malice would suggest, or official cruelty contrive, or official brutality inflict, was visited on a brave but submissive people." Hammond went on to highlight the extent, in his mind's eye, of the problem: "Ignorance in the judgment seat, corruption in the council chamber, rapacity at the receipt of customs, stupidity and fraud at the ballot-box, barbarism and brutality everywhere—the entire South one writhing, seething mass of rapine, debauchery and lust."[5]

A year later, in Memphis, Mississippi congressman John Sharp Williams was clear and graphic in his attack on the problem, the "so-called reconstruction," which was even worse than the four years of civil war. Williams described "those ten long years during every day and every night of which Southern womanhood was menaced and Southern manhood humiliated. You will remember the long, long carnival of folly, the saturnalia of vice and corruption, during which a black flood seemed all but to engulf ourselves as a race, our precious heritage from the past, our sweet and sacred hope for a future."[6] By the turn of the century, this racist view of the Reconstruction era was paramount; it would last for decades, due at least partly to its frequent repetition in city and town around the region at many ceremonial Lost Cause events.

The key objection southern speakers had to Reconstruction was what they perceived as "Negro rule," the bottom rail placed on the top rail, the threat of domination by newly freed slaves over their former masters and all other whites in the region. This attitude and perception was what the Redeemers capitalized on as Reconstruction began to fade. W. M. Hammond told his audience that the Radical Republicans "promoted ignorance over learning, and set brutality and lust to keep rule over innocence and virtue." The implied threat of blacks attacking innocent and virtuous white southern women was a frequent motif of southern oratory for decades, and it supported, defended, and justified lynching for more than three-quarters of a century.

Hammond went on: "They wrote negro suffrage and negro equality with bayonets in the code of every Southern State. They ravished the Federal Constitution and wrote it there." And then, the essence of the southern myth of Reconstruction: "They laid interdict after interdict on white supremacy and white control." John W. Daniel reminded veterans in New Orleans that "character and intelligence [were] disfranchised; the bottom rail on top; the slave became master." For Daniel, the government of the southern states was "a mixture of Sheol, Hades, hell fire, the black death and pandemonium." The "climax of crime," according to E. C. Walthall, "was completed when our new rulers armed the ignorant and deluded negroes with dangerous powers and set them in authority in the States." John Temple Graves refers to this racial argument when in 1876, he hoped that he would live to see the day "when the time-honored flag of Washington and Jefferson shall not be foul with the odors of civil rights and race amalgamation, but with the glorious matter of Constitutional Liberty flying on every fold."[7]

Jefferson Davis used the era of Reconstruction as justification for secession. As he said in 1878, "the course pursued by the Federal Government, after the war had ceased, vindicates the judgment of those who held separation to be necessary for the safety and freedom of the Southern States." Some of the orators compared what they saw as the unconstitutionality of the Civil War with the unconstitutionality of Reconstruction. Rev. Charles S. Vedder put it this way: "The conditions which followed the overthrow of the South were as much in defiance of the Constitution as had been the war which ended in that overthrow." The Charleston minister then quoted at length from Professor Roger Foster, a "lecturer on law in Yale University," who had written: "The Reconstruction Act must consequently be condemned as unconstitutional, founded in force, not law, and so tyrannical as to imperil the liberty of the entire nation should they be recognized as binding precedents. . . . It seems impossible to find any justification for the Reconstruction Acts in law, precedent, or consistency."[8] Vedder and many other Lost Cause orators in this era strongly endorsed these sentiments.

For many southerners, the worst aspect of Reconstruction was the traitorous behavior of some fellow southerners, the so-called scalawags, whites who joined forces with Republicans. According to James Black, "they basely bartered themselves for the spoils of office. They aligned themselves with the enemies of the people and their liberties." As Redemption began to turn the tide against Reconstruction, these evil men "insulted the presence of the virtuous and the brave by coming among them, and forever fixed upon their ignoble brows the stigma of a double treachery by proclaiming that they had joined our enemies to betray them."[9]

As Reconstruction drew to a close, Rev. Moses D. Hoge used the era to praise the southern people, as he reminded them that they "vindicated their valor and endurance during the conflict" and that since the war they had exhibited "their patience and self-control under the most trying circumstances." Their "dignity" and "heroic resignation to what they could not avert, have shown that subjugation itself could not conquer true greatness of soul." Another minister, Randolph McKim, also praised the white southerners for their "fortitude," "patience," and "courage," which, in spite of "those terrible years of Reconstruction—how much more bitter than the four years of war!"— had helped the South to emerge "more beautiful than ever." As David Blight shows, "the image of Reconstruction as black domination, radical ideology taken too far, would become one of the deepest strains of American historical consciousness in the next generation."[10]

This rhetorical story of the Reconstruction period remained in play for decades, as conservative southern Democrats used it with their constituents as a defense against any threats to the one-party system or to segregation. Modern scholarship rejects much of the story told by these Lost Cause orators, but as we will see in the next chapter, generations of white southerners have believed it all to be true.

"His was the proud mission to liberate his beloved and manacled Commonwealth": The Lost Cause View of Redemption

The "horrible excesses of Reconstruction" did not last indefinitely. Eventually, "the brief and disgraceful reign of inferiority and ignorance" ended; "forever" was the hope of Josiah A. P. Campbell, and "the superior race again controls the entire South." Redemption, the flip side of the mythological coin of Reconstruction as part of the Lost Cause narrative, edged onto center stage as the solid South redeemed itself from the "long period of tyranny and misrule." David Goldfield summed up the southern attitude regarding Redemption: "[It] offered the hope of setting things right again, of putting Yankees and blacks in their proper places: in the North and under the whites, respectively."[11] This redemption part of the myth was strongly reinforced by southern speakers in words that echoed for several generations as a cornerstone for the white-controlled, absolutely segregated "Solid South."

Redemption quickly gained the luster of the Confederacy and the whole Lost Cause legend. Throwing off all traces of black equality and northern control, white southerners quickly bought into the mythology and added it part and parcel to the Lost Cause. Charles C. Jones Jr. described the recently deceased Major General Martin W. Gary in words that were close to those he used to describe at other times other Confederate heroes and their wartime efforts: "His was the proud mission to liberate his beloved and manacled Commonwealth from the usurpation and the ruthless domination of the stranger, the uncivilized, and the plunderer." John Q. Marshall spoke of the "true sons of South Carolina" who responded "when the waves of political strife ran mountain high, threatening to engulf us in their dark bosom in ruin and destruction," and "made all true men believe and know that South Carolina should be ruled by South Carolinians."[12]

There was also a desire that those leaders in South Carolina and elsewhere should have strong and clear ties to the Confederacy and the Old South. The Redeemers, such as Hampton, were men "who had been trained in the old school in which the sons of the State were nurtured." Black, in 1886, praised the former Confederates whose "fortunes were destroyed, their fields desolated, their homes laid in ashes," but whose "invincible spirit and heroic resistance" led to the "peace, prosperity, and good government we enjoy today." John Sharp Williams stressed this continuity as well, as he bragged on the "superb spectacle," of "white men of the South standing from '65 to '74 and '75 quietly, determinedly, solidly, shoulder to shoulder in phalanx, as if the entire race were one man . . . praying for the opportunity which, in the providence of God, must come to overthrow the supremacy of 'veneered savages,' superficially 'Americanized Africans'—waiting to reassert politically and socially the supremacy of the English-speaking white race."[13] In short, racism was solidly at the heart of Lost Cause, Reconstruction, and Redemption narratives and was the tie to the Confederacy and the Old South that solidified that core belief and helped it live at least until mid-twentieth century and the civil rights movement across the South.

Jefferson Davis anchored his comments on Redemption in his lifelong belief in states' rights and local government. In an address to the Army of Tennessee just after the end of Reconstruction, Davis remarked: "Well may we rejoice in the regained possession of local self-government, in the power of the people to choose their representatives and to legislate uncontrolled by bayonets. . . . The revival of the time-honored doctrine of State sovereignty and the supremacy of the law will secure permanent peace, freedom and prosperity." W. Y. C. Humes, speaking in Memphis the year after Reconstruction had ended, echoed Davis's sentiments on the issue of local government. In spite of the evils of Reconstruction, in the end, "the Southern people have been restored to their full rights under the laws and constitution of the Union; they stand to-day on the same plane of civil rights as our Northern brothers; the filthy vermin who fed and fattened on our property, under the forms of law, have all fled; our local governments and domestic institutions are again our own." A recent historian of the New South, Edward Ayers, described how the Redeemers saw themselves in contrast to those who ruled during the Reconstruction era: they were "proponents of common sense, honesty, and caution where the Republicans offered foolishness, corruption, and impetuosity."[14] Only with Redemption could Reconciliation become a reality.

"It is our interest, our duty, and determination to maintain the Union, and to make every possible contribution to its prosperity and glory": The Duty of Reconciliation

Reconciliation did not come easily for the defeated South. Not only had southerners been surprised by their failure to establish a separate nation, but they were saddled with Reconstruction, and for some, at least, that era may have even been worse than the war. While the number of federal troops stationed in the South during the Reconstruction period was insufficient for their task, their symbolic presence angered white southerners and made reconciliation efforts difficult. John Hope Franklin believes that for some southerners, "military occupation was worse than defeat on the field of battle," and many of these speakers reflect that attitude.[15] Bitterness continued on both sides long after the war, as might be expected. Southerners still remembered—and Lost Cause orators frequently reminded them—the brutal Union generals who ground out the war in modern (that is, uncivilized, from the southern perspective) combat, especially Sherman, and the Confederacy's defeat due to sheer numbers, not to military or moral weakness. Reconciliation was advocated by many Lost Cause orators, but a careful reading of their speeches reveals that it did not take much to prick the skin and find the blood of southern defensive attitudes; the passion to protect the South flowed quickly and deeply.

There were still overtones of bitterness and resentment, which were identified by Lost Cause orators such as John B. Hood, W. Y. C. Humes, James C. C. Black, and Julian S. Carr. Hood made certain his audience in Charleston in 1872 understood that there were northerners who would try to block Reconciliation and continue to blame the South: "It is evident to the unbiased mind, that if the country is not restored to harmony and prosperity, it will not be the fault of the South. . . . [T]he people of New England, governed more by bitterness of feeling toward the former master than by love for the negro, will stand as the stumbling block. With a majority of Americans favoring peace and good-will to all, there will be a strong minority constantly probing the wound and arousing old enmities." Humes reminded his listeners in Memphis: "The great body of the Northern people cherished as bitter a hatred and animosity toward the South, engendered by the war, as ever was harbored in the breast of one people against another." Reinforcing the stereotypical view, he described the "pestilential swarm of venal adventurers from the North, like the locusts of Egypt," who invaded the South. Black took a pessimistic view as late as 1890 when he told his Atlanta audience that "the spirit of sectionalism that drenched the country in blood is not yet satisfied. There are men in high stations whose patriotism is too narrow and shallow to embrace every section of the country." Four years later, Carr believed there were still problems; however, there were "but few *rabid creatures* in the North from whose mouths flow the froth of sectional madness."[16]

Reconciliation was not yet fully a reality, but many Lost Cause speakers were doing their best to promote it. It is impossible to clearly define when Reconciliation began to be an acceptable goal of Lost Cause orators, but the various celebrations of the nation's one hundredth birthday in 1876 can be seen as a milestone on the road to reunion. By the mid-1870s, historian Rembert Patrick notes, "Northern public opinion was also veering toward sympathy for the white Southerner," and the compromise legislation in the presidential administration of Rutherford B. Hayes touched off a wave of reconciliation efforts such as the president's goodwill trip to the South and his participation in Confederate Memorial Day services in Tennessee, as described by Paul Buck in his landmark study *The Road to Reunion*.[17] By the end of the 1870s, the end of Reconstruction, the withdrawal of all federal troops, and the essential abandonment of the "Negro question" to southern solutions (namely, segregation), the ground was fertile for Reconciliation themes to enter into the Lost Cause orators' arsenal of arguments. For the next two decades or so, reconciliation was just as much a part of the rhetorical strategy as was praising Robert E. Lee.

It was easy to weave reconciliation into the rhetoric of the Lost Cause. After all, as we saw in chapter 3, duty and honor of the Confederate soldier was a cornerstone in the rebuilding effort for southern manhood after the defeat. Reconciliation themes drew on this prized southern value. Moses Hoge said simply and bluntly at the Jackson statue: "It is our interest, our duty, and determination to maintain the Union, and to make every possible contribution to its prosperity and glory." Jabez L. M. Curry spoke for himself when he told his Richmond audience: "Individually, as a Southern man and a Confederate soldier, I have felt that my highest duty to my section since the struggle ended, was to restore fraternity of spirit as well as political association."[18]

In his oration at Lee's mausoleum, John W. Daniel frequently invoked the value of southern duty to support the reestablished nation. He quoted Lee himself, who said in reference to men in general that "their conduct must conform to the new order of things," suggesting that former Confederates had to accept the new order in the South. J. C. C. Black, in his oration at the dedication of the statue to Benjamin H. Hill in Atlanta, said that the duty of former Confederates was to return "to their desolated homes like true cavaliers, willing to acknowledge their defeat, abide in good faith the terms of the surrender, accept all the legitimate results of the issue, respect the prowess of those who had conquered, and resume their relations to the government with all the duties those relations imposed."[19]

Patriotism for the reunited nation was frequently invoked; loyalty to the nation had not been crushed out of the southern memory by the war, and as we saw in the last chapter, Lost Cause orators appealed to pride in the contributions the South had made to the early history of the Republic. Graves, in his Memorial Day address in West Point, Georgia, reminded his listeners: "We cannot fail to know that we are and ought to be numbered among the Union of original States. We still claim, and justly, the heritage and honor of American citizens." Randolph McKim asserted to his audience in Nashville: "This is now for us an indissoluble Union of indestructible States. We are loyal to that starry banner. We remember that it was baptized with Southern blood when our forefathers first unfurled it to the breeze." The minister went on to remind his listeners that a southerner, Francis Key, "immortalized" the United States flag; a "southern soldier and statesman," George Washington, "established it in triumph"; and "Southern blood had again flowed in its defense in the Spanish war." General Thomas M. Logan bragged on the future of America at the reunion of the Hampton Legion in Columbia, South Carolina: "It requires neither prophet to foretell, nor oracle to pronounce, that there is a great future for the United States. . . . Truly, a vast empire is in process of formation." After the war, Logan was a part of that vast empire, as he was a successful railroad developer in South Carolina.[20]

Perhaps it should be expected, but Robert E. Lee was an often-used example as a model and mentor of reconciliation. Daniel's oration at the Washington and Lee mausoleum referred often to Lee's forgiving spirit. After the war, Lee was "reviled and harassed, yet never a word of bitterness escaped him; but, on the contrary, only counsels of forbearance, patience and diligent attention to works of restoration." Daniel used Lee's own words: "It should be the object of all to avoid controversy, to allay passion, and give scope to every kindly feeling." Again, "It is wisest not to keep open the sores of war, but to follow the example of those nations who have endeavored to obliterate the marks of civil strife, and to commit to oblivion the feelings it engendered." Late in the address, Daniel devoted an entire section to discussing Lee's forgiving spirit: "Lee had nothing in common with the little minds that know not how to forgive. His was the land that had been invaded; his the people who were cut down . . . ; his was the cause that perished. He was the General discrowned of his mighty place, and he the citizen disfranchised. Yet Lee forgave, and counselled all to forgive and forget."[21]

James W. Throckmorton, speaking to an 1889 reunion in Waco, Texas, presented examples of how the two sections were cooperating with each other, even over the graves of the dead. Throckmorton praised women of both sides: "The graves of Southern soldiers that died from wounds and disease in Northern prisons and hospitals are strewn with flowers by the wives and daughters of brave men who fell upon the battlefields of the South, and the graves of Northern soldiers who lie buried in the South are tenderly cared for by the fair women whose homes they invaded."[22]

John Temple Graves, at a Union Decoration Day program in Jacksonville, devoted his entire speech to the theme of reconciliation. Early in the speech he sets the tone: "The Grand Army of the Republic locking arms with the remnant of Confederate Veterans leads a great host of citizens who sing: 'My Country 'tis of Thee.'" This skillful juxtaposing of the "Grand Army of the Republic" with "*remnants* of the Confederate Veterans" leaves no doubt who was the victor. The entire ceremony was oriented toward reconciliation as participants decorated the resting places of both blue and gray with flowers. Both northerners and Confederates had a role in the ceremonies, and Graves's speech was a clear reflection of the occasion.

Graves depicted the nation as once again whole: "The bloody chasm is bridged by Northern heartiness and Southern warmth and mutual generosity, and the heart of Florida beats at last in loyal unison with the heart of Maine." He discussed a number of concrete examples of intersectional cooperation:

We recall with glowing memories that a generous regiment of Maine sent to Congress a memorial for the pension of the maimed and disabled veterans of the dead Confederacy. We remember that a gallant regiment of New York started those ringing cheers for Fitzhugh Lee in the great procession of the 4th of March. We can never forget, while memory lasts, that cultured, classic and chivalric Boston poured the rich tribute of flowers and welcome words in the lap of Stonewall Jackson's widow. These deeds have stirred the Southern heart, and we have tried to give back an answering throb in the sincere and heartfelt and universal sympathy that we have sent to the bedside of the North's great hero, dying in New York.

In concluding, Graves appealed to the whole nation to "chant the praises of our dead together" and "honor these men simply as soldiers who fought like lions, who endured like martyrs, and bore the separate flags of the cause they loved with an heroic faith, a matchless patience, a splendid patriotism that will live as long as the name of Jackson and the name of Grant."[23]

By 1896, Jabez L. M. Curry could cite the example of the building of a Confederate monument in Chicago as evidence that "the resentments and animosities and prejudices of the war are being effaced by healthier opinions and actions." Curry discussed the Atlanta Exposition, where northern governors and federal troops attended amid "profuse and cordial hospitality" that demonstrated "subsidence of antagonisms and prevalence of reconciliation and brotherhood." For Curry, "renewal of strife" would be a "irreparable calamity to both sections."[24]

Shortly after the turn of the century, Charles Vedder listed several reconciliatory events of the recent past that pointed to and supported reunion between the sections. Vedder pointed out that President McKinley had taken the position that "the whole county should charge itself with the care of Confederate graves," and perhaps even more amazing, President Theodore Roosevelt "is proud that his own near kin was represented in the Confederate forces." By 1911 it was possible for a southern speaker to allude to the fact that the "Secretary of War is an ex-Confederate soldier" and that the "Speaker of the House of Representatives is of Southern birth."[25]

The Spanish-American War provided many opportunities for southern speakers to extol the reunited country and boast again about the contributions the South had made to the national glory. Alfred M. Waddell had earlier forecast to an audience of Union veterans in New York City that "if it should come[,] the spectacle of a solid column composed of alternate regiments of ex-Union and ex-Confederate soldiers . . . would be a goodly sight to see. The thought of such a spectacle is inspiring and quickens the pulse." Rev. Randolph McKim lived to see that happen in the Cuban conflict and wrote: "Sectionalism is dead and buried. In the providence of God the Spanish war has drawn North and South together in bonds of genuine brotherhood. Their blood has watered the same soil; the common patriotism has glorified again the land of Washington. Men who faced one another in deadly conflict at Shiloh and Gettysburg rushed side by side under the Stars and Stripes up the heights of San Juan and El Caney." General William R. Cox told his audience on Confederate Memorial Day in 1911 that the first American killed in the Spanish-American War was a son of an ex-Confederate; that another son of an ex-Confederate was a successful spy during that war who "penetrated the lines of the enemy and secured the information most valuable to this government"; that still another son of a former Confederate "volunteered to fire the ships of Cevera"; and that a southern youth was the flag bearer "who raised the Stars and Stripes at Manila Bay." At the dedication of the Confederate monument on the Alabama state capitol grounds in 1898, H. A. Herbert reminded listeners that, as the state had sent thousands of brave men to the service of the Confederacy, "so now in our war with Spain she has given Richmond Pearson Hobson to the Navy and Joseph Wheeler to the Army of the United States."

Charles Vedder believed the Spanish-American War was the proof of southern love and patriotism for the reunited country. He praised the "Confederate officers and their sons, who bore themselves so magnificently there, proved as all others will, that . . . those who, holding in undying affection and reverence the flag which has gone down, array themselves in patriotic faithfulness for the defence and honor of the standard under which their sires fought in the American Revolution, the flag which waves over the whole land, and represents American liberty, and the prowess which can defend it in every clime to the remotest bounds of earth."[26]

Paul Buck, in his definitive study of the reconciliation process, asserts that by 1895 there were no real issues left between North and South. According to Buck, "The people of the United States constituted at last a nation integrated in interests and united in sentiment. . . . The reunited nation was a fact." Julian Carr summed it up, as he linked the past with the future: "The men of the South have no regrets to express for that past, but holding to it as a sacred treasure, they dedicate themselves, henceforth, to the perpetuation and glory of this Union." Lost Cause oratory was a major factor in bringing that reunion to reality, as these orations throughout the South reinforced the idea that the region was ready for it.[27]

While it might on the surface appear strange to hear these Lost Cause speakers advocating reunion, it fit perfectly into their agenda. By making the point that the South and the nation were ready for reconciliation, it was

easier for northern political leaders, even the "Bloody Shirt" orators, to accept the South's honoring the Confederacy through ritual, oratory, monuments, Confederate Memorial Day celebrations, and reunions. As Charles
Vedder could claim by 1901, "the name of Robert E. Lee is inscribed upon
our country's temple of fame."[28] By defending reconciliation and reunion,
the white leadership of the South was enabled to "win the peace" and establish a segregated South as the answer to the end of slavery and the "Negro question," as many orators described it. Defiance of the federal government and the North became increasingly rare, although it never died, and
we will see it resurface in the mid-twentieth century. It became more important for Lost Cause orators to promote reunion while still defending the justice and truth of the Confederacy and the story of its heroes. The advocacy
of reconciliation themes gave national legitimacy to the power of the Lost
Cause and was, therefore, an integral part of the southern rhetoric of the
era. Within the reunited nation, the South was able to develop its culture of
racial relationships—segregation—and maintain its political stance—states'
rights—far into the twentieth century. Lost Cause oratory played a leading
role in that culture and stance as the war receded into memory and the New
South took center stage.

"We have builded upon these wasted solitudes, an empire, boundless in resources . . . the wonder and admiration of the world": The New and Future South

Closely related to the reconciliation theme were the frequent attempts to bolster the pride and esteem of white southerners by praising the changes they
had wrought in the region since the Civil War and Reconstruction. Building on the New South boosterism sweeping the region, Lost Cause orators
painted a glowing picture of the South in the last decade of the nineteenth
century and the early years of the twentieth. The wave of the New South
was being felt around the region as early as 1876, when John Temple Graves
urged his Memorial Day listeners: "Work now to build again the land they
died to save, and make it bloom and blossom like the rose." Three years later,
Alfred M. Waddell pointed out to his North Carolina audience: "It is no ex-
aggeration to say that not only our former enemies, but we ourselves have
been astonished at the recuperative power displayed by our people since they
laid down their arms, and in this I find the chief hope on which our future rests." Almost a decade later, Graves drew quite a contrast between the
South in 1865 and the South of 1888: "Out of the wreck of our cherished institutions, out of the darkness of defeat, out of the ashes of desolation, with

the quickened energies of despair, we have builded upon these wasted soli-
tudes, an empire, boundless in resources, swelling with promise, incalculable
in wealth—the wonder and admiration of the world." Graves believed that
this contrast would not have occurred without the war, as the "feudal civilization of slavery and luxury" would have been "content with ourselves and
with our state," and the "iron might have slept forever in these noble hills,
and the granite towered in eternal loneliness among these delectable moun-
tains." But the South rebounded from the disaster of defeat and "gathered
strength for climbing to greatness and to glory."[29]

Comparing the post-Reconstruction South with the region's conditions
during Reconstruction was a favorite rhetorical tactic. James C. C. Black used
it as well as any. Praising his fellow southerners for their "manly, heroic efforts, under difficulties such as no other people ever encountered," Black
reminded them that they had "brought order out of Chaos, well regulated
government out of anarchy." The "ignorance and vice and greed and hate"
of those years was "supplanted by the peaceful supremacy of virtue and intelligence." The hardworking and virtuous southerner had "obliterated the
ravages of war by thriving towns and prosperous cities; restored your desolated homes and wasted fields until domestic peace blesses the hearthstone,
and generous rewards repay the toil of the husbandman." But that is not all:
"Braver and nobler than all this material greatness, you have preserved your
manhood. This is your highest and most enduring glory; this shall be the
richest heritage of your children."[30]

As one would imagine, the South had risen "Phoenix like" in many speeches
from Lost Cause orators. Julian S. Carr invoked this image on Confederate
Memorial Day in 1894: "And when we of the South recall her condition after
the War, and find that Phoenix like, she has arisen from the ashes of desolation, and stands to-day panoplied in the pride and power of progress sweeping onward to even greater prosperity . . . we know it is because her sons and
daughters have shown themselves as heroic in peace and prosperity, as they
were when lowered the war cloud darkest." General William R. Cox spoke
of the South's contented laborers, the peace between capital and labor in the
region, and content pervading her realms as evidence that "Phoenix like, the
South has risen from her ashes."[31]

Similar to their efforts to reestablish the pride and self-esteem of the defeated Confederate soldiers, Lost Cause speakers tried to build and enhance
the self-confidence of southerners trying to configure the postwar, post-
Reconstruction South. Charles Olmstead averred that "those lads of '61 to
'65 are the men upon whose stout shoulders has rested . . . the burden of rebuilding the waste places of the South." There was "on every hand ruin and

desolation, where to-day, is peace, prosperity and happiness." John W. Daniel also drew on this theme, as he had remarked in 1891: "In peace the Southern soldier has been an exemplar of good citizenship. Work has been his counter-sign, and with it he has passed through all the times of trial and tribulation." In Daniel's mind's eye, "the old Confederate is hewing his way through the forest of life with a keen broad axe on his strong right arm."[32]

Building on this newly regained regional and individual self-confidence reinforced by these orators, they began by the 1880s to counsel their white southern audiences with guidelines for present action and future prospects. As early as 1872, General John B. Hood urged Charleston veterans to "turn from the past, and meet with courage the mighty issues of the present and the future." At Jackson's statue dedication, Moses Hoge reminded his listen-ers: "We have a future to face, and in that future lies not only duty, and trial perhaps, but also *hope*." John Temple Graves admonished his audience on Confederate Memorial Day in 1888: "But . . . we cannot live in memories for-ever. There is a clamorous present and an unformed future. We must live the one and bravely mould the other."[33]

Lost Cause orators seemed almost obsessed with leaving a legacy for their children. Speech after speech developed this idea that a major goal was to communicate to future generations the bravery, the fulfillment of duty, the great memories of 1861–65, the heroism and devotion of the Confederacy and the Confederates, and what they stood for in their battle for their institu-tions and their interpretation of the Constitution. Rev. John Kershaw asserted that celebrating Confederate Memorial Day would mean nothing "unless we are found translating the virtues of our dead into action and consecrating ourselves to the perpetuation and emulation of the sincerity, courage, self-sacrifice and devotion to duty, which our soldier dead so grandly illustrated in their life and in their death." John Q. Marshall appealed to his Confederate audience to "hand down to your children, and children's children, the record you have made." Marshall warned his unit reunion that "he who hears and forgets will not be true to his name, nor true to his birth." Being worthy of the heritage and true to the tradition established by their Confederate ances-tors was a critical goal for the generations to come. General John Hood urged the Charleston survivors in 1872 to "teach the children of the brave men who fought and fell in defence of their homes what their fathers did; teach them that through mistakes we occupy our present position, that we are not con-quered; teach them all this for the sake of truth, manhood and the future, and that *sons may arise worthy of their sires*." He also reminded his listeners that the mission of his generation "should be to guide and teach the young how in the future to achieve greatness as a people" so that they could "add still greater renown to our much loved country of the South."[34]

Charles C. Jones Jr. bemoaned the fact in 1887 that soon there would be few left who could tell the glorious story of the Confederacy from firsthand experience. The historian in Jones urged his listeners, therefore, to undertake the obligation to "perpetuate in enduring form the true philosophy of events, the genuine circumstance of the action, the inspirations, the exalted aspirations, the patriotic impulses, the heroic endeavors, the illustrious achievements, and the grand memories which impart to the defensive war maintained by Confederates an importance, an interest, a dignity, an elevation, and a sanctity beyond compare in the history of kindred revolutions." That story had to be preserved for the retelling for generations to come, as "our children should be thoroughly taught the noble lessons inculcated by the lives and acts of those who died for country and for right." If future generations properly understand and observe the "principles and conduct of those who . . . illustrated the integrity, the virtues, and the valor of the Old South," then we can rest assured that the "manliness, the honor, and the courage of the future" will be guaranteed.[35]

On Confederate Memorial Day in 1876, John Temple Graves praised the eternal principles for which the Confederacy went to war and admonished the young men in his audience to "remember and cherish those that have come to you bathed in your fathers' blood." Twelve years later, speaking at a Memorial Day celebration of the "golden flood of prosperity" sweeping the South, Graves reminded his listeners that "we shall be recreant to memory and unworthy of all, if we forget to honor and to praise those whose bones and blood have been the brick and mortar of this splendid temple in whose glories they could not live to share."[36]

At the dedication of the Jefferson Davis Monument in New Orleans, the pageantry included five hundred schoolgirls—some dressed in red, some in blue, and some in white—arranged on the platform in the form of the battle flag of the Confederacy. As part of the program, they sang "Dixie" and "America." Later, Nicholas Bauer, the assistant superintendent of schools, addressed them specifically and reinforced in their young minds that they were those "to whom is intrusted the sacred duty of cherishing the memories of the days when the dark clouds of '61 spread over this beautiful Southland of ours." White southern children were almost always pressed into service in these Lost Cause rituals and celebrations as a means to impress upon them the reality of their "southernness" and to reinforce the tenets of the Lost Cause.[37]

Vindication was a strong part of the message for current audiences and future generations. "Comrades . . . be ready to give to your children, and who claim it, a reason for your faith; and that in such a manner as to vindicate the living and the dead from the charge of rebellion and treason," urged William Boggs in 1881. In 1888, Governor Peter Turney of Tennessee reminded his listeners that "our cause was worth all we sacrificed to it. Though lost, it deserves vindication. Its defense by our arms at least checked centralization. Understanding the principles of self-government, for which our comrades battled and died, our children will stand at their graves with love, admiration and approval of their course, and offer up the prayer, 'God bless and perpetuate their memories.'" Georgian Charles Jones, along with many other southern speakers, decried the fact that, as he saw it, "the historian too often busies himself so largely with laudations of the victor that justice is lamely meted out to the aims and the exploits of the vanquished." Jones called for "a general sentiment, an honest appreciation of fact, a faithful narrative of event, a true interpretation of purpose," to be "transmitted from sire to son," and which would be valuable in "forming the judgment, moulding the thought, and shaping the appreciation of the rising generation." "Let us see to it, my Comrades," pleaded Jones, "that we are not misinterpreted by our sons." J. L. M. Curry, while proposing to "keep the agreement entered into at Appomattox and Durham's Station," urged his Richmond audience near the turn of the century "to see to it that our children do not grow up with false notions of their fathers, and with disgraceful apologies for their conduct."[38]

Turney alluded to a concern of many of the Lost Cause speakers we have surveyed: the increasing centralization or the enhanced power of the federal government, which the outcome of the Civil War had speeded up. In the minds of many southerners, this product of the war must be reversed or, at least, held in check. This perception and attitude prevailed in the South through the twentieth century, perhaps finding its peak in the opposition to the civil rights movement, and is still finding its advocates in the first decade of the twenty-first century. James C. C. Black expresses this concern when he advises his audience to "cherish those essential principles that alone can save us from the encroachments of government that will be fatal to our free institutions."[39]

In the deeply conservative and tradition-bound South, it would be expected that some of the advice given by the Lost Cause orators would be to return to or preserve the values of the Old South. Part of that call for tradition involved a critique of the Gilded Age and what many southerners saw as a threat to the values of the past. Charles C. Jones Jr. was perhaps one of the most adamant of those who would hold true to traditional values as they saw them. In a speech to the Confederate Survivors' Association in Augusta,

Georgia, Jones alleged that the "moral and political standard of the present is not equal to that set up and zealously guarded by our fathers." Rather, the "effort to retrieve lost fortunes . . . the attempt to amass large moneys by spec-ulations" had resulted in the "lowering of the tone which marked our for-mer manly, conservative, patriarchal civilization." The standard that should be adhered to would be that of the Old South. Jones called his audience "to witness that the grand effort now is and should be to preserve inviolate the sentiments and to transmit unimpaired the characteristics of the Old South." For Jones, it is only in the "restoration of the good order, the decorum, the honesty, the veracity, the public confidence, the conservatism, the security to person and property, the high-toned conduct and the manliness of the past" that there is any hope for the "honor and lasting prosperity of the coming years." Jones is a good example of David Blight's observation that "the Lost Cause become a tonic against fear of social change, a preventative ideologi-cal medicine for the sick souls of the Gilded Age.[40]

A typical critique of the period comes from Rev. John Kershaw, who at-tacked those who "for lust of office sacrifice honor and violate conscience to feel for a passing moment the fickle breathe of popular applause; there are many more who are selling their souls for greed of gold . . . and many besides who make of self a god." For the minister, these men are "weak and crawling insects, fit only, and certain to be, trodden under foot of worthier represen-tatives of the race." Calling attention to the old Confederates, he maintains that "we would be worthy of their fame and example" if we should never be tempted to "sacrifice principle for policy, nor barter away our integrity, per-sonal, professional or social, for the seductions of a specious but more than questionable expediency." James C. C. Black reflects those sentiments when he warns his audience that the "greed of gain and lust of power are stand-ing menaces" and that the "highest offices are filled by the illegitimate use of money, thus corrupting the very fountains of government." John Sharp Wil-liams made one of the most direct attacks on the commercialism frowned on by many southern conservatives when he said in Memphis: "The man who surrenders his entire soul, or even subordinates his nature, who pros-titutes all of his energies, or his chief energies, to the business of piling one dollar upon another, who forgets that there are flowers and poetry, a past and a present for himself and for his race . . . would be bored to death in the kingdom of Heaven in twenty-four hours."[41]

One of the major concerns of the Lost Cause orators and of the many Ladies' Memorial Associations, the Daughters of the Confederacy, and the United Confederate Veterans was the fear that the history of the Civil War was being written by the North and that southern youth would be taught from textbooks that expressed the northern point of view. J. William Jones urged the UCV convention meeting in Houston in 1895 to see to it that "every Northern school history is banished from our schools, and every book slandering our Confederate people, our leaders, and our cause, is banished from our libraries and our homes." Landon Bell was still echoing that sentiment in 1929, when he admonished his audience that "we have need to see that the history of the Confederacy is not written in the future, as it has been in the past, by enemies of the cause for which the Confederate Soldiers laid down their lives." John B. Gordon, the longtime commander of the UCV, in his "Old South" lecture, delivered for years to audiences across the country, was a strong leader in this movement to ensure the "correctness" of the history of the Civil War and the South. In a version of the speech given in Augusta in 1887, Gordon reaffirmed to the veterans that "there is danger that the South may be inadequately represented, or wholly misrepresented in the future history of this country. Misrepresentation threatens the conquered always—the conquer never.... [I]n the average estimation of mankind, victory vindicates, while defeat dooms to misjudgment and thoughtless condemnation." So, therefore, Gordon urges his old comrades: "Let us strengthen the foundations of our future manhood and character by enhancing the self respect of southern youth. Let us ground that self respect in facts, not on the fictions of our history."[42]

While the postwar South was "blossoming like a rose," at least in the eyes of some of its orators, it was also creating a world of second-class citizenship and segregated discrimination for its black residents. Anyone in the late twentieth century and early twenty-first who does not understand the black southerner's objection to symbols of the Confederacy, which we will examine in the following chapter, need only read a few Lost Cause orations to see the racism and the drive to establish and defend white supremacy. Edward Pollard, who was one of the first to use the term Lost Cause, wrote in 1868, "This new cause—or rather the true question of the war revived—is the supremacy of the white race."[43] Orator after orator defended strongly the need to maintain the perceived superiority of the white over the black; a few examples will illustrate. Josiah A. P. Campbell, chief justice of the Mississippi Supreme Court, told an 1892 veterans' reunion in Jackson that the southern black was "doomed to inferiority forever.... [T]hey have no more capacity for a voice in public affairs, no more idea what is good for them or others, than children.... It devolves on us, the superior, the capable, the governing race, to do for them, to plan and shape for them, and so manage affairs as to bring about the best results for all." John Sharp Williams, speaking in Memphis in 1904, pointed out that the South fought for local self-government but that there was "even a greater cause. . . . This other thing for which we fought was the supremacy of the white man's civilization." Robert E. Lee Jr. praised the South in Richmond three years later and claimed that "generations yet unborn will rise and call her blessed for the determined fight which she has made, is making and will ever make to keep Anglo-Saxon blood untarnished and American citizenship pure and unbesmirched." Earlier in that speech he asserted that the black slave had been brought to the South "a wild, naked, shrieking, ash-besmeared savage," which the South "fed and clothed," "Christianized and civilized him."[44]

In several of these Lost Cause speeches one can find praise for the role of the Ku Klux Klan in defending white supremacy. Major General J. H. Martin, speaking to a reunion in Georgia in 1910, averred that "Africanizing the South" had been avoided by the "grand, invincible and invisible army that, Phoenix-like, arose from the remnants of the Confederate armies and under the mystic name of the Ku Klux Klan saved the South from negro domination and spoliation and established white control and supremacy." Eugene B. Gary, chief justice of the South Carolina Supreme Court, told a Confederate Memorial Day audience that "the civilization of the South, would have been destroyed, and we would have sunk to the level of Mexico and the Antilles if it had not been for the bravery and wisdom of the South, in daring to organize the KuKlux. The mysterious workings of that organization frightened the Negroes, kept them indoors at night, and checked them in their carnival of lawlessness."[45]

Katharine Du Pre Lumpkin clearly describes the link between the Lost Cause and the segregation and white supremacy that enveloped the South during this era. She wrote in her autobiography: "It was inconceivable, however, that any change could be allowed that altered the very present fact of the relation of superior white to inferior Negro. This we came to understand remained for us as it had been for our fathers, the very cornerstone of the South. It too was sanctified by the Lost Cause. Indeed, more than any other fact of our present, it told us our cause had not been lost, not in its entirety. It had been threatened by our Southern disaster. . . . No lesson of our history was taught us earlier, and none with greater urgency . . . 'either white supremacy or black domination.'"[46] We will see the results of this indoctrination in the next chapter.

6

The Persistence of a Myth

The Lost Cause in the Modern South

There is no question that Confederate ceremonial events and the rituals and rhetoric that created the cult of the Lost Cause made a deep and abiding impression on the white citizens of the post–Civil War South. A typical example of these celebrations and their impact on their communities occurred in Augusta, Georgia, in 1887. A newspaper reporter described the event: "The celebration of Memorial Day this year will certainly be on a grand scale, the Survivors' and Ladies' Association having entered into the movement with great earnestness and in thorough accord. All the railroads have arranged reduced rates, and thousands of visitors will be in the city." The organizing committee asked all of Augusta's stores to close for the day. The newspaper editorialized: "It is but right that our business men should accede, for April 26 is now really the only holiday into which the city enters with any extent."[1] With this much emphasis placed on the Memorial Day celebration and the involvement of the veterans' reunion groups, there is no doubt that these rituals created, enhanced, and solidified the southern white community and developed a sense of continuity in the face of overwhelming change. For some white southerners, this community continues in the early years of the twenty-first century. As David Goldfield concludes, for many southern whites in the twentieth century "the past had become so much part of them that it became their identity."[2] This identity is still alive and well.

The Lost Cause orators surveyed here are representatives of their type; they, and many hundreds not mentioned, through their rhetoric and rituals, transformed the violence, blood, and defeat of war into a symbol of regional unity, solidarity, and stability. Building on the South's traditional ties to the past and its honor of heritage, they helped bond white southerners into a culture that memorialized and reverenced the past. They helped create a white consensus regarding the past, a consensus that was expected to drive and guide the present and illuminate the future.

The Lost Cause generation expected no less, and it did all in its power to ensure this outcome. The historian of the United Daughters of the Confederacy, Mary Poppenheim, knew that at some point the people of the wartime generation would be gone, and "that era with its valor and its glory; its triumphs and its defeats; its heart-breaks and its sorrows; its loyalty and its devotion, will soon be a dream, a great adventure, but its influence on the South will be everlasting for the good of her people and through them, for the good of America."[3] Katherine Du Pre Lumpkin knew that her father's generation had a mission to accomplish, as it "became the preoccupation of their kind to preserve the old foundations at all costs."[4] That mission was largely carried out on warm April and May days when the white community gathered on city corners and town squares to celebrate the unveiling of the granite monuments honoring the Confederacy, or in a local cemetery covered with colorful spring flowers where tribute was paid to the dead on Memorial Day, or in the crowded and bustling arena where the old veterans gathered once again to share their war stories and hear the orators proclaim their wartime feats.

For the most part, the audiences that stood in front of the Lost Cause speakers had a broad and deep shared memory and heritage. The mention of Lee or Stuart, Jackson or Hill, Shiloh or Gettysburg, Chattanooga or Atlanta, Vicksburg or Antietam, all meant the same: "We were there," whether it was the aging veterans who really had been there, or the younger generations who had heard the tales over and over again from their fathers and uncles and grandfathers who were preoccupied with preserving the "old foundations at all costs." They were bonded both by blood spilled and by blood in the veins. Of course they remembered and passed it along like their very genes to their progeny and beyond, to all who would listen.

In one of the typical romantic rhetorical descriptions of the process of remembering, Stephen D. Lee described for his Richmond veterans over four decades after the guns were silent how glamorous and glorious the war had been. Lee depicted the "children and grandchildren" gathering about the old veterans and listening with "swelling hearts to the glorious story of the Confederacy." The younger generation rides "with Stuart, Hampton and Forrest. They march with Jackson, Cheatham, and Hood. They hear the thunder of Pelham's guns. They bear the body of Ashley in their arms. They listen to the hoof-beats of 'Traveler.' . . . We rejoice to remember these things. We know that our posterity will not forget them."[5]

Congressman John Sharp Williams, speaking on Confederate Memorial Day in 1904, told his Memphis audience that the ceremony would carry "forward into our children's lives and our children's children's lives of the sweet and brave memories of the men whose graves are bedecked, and whose cause is remembered." He said it was not really necessary for him to paint a nostalgic scene about the surrender at Appomattox (but he does anyway), "because the imagination of each old veteran here pictures it all for himself and every child has heard it so often that it presents itself in vivid coloring even to his mind."[6]

These speeches and ceremonies were, above all, designed to promote stability in an unstable time and to develop continuity with the past in the face of decades of turmoil, desolation, poverty, and social upheaval. That they succeeded is evident in the persistence of the mythology that was developed, believed in, and retained by many white southerners for all of the twentieth century and, for some, into the twenty-first. The mythology and stories of the Lost Cause resounded and echoed through the 1920s and 1930s when the United Daughters fought for the southern story and only the southern story to be told in the public school textbooks used across the region. It was promoted in the burgeoning mass media, especially with D. W. Griffith's film *Birth of a Nation* and with Margaret Mitchell's book and 1939 movie, *Gone with the Wind*. The 1946 Walt Disney movie *Song of the South,* based on the Uncle Remus tales of Joel Chandler Harris, perpetuated the mythology of the contented slave and an idyllic slave-master relationship. The Dixiecrat rebellion of 1948, in response to President Harry Truman's civil rights initiatives, echoed many of the Lost Cause themes and reflected those values instilled by the orators on Confederate Memorial Day, at veterans' reunions, and at monument dedications. The centennial of the Civil War coincided with the southern civil rights movement; the memories of the Confederacy were reinforced by the celebration of the centennial and were revitalized by the perceived threats to white supremacy raised by the sit-ins, the boycotts, and the marchers and protesters in Greensboro, Nashville, Birmingham, St. Augustine, Selma, and dozens of other southern cities and towns in the 1950s and 1960s.

During the heat of the civil rights movement, the rhetoric of the Lost Cause served as fundamental assumptions and assertions for a battery of segregationists. The rituals and oratory of the Lost Cause had bonded the white South together in a unified front that could be used against southern blacks as the institution of segregation was created in the late nineteenth century and later defended up through the middle of the twentieth. The children raised on the Lost Cause oratory of the 1870–1930 era became the white politicians, judges, and ministers who led the pro-segregation forces during the civil rights movement. Governors Ross Barnett, Orval Faubus, and George Wallace, Senator James Eastland, Judge Tom Brady, and many other white segregationists drew heavily on their memories and perceptions of the Confederacy, Reconstruction, and "The War" as they tried desperately to stop the tide of integration after the 1954 U.S. Supreme Court decision in *Brown v. Board of Education.*

The Confederate narratives were still current and effective during the 1990s as the region debated the value or the harm of flying the Confederate flag in public places. Confederate monuments are still being erected in the region, and repairs using public monies are being made on those a century and more old. Confederate Memorial Day is still celebrated in many cities, towns, and states across the South. Letters to the editor echo the Lost Cause orators as if their heyday were just yesterday. A June 15, 2001, letter to the *Charlotte Observer* regarding the Confederate flag issues roiling the Carolinas expressed clearly the point of view of one contemporary southerner about Reconstruction and sounded as if it were taken directly from any number of Lost Cause orations: "For Southerners it was hell on Earth at the hands of the U.S. government."

Debates still rage over the wearing of Confederate T-shirts and logos on clothing in high schools across the region, and the University of Mississippi continues to hear opposition to its Rebel name and mascot. The battles over allowing female cadets to attend The Citadel in Charleston, South Carolina; the 1997 federal court decision that ruled that the Confederate battle flag could not be banned from Maryland license plates; the court decision in North Carolina in 1999 that the Sons of Confederate Veterans was a civic organization and thus entitled to a special license plate; and the NAACP struggles in Kentucky to remove a statue of Jefferson Davis from the state capitol where it was placed in 1936—all of these reflect the gauntlet thrown down a hundred and more years ago by Lost Cause orators as they urged their audiences to recall "their sacred duty" to perpetuate "a love for the Cause for which we fought and the memory of the record made by the armies of the South."[7]

The symbols created and used by half a century of Lost Cause orators were powerful enough to last through the twentieth century and into the twenty-first. They drew their white audiences toward them and toward each other with words that adapted well to their audience's needs, attitudes, wants, dreams, emotions, values, and fears. Expressions such as "Southern womanhood," "our way of life," "states' rights," "white supremacy," "The South," "mongrelization," "outside agitators," and "damn Yankees" were emotionally

charged shorthand snapshots of a slice of the world confronting southerners, and the Lost Cause orators drove them home with telling and lasting effect. The legacy of this rhetoric in defense of the Confederacy, the South, and
the Lost Cause will be enduring in the public and private life of the South
for many years.

"We do not intend to acquiesce in the destruction of the IDEALs of our fathers by any party!": The Lost Cause in Segregation

The most vivid, bitter, and hard-fought battle using the symbols and mythology of the Lost Cause was the white dinosaurs' 1950s and 1960s defense
of segregation. Lost Cause oratory and the establishment of Jim Crow segregation flourished at the same time in the last two decades of the nineteenth
century and the first years of the twentieth, and each supported and ratio-
nalized the other. A malignant legacy of lynching and other violence, disfranchisement, and second-class citizenship followed. Lost Cause rhetoric
justified, vindicated, defended, and explained states' rights and white supremacy as enduring and fundamental planks of the "southern way of life."
That message was delivered and reinforced over and over by segregationists
like Ross Barnett, who declared to a Citizens' Council rally in 1960, "We do
not intend to acquiesce in the destruction of the IDEALs of our fathers by
any party!" David Blight shows that "the cause that was *not* lost . . . reverberated as part of the very heartbeat of the Jim Crow South." The issues might
be different (segregation, not slavery; Civil Rights Act or Voting Rights Act
or school integration, not Reconstruction), but the defenses thrown up by
the white South were the same as those in the previous century: states' rights,
the Constitution of our Fathers, republican government, delegated powers,
interposition. For the segregationists of the 1950s and 1960s, there was not
much distance between the Civil War and the civil rights movement as they
resurrected the rhetoric of the Lost Cause in their battles against integration
and change. The civil rights movement was just a contemporary example
of conflict brought to the South by "outsiders" who wished to change the
"southern way of life." Instead of abolitionists or General Sherman or Abe
Lincoln or carpetbaggers, it was the NAACP or the Communists or liberal
Democrats or the Kennedy clan. The very fact that there was a civil rights
movement shows that the nation was not yet one—even at that late date—
and that a large percentage of the population remained intent on keeping
black Americans "in their place." "Their place" may not have been slavery,
but it was certainly second-class citizenship; they were still on the outside,
looking in. Reconciliation was still not a full reality. David Goldfield dem-

onstrates that by the time of the civil rights movement, most of the South had become "fortified battlegrounds of the mind and spirit. . . . The press, political leaders, schools, and churches conspired to defend or at least tolerate white supremacy." This attitude was certainly not a uniquely southern trait; witness George Wallace's vote-getting power outside the South in his presidential campaigns in 1964, 1968, and 1972.[8]

In short, the South was still a defensive region, throwing up the bulwarks and manning the trenches against the Yankee. The speakers and audiences of the Lost Cause era would certainly have understood the rhetoric of those mid-twentieth-century speakers who drew their premises and evidence from the rhetoric of the defeated South. There was a straight line of descent from the Lost Cause to Coleman Blease, "Cotton Ed" Smith, or Theodore Bilbo of the 1920s and 1930s on through the segregationists who refused to bend to the sweeping changes that roared into the region in the 1950s and 1960s. Ross Barnett, Orval Faubus, George Wallace, and many other segregationists were the heirs of Stephen Lee, John W. Daniel, Charles C. Jones Jr., and many more orators who graced the platforms on Confederate Memorial Day, urging the Confederate veterans and their grandchildren to never forget, and dedicating the monuments to their valor and memory. James McBride Dabbs, a liberal white southerner, writing in the early years of the civil rights era, pointed out that the South defended segregation so strongly because it was so closely attached to the Old South, the Confederacy, the Lost Cause. "When we defend it," Dabbs asserted, "we defend the lives, hopes, customs of our fathers. This is the only thing we have left, the last beleaguered fortress of the Lost Cause." Later, Dabbs pointed out that the tradition of Reconstruction as created by the Lost Cause orators was what the white South of the 1950s feared: the ghosts of the southern Negro reemerging from the mythology of the Reconstruction era.[9] Certainly, the segregationist orators of the twentieth century knew how to tap into those ghosts for their political strength.

It is fair to say that white southerners as a whole by the twentieth century rejected the idea that the Civil War was fought to preserve slavery, despite what some of the region's leaders had clearly asserted. They did, however, hold onto the idea that it was fought over the rights of states, or "constitutional liberty," which they claimed was protected by the founders in both the Articles of Confederation and the Constitution. What have southerners really wanted or meant when they advocated "states' rights" or "constitutional liberty"? Generally, these were code words for local control of African Americans within the bounds of the South, protection of slavery before and during the war, and then establishment and perpetuation of rigid racial segregation after Reconstruction and into the twentieth century. On September 3, 1963, speaking to the Louisiana Committee for Free Electors, a group dedicated to defeating John F. Kennedy in the 1964 presidential election, Mississippi governor Ross Barnett summed up the call for state sovereignty: "The resumption and exercise of state sovereignty is indispensable to the preservation of human rights. My fellow Americans, I am convinced that once the right of a state to exercise exclusive jurisdiction over a local problem is lost, human rights, liberty and freedom will absolutely perish."[10]

Another southern governor, Orval Faubus of Arkansas, waved the flag of states' rights before that state's Democratic Convention in September 1958 as he told the delegates he believed that "back of all the struggle and turmoil . . . lies the usurpation of the powers of the states by the federal government and by the Supreme Court." Faubus did not promise victory in the battle, but he did promise his fellow Democrats he would "stand up and fight as best I could for the preservation of our Constitutional rights and the basic precepts of democracy."[11] As it turned out, the white South was fighting another lost cause.

Two weeks later, and a week before Little Rock citizens voted to close the public schools rather than integrate for the 1958 school year, Faubus was certain of his role: "It is my responsibility, and it is my purpose and determination, to defend the constitutional rights of the people of Arkansas to the full extent of my ability." The problem was clear for Faubus and his supporters: the "gradual, constant, and forcible usurpation of the powers of the States and the people, by the Federal Government and the United States Supreme Court." In words strongly reminiscent of the arguments of Lost Cause orators, Faubus described the conflict over segregation as the "violation of the rights guaranteed to the States by the Constitution."[12]

While the Arkansas governor drew early attention to the federal-versus-state battle over the Little Rock school desegregation crisis and his confrontation with President Eisenhower, who finally sent troops to monitor Central High during the 1957–58 school year, Mississippi's governor, Ross Barnett, was even more visible in the integration fight. In September 1962, James Meredith, a black Air Force veteran, enrolled at the University of Mississippi under the guns of soldiers and the watchful eye of the U.S. Justice Department, and over the strong and bitter opposition of Governor Barnett. In a radio and television speech to the citizens of his state, Barnett pulled out all the stops and in his assertions and wording called up the ghosts of the Lost Cause. Barnett blamed the federal government and, implicitly, the Kennedy administration for forcing this issue: "In the absence of Constitutional authority and without legislative action an ambitious Federal government, employing naked and arbitrary power has decided to deny us the right of self-determination in the conduct of the affairs of our sovereign State." Barnett decried the "now desecrated Constitution" that the founding fathers had "handed . . . to us in trust as our sacred heritage and for our preservation." For Barnett, "the last hope of our Constitutional form of government rests in the conscientious enforcement of state laws and the perpetuation of the sovereignty of the states." The governor proclaimed to his audience and the Kennedy administration that, "in obedience to legislative and constitutional sanction, I interpose the rights of the Sovereign State of Mississippi to enforce its laws and to regulate its own internal affairs without interference on the part of the Federal government or its officers." Proudly, Barnett asserted: "The State of Mississippi has become the keystone in the fight for State's Rights. Our nation's survival as a Republic of Sovereign States depends on what we do in this crisis." Reminding his listeners of the historically militant nature of the South and the nation, and the days of the Confederacy, Barnett recalled that "generations [have] defended their liberties with blood and sweat and tears at Valley Forge, at Shiloh and at Vicksburg, in the Argonne, at Guadalcanal and on the Heartbreak Hills of Korea."[13] There were doubtless some Mississippians in the range of his voice who may have added, "and we'll do it again in Oxford if we can." In the wake of Meredith's enrollment, two were killed in the riots on the Ole Miss campus, and Barnett was charged with contempt of court, fined ten thousand dollars a day, and sentenced to jail. He never paid the fine or served jail time.

A little less than a year later, Barnett challenged the proposed Civil Rights Act of 1963 in his speech to the Louisiana Committee for Free Electors, calling it "truly a wolf in sheep's clothing": "It is 10% Civil Rights and 90% extension of Federal executive power. It is the most far-reaching legislation ever proposed by any President of the United States. It will result in dictatorial control. It would destroy the free enterprise system—the bedrock of our economy—and would impose intolerable restrictions on the property rights and personal rights of every citizen." Barnett called for unified action to oppose the "complete Federal dictatorship which this legislation would set up."[14]

Southern governors led the charge in their states, and southern senators rallied behind their constituents' values and demands in Washington. Mississippi senator James Eastland spoke early and often about his impressions of the misuse of power by the U.S. Supreme Court. In 1955, speaking to a meeting of the Association of Citizens' Councils of Mississippi in Jackson, Senator Eastland attacked the Court's decision in *Brown* the year before: "This is an attack upon the sovereignty of the States, and a State has the le-

gal right and the legal duty to protect its sovereignty. It is obligated to protect and preserve its powers." Seven years later, segregation was still a constitutional question for the Mississippian, who asserted that "the Supreme
Court of the United States has infringed, invaded and usurped the powers
vested by the Constitution in the legislative branch of the Federal Government." Eastland warned of not just the Court's unconstitutional actions but
also that "the executive branch . . . has invaded and usurped the power of
the legislative branch in creating rules of law and conduct that are not to be
found in any statute law of the United States and cannot be justified by any
remote constitutional authority."[15]

Strom Thurmond of South Carolina, who had been the Dixiecrat Party
candidate for the presidency in 1948, carried the flag for the states' righters
for many years. In 1965 he told a chamber of commerce audience in Aberdeen, South Dakota: "Already our political and social structures have under-
gone drastic changes from the individual-based system envisioned by the
Constitution." Senator Thurmond urged the chamber to "fight for a return
to the Constitution, for it is the best political charter yet devised by which
men can govern themselves." The Supreme Court "has, of course, been the
primary instrument in these drastic departures from the Constitution."[16]

One of the strategies of the southern states' rights leadership was to take
their message across the nation. White southerners believed they had a sym-
pathetic ear in at least the Midwest and far West. Like Thurmond's foray into
South Dakota, many others went to western and midwestern venues to spread
their gospel. William J. Simmons, the editor of publications for the Citizens' Council, spoke in 1958 to an audience at a annual farmers-merchants
banquet in Oakland, Iowa. He praised his listeners and proclaimed that the
Midwest and the South "are both dynamic strongholds of States' Rights and
of responsible local self-government." Simmons paraded the party line, reminding the gathering that America is not a democracy, but "a republic of
48 sovereign states. . . . The Constitution was therefore ratified by the States
acting in their sovereign capacities as independent, separate political communities." Simmons warned his listeners: "If our States' Rights are usurped
with impunity, are yours safe?"[17]

Thomas Pickens Brady, an associate justice of the Mississippi Supreme
Court, took the message of states' rights to the West Coast as he spoke on
October 4, 1957, to the Commonwealth Club of California in San Francisco.
Linking segregation and states' rights, Brady discussed the role of the Citi-
zens' Councils and told his audience: "Primarily, the Councils are dedicated
to the preservation of segregation and the sovereign rights of the States of

this Union." Attacking the recently enacted Civil Rights Act of 1957, the judge quoted a fellow Mississippian, Congressman William Colmer, who in a speech on the floor of Congress articulated the goals of that act as "the complete destruction of the sovereignty of the States and the centralization of all power of the people in our strong centralized government under the dome of the Capitol in Washington."[18]

Not only did the segregationists continue the Lost Cause orators' theme regarding the centrality of states' rights to the history and heritage of the South, but they also continued and reinforced the Reconstruction mythology that had been created and defended by the late-nineteenth-century white leadership. W. M. Caskey, a professor of history at Mississippi College, delivered the "Mississippi Day" address at Valley Forge, Pennsylvania, on May 15, 1960, in which he attacked the "ruthless architects of that period of misrule and corruption" and called Reconstruction that "negro-carpetbag-scalawag period of supremacy, and corrupt misrule." Ross Barnett told of the "white citizens of New Orleans [who] rose up in arms against the tyrannical rule of the Carpetbaggers"; once again (in 1960), the Crescent City and the "entire South" were at the mercy of the "NAACP and other modern-day Carpetbaggers." He concluded that the white South "will not surrender ourselves to endure another siege of Carpetbag rule!" Then he played his trump card—his and his audience's relationship to the Confederate generation: "Your grandfather and mine kept faith, even beneath the conqueror's boot. In the great city of New Orleans—and throughout your state and mine—loyal Southerners remained true to their principles, even while enduring the cruel excesses of the Reconstruction era."[19]

Judge Brady also tied his appeal to his family heritage: "My grandfather was a Captain in the Mississippi Rifles. He fought for four years in the War Between the States. He buried his brother who was killed by his side at Vicksburg. From my grandfather's lips, as millions of other Southerners heard from their grandfather's lips, I obtained a vivid description of the first Reconstruction Era." Brady's description of his grandfather was indeed vivid; it was right out of innumerable Lost Cause orations of the previous century: "The homes, cotton and corn fields, which had escaped the scourge of war were destroyed under the Negro Carpetbag military rule which lasted 3½ years in Mississippi. Drunken, marauding bands of crazed Negroes shot and broke into homes, raping and killing the women and children whom they dragged screaming from their flaming homes." And then, in a critical point that illustrates the enduring legend of the Lost Cause and its impact on the region decades after the end of Reconstruction: "The crackle of the flames and the groans and screams of the helpless victims, though not loud, *are still audible in the minds of Southerners* [emphasis added]."[20] Audible they were, and for a sizable number they were still audible in 2010. When will they die?

But a state supreme court justice was not the only southern leader to recall Reconstruction. James E. Byrnes, former South Carolina governor and U.S. senator from the Palmetto State, reminded his listeners in Bennettsville that "the leaders of the two political parties have no conception of the feelings of millions of white Southerners in this matter." In fact, they "accept the optimistic generalities of a few writers who are regarded today just as were the scalawags who betrayed their neighbors in Reconstruction Days."[21] Brynes's speech was delivered at the height of the Little Rock Central High School crisis in September 1957, so it doubtless received a warm welcome from his fellow South Carolinians as the 101st Airborne Division occupied the campus of Central High and the Arkansas National Guard was federalized by President Dwight Eisenhower.

Iowa farmers and merchants heard William Simmons use the mythology of Reconstruction to support his case for segregation: "The dark days of Reconstruction lasted over a decade. The South was under military occupation. The white people were disfranchised. Negro supremacy as virtually complete." In Simmons's mind, the "Negro-carpetbagger rule" had "brought possibly as much economic devastation to our region as four years of war." He concluded later that the white South could not permit the NAACP "to gain comparable power in our section. It would mean a repetition of the Reconstruction era in the South."[22]

A final example of many that could be offered is George Wallace's infamous inaugural address of 1963, when the governor proclaimed, "Segregation now . . . segregation tomorrow . . . segregation forever." Wallace reinforced the defense of segregation from the white perspective a bit later in the speech when he painted the usual Lost Cause version of the Reconstruction era; this time, from the prestigious pulpit of the inaugural of a state's governor, he painted the verbal picture:

[A]fter the great War Between the States, our people faced a desolate land of burned universities, destroyed crops and homes, with manpower depleted and crippled, and even the mule, which was required to work the land was so scarce that whole communities shared one animal to make the spring plowing. There were no government hand-outs, no Marshall Plan aid, no coddling to make sure that *our* people would not suffer; instead the South was set upon by the vulturous carpetbagger and federal troops, all loyal Southerners were denied the vote at the

point of bayonet. . . . There was no money, no food and no hope of either. But our grandfathers bent their knee only in church and bowed
their head only to God . . . They dug sweet roots from the ground with
their bare hands and boiled them in the old iron pots . . . they gathered
poke salad from the woods and acorns from the ground. They fought.
They followed no false doctrine . . . they knew what they wanted . . . and
they fought for freedom! They came up from their knees in the greatest display of sheer nerve, grit and guts that has ever been set down in
the pages of written history . . . and they won![23]

The Lost Cause orators had done their job well—those memories of the
Reconstruction era had been drilled deeply into the hearts and minds of
many white southerners and were at the beck and call of segregationists who
wanted to use them to support their point of view.

The southern white leadership that adamantly opposed and bitterly fought
the civil rights movement during the 1950s and 1960s had its cadre of scapegoats for the regional ills and travails through which they were passing, just
as the Lost Cause orators had theirs. In many respects, they were similar.
The South has been a defensive region throughout much of its history. Before the Civil War, the rhetorical targets were the northern slave traders
who had brought the slaves to the country, the abolitionists, the Republican
Party, Abraham Lincoln, Congress, and the North, especially "Yankees," in
general. In the late nineteenth and early twentieth century, oratorical battles
were waged against the Republican Party, Congress, Yankees, carpetbaggers,
scalawags, and "Negro domination." In the mid-twentieth century the segregationists rallied against a general target: "outside agitators," which brought
back memories of the abolitionists and the carpetbaggers. There was a list
of familiar demons: the liberal Democrats, Congress, the Kennedy administration, the Supreme Court and the federal government in general, the liberal media, the NAACP, national foundations and organizations that supported the movement, and the biggest target: Communists.

Senator Eastland believed that the "South today is the victim of forces
and influences that originated far from its own borders." In Jackson, Mississippi, Mayor Allen C. Thompson blamed the "outside troublemakers" for attacking his city with their "Freedom Riders" strategy. Judge Brady warned
his San Francisco audience about the "left-wing minority groups" creating
so much havoc back home in Mississippi. In his speech on the James Meredith crisis at Ole Miss, Governor Barnett attacked the "professional agitators," the "unfriendly liberal press," "other troublemakers," and "paid propa-
gandists" for the problems at Oxford.[24] "Outside agitators" (one of the most

favored devil terms used by the white defenders of segregation) just needed
to leave the region alone and let the South take care of itself.

Governor Wallace reminded his inaugural audience that the region was
perfectly capable of even national leadership: a "*Southerner,* Peyton Randolph, presided over the Continental Congress . . . a *Southerner,* Thomas
Jefferson, wrote the Declaration of Independence . . . a *Southerner,* George
Washington, is the Father of our Country . . . a *Southerner,* James Madison,
authored our Constitution . . . a *Southerner,* George Mason, authored the
Bill of Rights, and it was a *Southerner,* who said, 'Give me liberty or give me
death,' Patrick Henry." Wallace asserted that "Southerners played a most significant part in creating this great divinely inspired system of freedom . . .
and as God is our witness, Southerners will save it."[25] No help needed.

But when the racist leadership wanted to be more specific than simply
attacking "outsiders," they had many concrete targets. The Supreme Court
and other federal courts were all one bull's-eye for southern segregationists.
U.S. senator Sam J. Ervin Jr. attacked the Court in a speech at Harvard Law
School just over a year after the *Brown* decision. The North Carolinian asserted that "on many occasions during recent years the Supreme Court has to
all intents and purposes usurped the power of the Congress and the States to
amend the Constitution." Orval Faubus blamed the Little Rock Central High
School crisis on the integration plans "being forced upon us by the Federal
Courts." This "illegal usurpation of powers by the U.S. Supreme Court and
the federal government" was for Faubus and the southern leadership one of
the major sources of conflict. Eastland, and many other southerners, warned
the rest of the country that "when the Supreme Court destroys local self-
government in the South, it also destroys it in the North."[26]

The U.S. Supreme Court and the federal courts were part of a larger issue, the rapidly increasing power of the central government, which had been
a threat to southerners since at least the days of the Nullification Crisis in
South Carolina almost a century and a half earlier. Barnett defined his vision
of the problem in 1963: "The real goal of this left-wing conspiracy which attempts to control your emotions with this 'race issue' is the concentration
of all effective power in the central government at Washington." Five years
earlier, William Simmons had focused on the same issue in his Midwest address with an even more specific charge: "Since 1932 the New Deal, the Fair
Deal, and all the other deals have never wavered from one course, however
soothing the words or how alluring the promises. That unswerving course
is the steady march toward an all powerful centralized government." Judge
Brady also traced the problem back to the era of the Great Depression: "Beginning with the administration of F.D.R., the South viewed with alarm the

birth of the welfare state, and the growth of the 130 Communist-front organizations which nourish it."[27]

Attacking the "Warren Court" was part and parcel of the broader, but at
the peak of the cold war era the more serious problem for many white southerners was the influence of the Communist Party on the trend toward centralized power and its support for the civil rights movement. Most, if not
all, of the segregationist orators pinned the blame for the racial unrest and
the push for racial integration squarely on the backs of the Communists and
Communist-front organizations and their influence on the media, the courts,
and the liberal wing of the Democratic Party. Within months of the *Brown*
decision, Senator Eastland blamed the Court for responding "to a radical pro-
Communist political movement in this country. I do not have to tell you that
this thing is broader and deeper than the N.A.A.C.P." He went on to link the
NAACP with "church groups, radical organizations, labor unions and liberal
groups of all shades of Red. They run from the blood red of the Communist Party to the almost equally Red of the National Council of Churches of
Christ in the U.S.A." The senator's Mississippi compatriot, Judge Brady, proclaimed to his San Francisco audience in 1957 that southerners "realize and
firmly believe that the resurgence of demand and effort for the advancement
of the Negro politically and socially in the last thirty years was conceived
and promoted by world-wide communism."[28]

Governor Faubus cited the Communist ties of two of the sources used
by the Supreme Court in its *Brown* ruling, charging that Theodore Brameld
had been cited by the House Committee on Unamerican Activities as having been a member of "no less than 10 organizations declared to be Com-
munistic, Communist-front, or Communist-dominated." Faubus also cited
E. Franklin Frazier, who "has at least 18 citations of connections with Communist causes in the United States." William Simmons broadened that charge
by pointing out that W. E. B. DuBois, a founder and leader of the NAACP,
"has one of the longest records of pro-Communist activity of any person
in the country." Furthermore, "the public record of activities of many top
N.A.A.C.P. leaders in Communist-front enterprises is long, and it is copi-
ously documented." He goes on to list the Urban League, the Fund for the
Republic, the Southern Regional Council, and the Southern Conference for
Human Welfare as being heavily influenced by Communist leadership and
concludes there is "deep involvement of the Communists in the race incita-
tion and integration controversy in this country."[29]

Almost eight years later, James Eastland was still blaming the Communist-
influenced Supreme Court for the racial disharmony in the South. In a Senate speech in 1962 titled "Is the Supreme Court Pro-Communist?" he left no

doubt about his answer. According to him, the Supreme Court lends "aid and comfort to the conspiracy that is dedicated to the overthrow and destruction of our system of government itself." Chief Justice Earl Warren bore the brunt of Eastland's attacks (and throughout the South, highway billboards called for Warren's impeachment). The Mississippian identified "70 cases or more involving Communist or subversive activities in one form or another" that had come before the Court in the years that Warren had been chief justice. According to the senator, forty-six of these decisions sustained the Communist position, while only twenty-four opposed that point of view.[30] As the cold war almost daily threatened to become a hot war, and fear of Soviet power swept the country in the 1950s and 1960s, Americans in general, and the defensive South in particular, were eager and willing to point their fingers at the Communist conspiracy and blame the "Commies" for most, if not all, of the nation's ills. The white southern leadership played that card to the maximum.

The fundamental fact of southern life that the segregationists fought so hard to retain was the "determination on the part of the white people to resort to every legal means to prevent the mixing of the races," in the words of South Carolinian James Brynes. As William Simmons put it, the Citizens' Councils are "stopping race mixing in its tracks." This "sacred heritage" of a white South was the be-all and end-all as far as Ross Barnett was concerned. He proudly proclaimed to an audience in 1960: "Ross Barnett is a MISSISSIPPI SEGREGATIONIST AND PROUD OF IT! and I will do everything within my power to preserve our sacred heritage."[31] Many white southerners like Barnett were trapped by Lost Cause rhetoric and the racist institutions and restrictions that had grown out of it in the last decades of the nineteenth century and the early decades of the twentieth. In a tribute to the power of rhetoric, whether for good or ill, only a few were able to escape from that world until the late 1960s and early 1970s, when governors such as Florida's Reuben Askew and North Carolina's James Holshouser were elected on nonracist platforms.

Although segregation was the battlefield of the 1950s and 1960s, various issues festered for years. Many may have thought that the Civil War was truly and finally over with the passage of the Civil Rights Act of 1964 and the Voting Rights Act of 1965. In general, white southerners accepted the new order and the white supremacy dinosaurs were replaced in southern governors' mansions throughout the region beginning soon after these landmark bills became the law of the land. Blacks across the region began voting their peers into office in ever-increasing numbers, and schools were integrated across the South with little or no fanfare. But it was only a mirage, as issues still smoldered like a fire in a compost pile or a sawmill's mountain of sawdust—just below the surface.

"This is all about states' rights": The Lost Cause and Confederate Symbols

Lieutenant Colonel Oliver North, speaking as a delegate to the Virginia Republican Convention in 1994, was referring to the struggles over the Confederate flag when he said: "This is all about states' rights, and limiting the federal government. And I can tell you this: you're going to see a whole lot more of it."[32] He was right; there was "a whole lot more of it" as the century rolled over. The issue is still by no means settled. On the one hand, many white southerners consider the Confederate flag a symbol of their regional and family heritage, and they see it as honoring the courage and prowess of their ancestors. For this group there is a strong desire to preserve and respect the best qualities of southern life they believe are inherent in southern culture. Many of them also see themselves as a last-ditch defense against modern influences such as an ever-growing federal government, the "corporation" (defined in many ways), a loosening of morals, and a decline in the values of family and home.

On the other hand, many African Americans view the Confederate flag as a symbol of slavery and racism and demand that it be banned from public view; for them, its only appropriate setting is a museum. They claim those who wish to protect and defend their view of southern life are racists who use the Confederate flag, Confederate Memorial Day, groups such as the United Daughters of the Confederacy (UDC) and the Sons of Confederate Veterans (SCV), and Confederate monuments as offensive reminders of the worst in southern culture: slavery, segregation, and continued racism. On the one side, the flag represents Lee, Jackson, Davis, great-grandfathers, Bull Run, and the ideals, honor, and valor of their ancestors. On the other side, it represents the Klan, poor schools and medical care, segregated housing and transportation, and generally, second-class citizenship. It is impossible to deny that since the 1950s the Confederate flag has been used by the segregationist Citizens' Councils, the Ku Klux Klan, and state and local governments as an act of defiance toward the federal government—of thumbing the white South's collective nose at the Warren Court and the Kennedy administration in the 1960s. This defiance has continued in the early years of the twenty-first century by various white supremacy groups that use the Confederate flag as their symbol. These polar opposites have fueled boycotts and protests from both sides and have led to statewide votes, legislative enactments, and gubernatorial decrees regarding whether, when, where, and how the Confederate flag is to be flown in public places around the South.

It is perhaps in South Carolina that the most polarized debate has occurred. The state chapter of the NAACP called for a boycott of the state as long as the flag was flying on the statehouse grounds. The flag had been posted there in 1962, at the peak of the civil rights movement across the South, but in 2000 there had been a compromise of sorts, as the flag was moved from the top of the statehouse and raised on a flagpole on the grounds. Still too visible, said the NAACP, and it called for the boycott. In neighboring Georgia, the governor changed the state flag after protests over the Confederate battle emblem on the previous state flag, which had been redesigned in 1956 in a protest over the *Brown* decision. The Heritage Defense Fund collected a "low- to mid-six-figure" fund to fight the removal of the Confederate insignia from the state flag, and the membership in the Georgia SCV grew from 350 to 3,800 members; its commander, attorney Allen Trapp Jr., challenged the state: "This is a line in the sand. For the past 15 years anything Southern, anything Confederate has been subject to vicious attack." Later, the voters of Georgia chose a flag design similar to the first Confederate national flag.[33] Mississippi's residents voted overwhelmingly to keep the state flag, which includes the Confederate battle emblem, and rejected a proposed flag without the emblem. Even the border state of Missouri participated in the debates; its Department of Natural Resources removed Confederate flags from the Confederate Memorial State Historic Site and the Fort Davidson State Historic Site.

This furor over the flag is not new. A full century earlier, the national convention of the Grand Army of the Republic had proclaimed that displaying the Confederate flag "[is] an affront to patriotism, encourages disloyalty, and lessens respect for our government." A year later, Order no. 4 prohibited GAR members from participating in an event at which the Confederate flag was on display.[34] In Dixie, former Confederates and their kin took the opposite tack and promoted the flag at every opportunity. At the 1899 United Confederate Veterans (UCV) reunion, General Gordon had asked that "as many historic Confederate Battle Flags as possible be brought and used on the parade. As a special guard of honor to such flags all the members of any command of which the battle flag was the colors, will parade with their colors and not with their [UCV] camp. . . . It is desired to give the highest dignity and honor to these worthy emblems of Southern valor."[35]

A brief look back at some of our Lost Cause orators clearly shows their devotion to the Confederate flag and how their oratory provided the basis for the deeply held feelings of white southerners a century later. Randolph

McKim, speaking to a 1904 veterans' reunion in Nashville, spoke of the divided loyalties of the South: on the one hand, to the national flag of the Stars and Stripes, but at the same time, "the offering of our love and loyalty to the memory of the flag of the Southern Confederacy!"[36] McKim's statement defines one side of the contemporary debate: those who see the flag as a symbol of an honored tradition and history.

In that same year of 1904, halfway across the state of Tennessee, Congressman John Sharp Williams defined the other, less glorious, and indefensible side of the issue: the racism seen by modern African Americans. In his address to a group of Confederate veterans, Williams said this about the battle flag: "Once a year in the resurrection season of nature, we shall unfurl it, unfurl it as a symbol of the cause which it represented, and still represents, as the symbol of the solidity of its people in behalf of local self-government and in behalf of the perpetuation of the supremacy of the white man's ethics, his law, the precious fruits of his literacy and industrial attainment— in a word, his civilization." Williams reflected on how this respect would be passed down: "We shall place it in the hands of little children, that it may symbolize in their hands the perpetuation of the annual resurrection of those memories to our children and to their children's children. . . . It is the symbol today of something grander even than the immortality of the individual, to-wit: the immortality of the race, its culture, its ideals and that body of acquired sentiment which we call civilization."[37]

Katharine Du Pre Lumpkin recalled in her autobiography a Confederate reunion she witnessed a year before Williams's speech at which the flags were literally handed to the younger generation, just as Williams had predicted: "Confederate flags. They were everywhere, by the thousands, of every size. People thronging Main Street carried flags. A few might also have South Carolina's banner. . . . but all would have Confederate flags . . . a huge Confederate banner [was spread across the face of the state capitol building]. . . . [B]oth Opera House and City Hall were festooned and flag-draped."[38] The children of the Confederacy certainly could not have missed the point Williams and other orators were making: the flag reflects all sides of their heritage—the good, the bad, and the ugly.

By the late 1940s, the Confederate battle flag was representing the southern region in many ways. It began to be raised as part of the white southern protest over President Truman's civil rights initiatives such as desegregating the military forces. It became the symbol of the "Dixiecrats," officially known as the States' Rights Party, which ran Strom Thurmond and Fielding Wright for the presidency and vice-presidency in 1948. According to the Confederate battle flag's leading historian, John Coski, a "flag fad" raged over the region and it became an endeared symbol for a generation of white southern college students, especially at the University of Mississippi. When the civil rights movement began in earnest in the mid-1950s, the Ku Klux Klan and other defenders of segregation and racism quickly pressed the flag into service. In 1963 George Wallace ordered it flown over the capitol in Montgomery as he preached "segregation now . . . segregation tomorrow . . . segregation forever" and stood in the schoolhouse door at the University of Alabama to stall integration there.

About three decades after the civil rights movement, the Confederate flag was still a burning issue. The NAACP passed a resolution in March 1987 that declared the "Confederate Battle Flag to be a symbol of divisiveness, racial animosity, and an insult to black people though the region: . . . [and] requests the States of South Carolina and Alabama . . . to remove the Confederate Battle Flag from the domes of their Capitol Buildings; and . . . requests the State of Georgia to return to its standard state flag of pre-1956; and . . . the State of Mississippi to return to its standard State flag of pre-1894."[39]

In 1999 the NAACP unanimously approved a tourism boycott of South Carolina until the Confederate battle flag was removed from the capitol building; the tactic was aimed at the estimated $280 million spent annually by black tourists in South Carolina.[40] The debate quickly focused on the economic issues, as some South Carolinians feared that other states would use the flag issue to attract industry and businesses to move to their states rather than to South Carolina. Business leaders in the Palmetto State were leaders in the campaign to have the flag removed from the dome of the statehouse. As the chairwoman of the state chamber of commerce remarked, "If we're going to be part of the next millennium, we have to move that flag off our Statehouse dome, and put it in a place of honor elsewhere." Bernard E. Powers Jr., a history professor at the College of Charleston, expressed the conventional wisdom of white South Carolina's leadership: "You can't go on celebrating the oppression of African-Americans and expect to attract outside dollars and corporate interests." John S. Rainey, a former chairman of the state-owned water and electric utility, took the higher ground, observing, "I think this is about more than money. It's about doing the right thing, the honorable thing. There is a sea change going on in South Carolina, an awakening to what we can be if we really start tackling the old, hard issues."[41]

But this was not a universal feeling around the state. There were echoes of the Lost Cause in this debate almost a century after Confederate veterans were in the grave. State sovereignty was not a dead issue at the turn of the twenty-first century. Many whites across the region saw the debate turning on this concept raised many times in U.S. history, but nowhere as eloquently and forcefully as in the antebellum South and after Appomattox by the Lost Cause orators as we saw in chapter 3. The state legislature had raised the flag in commemoration of the Civil War Centennial in 1961, and it was left flying after the Centennial, doubtless as a reminder for white and black South Carolinians alike during the raging civil rights movement of the mid-1960s. Walter Edgar, director of the Institute for Southern Studies at the University of South Carolina, remarked in early 2000: "This is a state that has always believed it should determine its own affairs."[42]

The pressure for change was mounting, however, as an anti-flag rally drew almost fifty thousand people on January 17, 2000, Martin Luther King Jr. Day. On July 1, 2000, the flag was removed from the dome of the capitol and moved to a flagpole near the state's Confederate monument on the grounds of the statehouse at the corner of Main and Gervais Streets. At the time it was moved, a group of several hundred African Americans picketed and protested having it anywhere on the grounds, and a number of supporters of the flag formed a line near the flag to protect it from the protesters. The NAACP called for the tourist boycott to continue as long as the flag was anywhere on the capitol grounds.[43]

As the boycott continued into 2002, NAACP president Kweisi Mfume visited the protesters at the South Carolina Welcome Station on I-77 near Fort Mills, South Carolina. More than one hundred demonstrators were on "Border Patrol" to discourage people from spending money in South Carolina; their motto was, "Don't Stop, Don't Shop, Until the Flag Drops." Several counter-protesters waved Confederate flags around the Welcome Center. Eight other South Carolina Welcome Stations had their own "Border Patrols" to pass out literature and support the boycott. Of course, the flag supporters were not to be outdone, and they formed their own version of "Border Patrols," led by a "white civil rights" group called European-American Unity and Rights Organization (EURO), based in New Orleans. EURO asked members to meet at the South Carolina visitors' centers "to show good ol' fashioned Southern hospitality," said Vincent Breeding, the national director.[44]

A sideshow to the serious debate was the "biggest Confederate flag in Christendom" bought and flown in Columbia by Maurice Bessinger, a well-known entrepreneur and owner of a chain of barbecue restaurants called Piggy Park. As a result of his continued loud and visible protest of the protesters and his vocal support of the Confederate flag, Wal-Mart and other merchants stopped carrying Bessinger's line of barbecue sauce. In addition, the parent company of South Carolina Electric and Gas issued an edict that employees could not park company vehicles at a Piggy Park restaurant.[45]

In Mississippi a vote was held to determine the flag design for the state.

Two designs were on the ballot: one, designed by a biracial commission, which was a circle of twenty white stars on a blue background; the other was thirteen white stars on a blue cross over a red field. The Confederate battle emblem won with 65 percent of the vote.[46] Like other debates over the flag and the "flag wars" documented by John Coski, Mississippians were clearly saying to the NAACP or any others who opposed the flag, "Leave us alone, let us do our own thing." The state sovereignty issues of the Lost Cause orators surfaced all over again.

The flag debate included the high school generation as well. At Cherokee High School in Canton, Georgia, T-shirts sporting the image of the Confederate flag were banned from campus in 2003. Two black families had found them offensive, and the school authorities agreed, saying, "The rebel flag's modern association with white supremacists makes it a flashpoint for racial confrontation." The American Civil Liberties Union took the white students' side, arguing that their First Amendment rights were being trampled in the name of political correctness. Student Ree Simpson, a senior, told a reporter, "I'm a country girl. I can't help it. I love the South. If people want to call me a redneck, let them." In North Carolina, thirteen students (out of 1,510 enrolled) were sent home in 2004 for wearing Confederate flag shirts at South Caldwell High School. Predictably, several students and their parents believed that "the move is a violation of their right to free speech." In Kentucky, Jacqueline Duty sued her school for violating her free speech rights when she was banned from her high school prom because her dress was patterned after the Confederate battle flag.[47]

Debate surfaced on the internet in 2003 when the question arose of which flags should be flown in the procession honoring the eight crew members of the Confederate submarine *Hunley*, whose remains had been found in the sunken and recently retrieved submarine. More than twenty thousand people signed the online petition to ban the U.S. flag from the proceedings. After all, that flag was the symbol of the "eternal enemy" of the submarine's crew. The bodies lay in state at the statehouse for three days, then a four-and-a-half-mile-long procession with four horse-drawn caissons took the bodies to their final resting place in Magnolia Cemetery, escorted by more than twenty thousand Civil War reenactors dressed in Confederate and Union uniforms.[48]

The Confederate flag even became embroiled in the 2004 presidential campaign when Democratic Party candidate Howard Dean commented that he would like to be the "candidate for guys with Confederate flags in their pickup trucks." The other Democratic candidates denounced Dean's remark. John Kerry called it pandering to "lovers of the Confederate flag" and proclaimed that he would rather be the candidate "of the NAACP than the NRA"

(National Rifle Association). John Edwards, the Democratic candidate from North Carolina, responded to Dean's remarks with a classic Lost Cause–tinged retort: "Let me tell you, the last thing we need in the South is somebody like you coming down and telling us what we need to do"—shades of the abolitionists and more recently, all those "outside agitators," decried by Ross Barnett and George Wallace.[49]

The flag controversy has touched higher education as well. East Carolina University M.B.A. graduate James E. Hickmon authored a website, "My Dixie Forever," that flew an animated Confederate flag. Peter A. Kalajian, a student writer for the *East Carolinian,* the student newspaper at that university, wrote an opinion piece on October 14, 2004, calling Hickmon's flag a symbol of "racist propaganda." Hickmon organized a petition campaign calling for disciplinary action against Kalajian and the student editor, Amanda Q. Lingerfelt, for attempting "to incite racial animosities towards descendants of Confederate veterans." Within a few days, 250 had signed the online petition. Hickmon also stopped his donations to East Carolina and began donating to Wake Forest University, where he received a law degree. His website had a map that could automatically be sent to Kalajian directing him to Bangor, Maine. "Help Peter find his way back North," said the legend on the map.[50]

In the fall of 2004 yet another Confederate flag debate erupted. A flag flying in Charlotte-owned Elmwood Cemetery was challenged by city council member Warren Turner, who asked that it be taken down so as not to make it appear that the city endorses the flag. Giving the traditional Lost Cause defense, supporters of the flag argued that it simply honors the history and heritage of the Confederate soldiers buried in the cemetery. In November 2004 about fifty people demonstrated in defense of the flag, and Mark Palmer, president of the Historic Preservation of Elmwood/Pinewood Cemetery, Inc., said, "We feel like history should be left alone." After a public hearing on the issue, a proposal was made to the city to take the flag down, display it in a glass case, and fly it on special days. It would be replaced with another Confederate-era flag, such as the North Carolina State Flag of 1861. Flag supporters protested the plan, and Alexander Palmer, who has relatives buried at Elmwood, told the city council, in words right out of the Lost Cause era, "This flag represents what these men fought and died under. It represents their beliefs. They have the right to have it flown over their headstones." He further said he had more than fifteen hundred signatures from people who want the flag to stay in place.

After an editorial in the Charlotte newspaper on the issue, several letters to the editor appeared. The pro-flag letters could have been composed in

1890 or 1910 had this been an issue at that time; the Lost Cause was alive in 2005. Rev. Bill Swann pointed out: "The battle flag wasn't a political flag. It never flew over slavery a single day, while the U.S. flag flew over slavery for 89 years." Joy Shivar wrote the editor: "What a defeat for free speech. . . . It is ok to burn an American flag in public streets but not ok to fly the Confederate flag over Confederate graves." And Michael C. Tuggle claimed that "far more folks display the battle flag as a symbol of Southern pride and culture than use it as an emblem of hate." Finally, after eight months of debate, City Manager Pam Syfert ordered it removed and the flagpole taken down. That did not calm the debate, as some quickly charged vandalism, as the flag and flagpole were private property donated by the United Daughters of the Confederacy.[51]

Reverence for the Confederate flag continues well into the twenty-first century. In April 2006 a ceremony was held on the grounds of the Arkansas State Capitol commemorating Confederate Flag Day, which in Arkansas is the Saturday before Easter Sunday. The ceremony included a speech by Chuck Rand, commander of the Army of the Trans-Mississippi Sons of Confederate Veterans; a reading of a list of names of some of those who died in the Civil War; and a group of Confederate reenactors firing a salute to the flag.[52]

Many other examples could be given of events celebrating the flag and the Confederacy and of debates and lawsuits over the public exposure of the flag. This issue, unfortunately, shows that the Union is not fully reconciled, nor will it be for some time to come. An Atlanta factory worker perhaps summed up in 1987 the modern Lost Cause version of the flag debate: "[The flag] ain't got nothing to do with hating black people or any of that KKK stuff. All they mean to me is 'get the hell off my back and leave me the hell alone.'" Put a little less crudely is University of South Carolina history professor Clyde N. Wilson's perception that "for most of these good Americans [SCVs, UDC members, Civil War Roundtable members, and others], the flag is a symbol not of white supremacy, but of identification with their own ancestors and heritage and an affirmation of their own identity." On the other side, James Forman Jr., son of a key player in the 1960s civil rights movement and a professor at Georgetown University Law School, sums up the feeling of many black southerners when they see the flag: "My eyes close tightly, my fists clinch, and I slowly force from my mind images of the flag, of the Ku Klux Klan, of Bull Connor and George Wallace-of black people in chains, hanging from trees, kept illiterate, denied the opportunity to vote."[53]

Perhaps James K. Flynn, an independent writer, columnist, and radio producer in Charlotte, North Carolina, has proposed the way this story should end. After suggesting a new design for the flag to depict Confederate heritage and suggesting that the battle flag be relegated to museums and historical reenactments, Flynn wrote in a column at the height of the debate over the flag in Elmwood Cemetery: "Unfortunately for the heritage side . . . the perception of any flag of the Confederacy is too entrenched in images of slavery—along with the Ku Klux Klan, outlaw bikers and other mouth-breathing, knuckle-dragging bigots—to ever be wholly viable as a symbol of heritage. But this is America, land of the free and home of the Bill of Rights. It is imperative that those who wish to venerate their Confederate ancestors have the right to do so."[54] As the ubiquitous Confederate beach towels and T-shirts, plastic statuettes of Robert E. Lee and Stonewall Jackson, and "Forgit Hell!" bumper stickers found at many convenience stores along southern interstates and in tacky tourist shops across the region attest, they are likely to defend that right for many years to come.

"Today we honor our Confederate ancestors. We are Southerners. We make no apology for our ancestors. This is who we are": The Lost Cause on Confederate Memorial Day

Some twenty-first-century white southerners carry on the Confederate Memorial Day tradition. This comment about "our Confederate ancestors" was made by Sissy Piechocinsky, president of the local UDC chapter, at the 2003 Confederate Memorial Day observance in Savannah, Georgia. This particular event was better organized than many I have witnessed around the region over the years. Often, a sole orator, a couple of musicians, and several reenactors firing their Civil War–era guns or a cannon will celebrate the day for a few UDC and SCV observers or curiosity seekers. In Savannah's Forest Park, reenactors from the Eighth Georgia Cavalry and the Twenty-Second Georgia Artillery participated, along with Jim Adams, portraying Robert E. Lee. Pastor John Weaver, the national chaplain of the SCV, was the keynote speaker, and the newspaper account praised his "impassioned speech on the theme of sacrifice—how the South's soldiers sacrificed their lives for what they believed in." Karen Coates, a prospective member of the UDC, commented right out of the nineteenth century: "I was born and raised Southern. It is my culture, my heritage."[55]

Two years earlier at Elmwood Cemetery in Charlotte, North Carolina—the site of the Confederate flag debate—May 6, 2001, was celebrated as Confederate Memorial Day, sponsored by the E. A. Ross Camp, Sons of Confederate Veterans. One of the speakers, who was not identified, could have been reading straight from a Lost Cause oration from a century-earlier Confederate Memorial Day, as he remarked: "We turn to memories of duty, honor and sacrifice of the men in the gray-clad armies who gave their lives fighting for something they believed in equally as much as veterans of other wars—the constitutional right of citizens to determine their form of government." The *Pensacola News-Journal* reported on the Confederate Memorial Day celebration on May 13, 1995, in Georgetown, South Carolina. The Palmetto State celebrates the day statewide on May 10, the date of the last surrender of southern troops and the capture of Jefferson Davis, but in 1995 Georgetown saved it until Saturday, May 13. Fifty reenactors in gray uniforms marched down Screven Street to the Old Baptist Cemetery, where the town's Confederate monument is located. More reenactors were there with a cannon, which they fired in memory of the Lost Cause. Orator of the day, Paige Sawyer, declared in appropriate style, "They may be dead, but their legacy will continue for generations to come." Jacob F. Strait, a seventy-four-year-old whose father fought in the Civil War at age fourteen, shed some emotional light on the event and its meaning for him: "They burned down my grandmother's home place and butchered her cow. We have to remember it."[56]

Around the South, Alabama, Georgia, and Mississippi observe Confederate Memorial Day on April 26, the day General Joseph Johnston surrendered his army to General William Sherman in North Carolina. Texas celebrates Robert E. Lee's birthday, January 19, as Confederate Heroes Day, and Alabama takes another state holiday on Jefferson Davis's birthday, June 3.

In Mississippi, Confederate Memorial Day demonstrates why black southerners can and do object to the recalling of the Confederacy. As the civil rights movement gained momentum, the April 25, 1961, observance of the day marked the ninety-sixth anniversary of the first "Decoration Day" held in Columbus, Mississippi, in 1866. According to the newspaper report a day before the event, the featured speaker, Hunter Gholson, an attorney from Columbus, was planning to draw a comparison "between the struggles of the South during the 1860s and the battle facing it in the 1960s." Seventeen years later, one of white Mississippi's "heroes" of the opposition to the civil rights movement, former governor Ross Barnett, was the orator of the day in Jackson. Barnett's father had joined the Confederate army at age sixteen, so the war was still real for Governor Barnett, as he asserted to about one hundred persons in the audience: "The desolation of the war still lie so heavily upon many people of our beloved land, and the wounds and those hearts which were called upon to give their dearest treasures upon the bloody fields of battle are all very, very tender. Our soldiers came home not as a conquering people, but they came home with courage, in the face of disaster, in the face of suffering, with a country desolated and in ruins, and we are here today simply to testify before the world that we are faithful to our dead." The event was sponsored by two UDC chapters, one SCV chapter, a chapter of the Children of the Confederacy, and a unit of the Military Order of the Stars and Bars.[57]

If the memories of the Confederacy ever fade from recollections of white southerners, a case could be made for Mississippi as the location where that will happen last. Confederate organizations and their ceremonies remain strong across the state, and they are still following the same pattern of ritual and celebration that the Ladies' Memorial Associations and, later, the Daughters of the Confederacy created in the late nineteenth century. A copy of the program for a 1982 event at the Greenwood Cemetery in Jackson shows this clearly. The order of business was initiated by children decorating Confederate graves, followed by the Pledge of Allegiance to the American flag and salutes to the flag of Mississippi and, of course, to the Confederate flag. Next, a wreath was placed on the Confederate monument, and eleven remaining "Real Daughters" and three "Real Sons" (including former governor Barnett) were recognized. A memorial poem was read, followed by the featured orator of the day, John E. Aldridge, the judge advocate of the Mississippi chapter of the SCV. "Dixie" was then sung, there were rifle salutes, the colors were retired, a benediction was pronounced, and "Taps" was played by a local bugler.[58] Charles C. Jones Jr. or John B. Gordon would have felt right at home.

It would seem that some of the celebrants at these events and those who are standing for preserving the Confederate heritage as a tribute to their ancestors and tradition know they are fighting an uphill battle, and one perhaps not likely to be won. Mollie Watkins, president of Chapter 77 of the UDC in Vicksburg, acknowledged the protests and scorn directed toward their efforts, as she told a reporter in 1986: "We receive some criticism from time to time, usually from people who know nothing about it. They feel like we are bigots. Black people look down their noses at us." Senator Mike Gunn of Mississippi, the speaker at the 1997 Confederate Memorial Day event in Oxford, Mississippi, expressed the feelings of many when he told the audience: "There is a national conspiracy to exterminate the vestiges of our heritage"; one can easily visualize and hear a round of applause from the audience.[59]

"It's our history": The Lost Cause and Confederate Monuments

In the early twenty-first century, Confederate monuments continue to be reference points for discussion of the legacy of the Confederacy and the Civil War. New monuments are being built and old ones are being repaired and restored. Sanford, North Carolina, is raising money for a Lee memorial to be built by sculptor Gary Casteel, which will be placed between the old and the new courthouses in Sanford. It was dedicated in 2007, on the two hundredth anniversary of Lee's birth. The funds are being raised through golf tournaments, seminars, and private contributions. Casteel is also working on a monument to Confederate general A. P. Hill to be erected in Hill's hometown of Culpepper, Virginia. T-shirts and other Confederate memorabilia are being sold to finance this monument. Colquitt, Georgia, dedicated a new monument to the Confederate soldiers and sailors from Miller County on April 13, 2003. The monument was sponsored by the Decatur Grays Camp 1689 of the SCV "in honor of their ancestors who sacrificed for states rights and Southern independence." Benjamin David Hunter, age ninety, a "real son" of the Confederacy, unveiled the monument.[60]

In some situations, state or local public funds are being spent to repair old monuments or establish new ones. Maryland, for instance, inventoried its 400 monuments, of which 101 are related to the Civil War. A fund-raising effort and a state grant of seventy-five thousand dollars made possible a new Maryland monument placed on the Gettysburg battlefield in 1994. From 1989 through 2002, the state's Military Monuments Commission sponsored conservation treatment of 93 military memorials and oversaw restoration of more than 300, many of which were Confederate. On May 12, 2007, Georgetown, Delaware, hardly a well-known hotbed of Confederate sentiment, dedicated an obelisk to the two thousand Delaware citizens who fought in Confederate units. In 2008 the Laurens, South Carolina, SCV dedicated a monument to McGowan's Brigade at Spottsylvania, Virginia, in the "Bloody Angle," where it will "honor our ancestors who . . . held off Union forces for almost 20 hours while General Lee formed a second line of defense."[61]

In Smithfield, Tennessee, the SCV dedicated a new Confederate monument on Monday, May 26, 1997. An equestrian statue of Confederate general James Longstreet was dedicated at Gettysburg on July 3, 1998. Rex Hovey, a retired Charlotte, North Carolina, firefighter and Civil War reenactor, promoted a campaign to raise eighty-five thousand dollars for a monument near Boonsboro, Maryland, where many Carolinians died in the Battle of South Mountain. The new monument was dedicated on the battlefield on Saturday, October 18, 2003. While many monuments depict an anonymous soldier or sailor, this one honors the story of a flag-bearer who saved his surrounded comrades by jumping onto a fence and waving the flag, which attracted the attention of the Union forces and allowed his fellow Confederates to escape. The monument represents a fallen flag-bearer. Catawba County, North Carolina, plans to build a Confederate monument to place on the grounds of the old courthouse, near another Confederate monument dedicated in 1907 in Newton. Three hundred names of Confederates from the county who died in the Civil War will be engraved on the monument. The SCV is raising the funds for the monument, and the president of SCV Camp 489 in Hickory, North Carolina, says the monument is needed: "With the many cultures that are here now, they need to know who these men were." The twenty-five-ton granite monument to Confederate general P. G. T. Beauregard in Washington Park in Charleston, South Carolina, had begun to lean backward over the years since it was built in 1904. The city government paid for the repair of the statue, and Mayor Joseph Riley commented, "Monuments are an important part of the public realm in our city and we wanted to have it correct." Plans were in place to clean the statue in the spring of 2005.[62]

A Confederate statue in Arkadelphia, Arkansas, was repaired and placed back on the Clark County Courthouse lawn in 2002, after a tornado swept through the central Arkansas town on March 1, 1997, and damaged the monument. The Arkansas UDC paid twenty thousand dollars for the restoration of what is believed to be the oldest Confederate monument in the state, originally erected in 1911. Other monuments were damaged across Arkansas by a December 2000 ice storm. Pamela Trammell, president of the Arkansas UDC, remarked at the rededication of the monument in Arkadelphia, "It's our history. Without our history, we lose so much. If our kids are going to remember, we've got to put them back up."[63]

As might be imagined, debates over monuments and repairs continue even today. In Selma, Alabama, the famed starting point of one of the defining moments of the civil rights movement, the Selma-to-Montgomery March, a new monument to Confederate general Nathan Bedford Forrest was erected on city property. After much debate, the city council voted five to four to move it to the local cemetery where many Confederate soldiers were buried. In Charlotte, a college student, Laura Crawford, noticed a Confederate monument near the campus of Central Piedmont Community College. She began to pass out flyers and call her professors' and fellow students' attention to the monument and call for its removal. University of North Carolina–Charlotte professor Dan Morrill argued, "To say we should eradicate artifacts that document something we don't agree with, that's a very dangerous set of notions." In Franklin, Tennessee, and Walterboro, South Carolina, black leaders have asked that Confederate monuments on public property be torn down or removed. Preservationist Ernest B. Furgurson agrees with Professor Morrill: "Correcting history by erasing it is an exercise best left today to leaders in China, Korea, and Cuba, countries where mind control is an official function of the government." He goes on to offer what is perhaps the best solution to this debate: "Here, it seems, is where the campaign for civility and the correction of history should draw a line: no flag waving, no taunting, no sentimental fairy tales about happy slaves—but agreement that our past was both light and dark, and that the tangible memorials of it be left in peace to remind us of that. To tear them down is to pretend the past never happened, to substitute this generation's propriety for the whitewash that was fashionable back when."[64]

Conclusion

It is highly unlikely that discussion and debate over Confederate symbols will disappear anytime soon. For many contemporary white southerners, Appomattox, Shiloh, Gettysburg, Robert E. Lee, Stonewall Jackson, J. E. B. Stuart, and all the other battles and heroes of the war are as real as the morning sunrise, and just as permanent. For almost 150 years, white southerners have been trying to make some sense out of that war and the bitter defeat, and to claim kinship to what happened so dramatically between 1861 and 1865. Shelby Foote said it well in the Ken Burns documentary on the Civil War when he remarked: "And it is very necessary, if you're going to understand the American character in the twentieth century, to learn about this enormous catastrophe of the nineteenth century. It was the crossroads of our being, and it was a hell of a crossroads."[65]

The sesquicentennial of the Civil War will likely generate another landslide of books, battlefield tours, videos, movies, and, certainly, debates over the Confederate battle flag, Confederate Memorial Day, and Confederate monuments. The Lost Cause orators surveyed here laid a powerful and firm foundation for those who want to attach themselves to their past history and heritage. But there can be hope for an honest celebration of the 150th anniversary. An example is the state of Arkansas, which in 2007 created a statewide Civil War Sesquicentennial Commission to "assist the Department of Arkansas Heritage in promoting the observance, cooperate with other groups in the observance, help make sure any observance is *inclusive of all people affected by the Civil War* [emphasis added]."[66] Members of the panel must have a background in Arkansas history, black history, or Civil War history. Obviously, the 150th anniversary of the war will be a major attraction, not just for Arkansas, but likely throughout the region and even nationally. The Civil War lives on in American memory.

But it is time for the debates to move into serious discussion and positive action. Reuben Greenberg, the Jewish, black police chief of Charleston, South Carolina, remarked in 1995: "It took four years to fight that war, and may take another hundred to exorcise all the demons it let loose." Dotsy Boineau, the curator of the Confederate Relic Room and Museum in Columbia,

South Carolina, talked about those demons when she told Tony Horwitz: "We don't forget the War, and in the case of Sherman, we don't forgive. Some of us aren't even sure yet that we want to be part of the Union." Her demons are not as vicious as those of Eugene "Bull" Connor, who roared to the Selma, Alabama, Citizens' Council in April 1960: "We are on the one-yard line. Our backs are to the wall. Do we let them go over for a touchdown, or do we raise the Confederate flag as did our forefathers and tell them. . . . 'You shall not pass!' "[67] But they are similar. During the sesquicentennial we will doubtless hear some of the same rhetoric of hatred, bitterness, and injustice by those who use Confederate symbols and myths to support their bigotry. But perhaps we will have begun to see our better angels, and as the Arkansas commission urges, this observance will be inclusive of all points of view and the experiences of all of us affected by the Civil War—in short, all of us, for, as Robert Penn Warren pointed out, "the Civil War is, for the American imagination, the great single event of our history."[68]

The time is past due for taking the approach raised by Franklin Forts: "For southerners to begin a new dialogue on their symbols will require openness to the other—in a word—tolerance." Perhaps at long last, that is about to come about. In the debate over the revision of the Georgia state flag, Tyrone Brooks, a black Georgia state representative from Atlanta, who fought for years to abolish Confederate symbols from public venues, told a reporter, "What I finally had to acknowledge was that Confederate history is a part of our history. We cannot erase it, and it needs to be preserved for history's sake. Just like I have no intention of removing the statues of Robert E. Lee or Stonewall Jackson, because as long as they're there, they will help us remember not to repeat our history." Calvin Smyre, another black Georgia legislator, said, "You have to look across the table and realize that just because someone has a different view of history doesn't mean they hate you." Hodding Carter III wrote in 1996 without a trace of rancor or hate: "In Greenville, Mississippi, where and when I grew up, the past was neither prologue nor even really past. It was absorbed whole as explanation and justification of the present, history and life woven together by an unbroken thread of context." He goes on to write: " 'Our way of life' turns out to have encompassed more than the meets and bounds of institutionalized racism. If we are lucky, at least some of the old heritage will last longer than the remnants of white supremacy. For me it has and will."[69]

Around the South, the past is alive and vivid to many contemporary southerners, black and white. It intrudes upon our lives, infiltrates the present, and attempts to shape, influence, and persuade the future. The Lost Cause orators and orations, the monuments, the reunions, the reenactors, the celebrations of Confederate Memorial Day or Robert E. Lee's birthday—all this and more attest to our heritage as a region, just as do the marks and remnants of slavery and segregation, and discrimination and racial injustice. All of this and more is part of our life story of the South, and this narrative should be—must be—shared and protected, explicated and understood by all of us in the South, as well as by all Americans who care about our nation and our people. Understanding more about how we got this way, by reading and understanding the rhetoric of the Lost Cause, will go a long way toward creating the tolerance Franklin Forts wrote about.

Notes

Introduction

1. Goldfield, *Still Fighting the Civil War*, 16.

2. Hariman, "Afterword," 164.

3. See J. O. Robertson, *American Myth, American Reality*, for an extended overview of the role of myth in America. The definitive study of American memory is Kammen, *Mystic Chords of Memory*.

4. Lumpkin, *Making of a Southerner*, 112.

5. For an overall analysis of the development of the Lost Cause mythology, see Foster, *Ghosts of the Confederacy*; Osterweis, *Myth of the Lost Cause*; and C. R. Wilson, *Baptized in Blood*. The following works shed considerable light into many nooks and crannies of the Lost Cause and have informed my thinking about this cultural artifact: W. C. Davis, *The Cause Lost*; Mills and Simpson, *Monuments to the Lost Cause*; Neff, *Honoring the Civil War Dead*; and Blight, *Race and Reunion*. None of these works on various aspects of the Lost Cause phenomenon, however, focus as sharply as I do on the relevant ceremonial public address and ritual, which I contend was the major influence shaping the culture of the post–Civil War South.

6. Herrington, "Civil War History Is an Enduring Tourist Lure," A8; "Crewmen of Recovered Confederate Sub Are Honored at Burial"; Doug Gross, "Georgia Keying on Civil War's 150th to Boost Tourism," *Southeast Missourian* (Cape Girardeau), March 5, 2007, 5A; Horwitz, *Confederates in the Attic*, 9.

Chapter 1

1. Quoted in Carleton, "Celebrity Cult," 137.

2. Boorstin, *Genius of American Politics*, 155, 156; Boorstin, *The Americans*, 307, 308, 312.

3. Baskerville, *The People's Voice*, 2; Sydnor, *Gentlemen Freeholders*, 115.

4. Braden, *Oral Tradition in the South*, 26–28.

5. Brown, *The Lower South*, 127, 125.

6. Hollis, *University of South Carolina*, 1:260; Preston quoted in *The South in the Building of the Nation*, 9:167.

7. Cash, *Mind of the South*, 53; Freehling, *The Road to Disunion*, 48; Owsley, *Plain Folk*, 140; Gaines, *Southern Oratory*, 1.

8. R. Davis, *Recollections*, 69; Thornwell quoted in Eubanks, "Rhetoric of the Nullifiers," 32; Hollis, *University of South Carolina*, 1:230; Gaines, *Southern Oratory*, 2.

9. Green, *History of the University of South Carolina*, 267; Weaver, *Southern Tradition at Bay*, 80; Braden, *Oral Tradition in the South*, 38; Taylor, *Ante-Bellum South Carolina*, 129; Coulter, *College Life in the Old South*, 163.

10. Cash, *Mind of the South*, 99; Weaver, *Southern Tradition at Bay*, 73; Hollis, *University of South Carolina*, 1:255–56; Dabney, *Liberalism in the South*, 80; Wyatt-Brown, *Southern Honor*, 47.

11. Lumpkin, *Making of a Southerner*, 125.

12. Wyatt-Brown, *Southern Honor*, 330.

13. Aristotle, *On Rhetoric*, 47–50.

14. Condit, "Functions of Epideictic," 292.

15. Groppe, "Ritualistic Language," 63; W. L. Warner, *American Life*, 3; Johnson, "Non-Aristotelian Nature," 272; Brandt, *Rhetoric of Argumentation*, 13; Walker, "Aristotle's Lyric," 7.

16. Condit, "Functions of Epideictic," 284, 288, 289, 290, 291.

17. Perelman and Olbrechts-Tyteca, *The New Rhetoric*, 50, 51; Perelman, *The Realm of Rhetoric*, 20.

18. Sullivan, "Ethos of Epideictic Encounter," 124, 128.

19. Johnson, "Non-Aristotelian Nature," 273; Brandt, *Rhetoric of Argumentation*, 13; Corbett, *Classical Rhetoric*, 29.

20. Chase, "Classical Conception of Epideictic," 295, 296; Brandt, *Rhetoric of Argumentation*, 12–13.

21. Mayo, *War Memorials as Political Landscape*, 5.

22. C. C. Jones, "Oration," 20, 29; Capers, "Address on Memorial Day," 6; Anderson, "Address at Dedication of Lee Monument," 313; E. P. Cox, "Address to R. E. Lee Camp Confederate Veterans," 296.

23. Andrews, "Oaths Registered in Heaven," 96.

24. Braden, " 'Repining Over an Irreversible Past,' " 277.

25. Mayo, *War Memorials as Political Landscape*, 11.

26. Wolfe, "Chickamauga," 201–2.

27. Shuptrine and Dickey, *Jericho*, 16; Gronbeck, "Rhetorics of the Past," 57; Bodnar, *Remaking America*, 15.

28. Weaver, *Southern Tradition at Bay*, 224.

29. Blight, *Race and Reunion*, 19.

30. Crump, "Speech at Reunion," 1; Williams, "Address to Company 'A,' " 3.

31. Nolan, "Anatomy of the Myth," 12; Osterweis, *Myth of the Lost Cause*, 57.

Chapter 2

1. Turner, *Celebration*, 11–12; Lewis, *History*, 13; Mayo, *War Memorials as Political Landscape*, 50.

2. For a brief but thorough survey of the topic, see Foster, "Lost Cause Myth," 1134–35; for a full treatment of the subject see Foster's *Ghosts of the Confederacy*.

3. Blight, "Decoration Days," 100.

4. Buck, *The Road to Reunion*, 120. In 1966 Congress declared Waterloo, New York, the birthplace of Memorial Day, due to a May 5, 1866, ceremony honoring local veterans, but according to the Department of Veterans Affairs, "approximately 25 places have been named in connection with the origin of Memorial Day, many of them in the South where most of the war dead were buried." http://www.va.gov/feature/celebrate/memday.95p.

5. Blight, *Race and Reunion*, 70; "The First Confederate Memorial Day," 369; Hardy, "Credit for Memorial Day Could Go to Confederate Nurse, Spy"; Kilmer, "The Origin of Memorial Day," 2–3; Negri, *Civil War Poetry*, 78; S. Martin, "Confederate Memorial Day," 10.

6. Benning, *Origin of Memorial Day*, 7, 18, 22, 24–25.

7. Ibid., 7, 22; Albanese, "Requiem for Memorial Day," 389.

8. Benning, *Origin of Memorial Day*, 10, 17.

9. Bishir, "'A Strong Force of Ladies,'" 455, 456–57, 461.

10. Porcher, *Brief History*, 5–7.

11. Kammen, *Mystic Chords of Memory*, 103; S. Martin, "Confederate Memorial Day," 10.

12. Kinney, "'If Vanquished I Am Still Victorious,'" 239.

13. "Memorial Day," *Raleigh News and Observer*. In her delightful description of Decoration Day, Margaret Inman Meaders expresses how some in the South needed this celebration: "The defeated have left to them only the transforming of grief into glory. Losses can be endured only when wreathed in laurel. Memories must march to drums; and fear, be beaten down by fifes. Pride must be reborn before its earlier death can be admitted." Meaders, "Postscript to Appomattox," 298–99.

14. "Shall Memorial Day Be Changed?," 4.

15. Letter to the editor, *Atlanta Constitution*, April 26, 1887, 4; "Suggested by the Day," 4.

16. Benning, *Origin of Memorial Day*, 25, 19.

17. Davies, *Patriotism on Parade*, 257; Bishir, "'A Strong Force of Ladies,'" 467, 469; Kinney, "'If Vanquished I Am Still Victorious,'" 244–45.

18. Turner, *Celebration*, 12; Braden, "Myths in a Rhetorical Context," 81.

19. *Norfolk Virginian*, June 5, 1891; Rutledge, "Memorial Day Address"; Kinney, "'If Vanquished I Am Still Victorious,'" 241; unidentified Atlanta newspaper clipping dated April 27, 1874, in *Confederate Pamphlets*; *Norfolk Virginian*, June 5, 1891, 2; Benning, *Origin of Memorial Day*, 16.

20. "Memorial Day," *Newbernian.*

21. Waddell, "Memorial Day Address."

22. See, for example, M. S. Wheeler's *New Women of the New South* for a thorough discussion of the opposition in the South to even such a fundamental public right as the ballot. Scott, *The Southern Lady,* is the classic study of the evolution of women's public role in the South.

23. Van Zelm, "Virginia Women as Public Citizens," 88; Whites, "'Stand by Your Man,'" 141. See K. L. Cox's *Dixie's Daughters* for a thorough and persuasive discussion of the critical leading role of women in promoting the Lost Cause. Goldfield, *Still Fighting the Civil War,* 97.

24. "Memorial Day," *Augusta (GA) Daily Chronicle and Sentinel.*

25. Bisher, "'A Strong Force of Ladies,'" 458; Daniel, "Memorial Day Address."

26. Graves, "Memorial Address"; Capers, "Address on Memorial Day," 17–18.

27. Davies, *Patriotism on Parade,* 276.

28. Benning, *Origin of Memorial Day,* 5, 6, 7, 24; Porcher, *Brief History,* 8.

29. Graves, "Memorial Address"; Black, "Anniversary Address," 3; Carr, "To the Confederate Soldiers," 3.

30. Emerson, *Historic Southern Monuments,* 97.

31. "Pensacolians Decorate Graves of the Blue and the Gray," *Pensacola Journal,* April 26, 1983.

32. While it is as impossible to accurately determine when and where the first veterans reunion was held as is it to ascertain when Memorial Day began, Lumpkin asserts that her father's unit, the Third Georgia Regiment, held the first reunion in Union Point, Georgia, in 1874. Lumpkin, *Making of a Southerner,* 111; Blight, *Race and Reunion,* 209.

33. *Charleston (SC) News and Courier,* February 20, 1879, clipping in Holmes Scrapbook on Palmetto Guard, South Carolina Historical Society, Charleston.

34. Hattaway, "Clio's Southern Soldiers," 214.

35. C. C. Jones, *Memorial History of Georgia,* 297–98, quoted in Towns, "Ceremonial Speaking," 134; "Memorial Day," *Augusta (GA) Chronicle.*

36. "Orr's Rifles Reunion."

37. *Ceremonies and Speeches,* 3; "Annual Reunion of the Virginia Division," 283–84.

38. Lumpkin, *Making of a Southerner,* 112.

39. Philpott, *Sponsor Souvenir Album,* 19.

40. Ibid., 23–31.

41. Headquarters, South Carolina Division, United Confederate Veterans, General Order No. 41, Charleston, S.C., April 6, 1899, copy in collection of South Carolina Historical Society, Charleston.

42. *Information for Veterans and Visitors U.C.V. Reunion, Charleston, S.C., May 10–13, 1899,* copy of information pamphlet in collection of South Carolina Historical Society, Charleston. This same pamphlet listed prices of hotels (single rooms, one person, $5; double rooms, two persons, $3 to $4; four persons, $2 to $3.75), boardinghouses ($1 to $2.50), private homes (50 cents for lodging only and up to $2.50 for

lodging and three meals), and carriages (25 cents from the train station to hotels and 50 cents to private homes). The veterans were also reminded that excursion boats would be running to Fort Sumter, Fort Moutrie, and Fort Johnson in Charleston harbor.

43. Lumpkin, *Making of a Southerner,* 115–16.

44. Hanley, "The Gray Reunion," 42–63.

45. Winberry, "'Lest We Forget,'" 114; Poppenheim et al., *History of the UDC,* 49; Coulter, "Confederate Monument in Athens, Georgia," 235. The quotation in the title of this section is from Poppenheim et al. For photographs of hundreds of these monuments, see Widener, *Confederate Monuments.*

46. Towns, "Honoring the Confederacy in Northwest Florida."

47. F. Wheeler, "'Our Confederate Dead,'" 391; Poppenheim et al., *History of the UDC,* 49 (for an interesting and useful essay on Poppenheim, see Bland, "Promoting Tradition, Embracing Change"); Hale, *Memories in Marble;* Seigler, *Guide to Confederate Monuments,* 331–41.

48. Hale, *Memories in Marble;* Kammen, *Mystic Chords of Memory,* 117; *Edgefield (SC) Advertiser,* March 20, 1879, clipping in Holmes Scrapbook of Palmetto Guard, South Carolina Historical Society, Charleston; Huff, "The Democratization of Art," AH-4; *Tallahassee (FL) Daily Democrat,* April 27, 1922; C. R. Wilson, *Baptized in Blood,* 19. The commander of the Confederate forces was General William Miller, whose grave in Pensacola was marked with a marble military headstone in St. John's Cemetery on June 9, 1960, by a loyal group of UDC members and local historian T. T. Wentworth Jr. *Pensacola Journal,* June 10, 1960.

49. Quoted in Davies, *Patriotism on Parade,* 256; McKim, "Motives and Aims," 4; *Dedication of Monument to Confederate Dead.*

50. Foster, *Ghosts of the Confederacy,* 40–44.

51. Porcher, *Brief History,* 9.

52. Piehler, *Remembering War the American Way,* 9, 64; C. R. Wilson, *Baptized in Blood,* 19.

53. The southern propensity for lengthy orations was well accepted throughout the region. After Lucius Q. C. Lamar delivered a three-hour oration at the dedication of the John C. Calhoun monument in Charleston, South Carolina, President Grover Cleveland complained that it was too long. Lamar replied: "No, Mr. President; a Southern audience expects three hours, and would be better satisfied with five." Quoted in Dickey and Streeter, "Lucius Q. C. Lamar," 216. Comment on Marshall's address in *Atlanta Constitution,* October 28, 1887. Reference to Bate's speech in Moffatt, "A Tale of Two Monuments," 8–9. Hardee reference in unknown, undated newspaper clipping, Mrs. John C. Packard Scrapbook, Marianna, Florida, author's files.

54. "Memorial Day," *Augusta (GA) Daily Chronicle and Sentinel,* 2.

55. Poppenheim et al., *History of the UDC,* 49.

56. Allen, *Historical Sketch,* 17; Daniel, "Oration at the Inauguration," 81. For a comprehensive examination of the creation of the Lee Mausoleum and its meaning

to the white South in 1873 and for many years afterward, see Lawton, "Constructing the Cause."

57. "The Hero Dead," 3, 4.

58. S. Davis, "Empty Eyes, Marble Hand," 17; Mayo, *War Memorials as Political Landscape,* 186.

59. Mayo, *War Memorials as Political Landscape,* 17.

60. Faulkner, *The Sound and the Fury,* 335.

61. Haardt, "Southern Credo," 110.

Chapter 3

1. Black, "Anniversary Address," 17. Black, a Kentucky native, had served in the Confederate army as a private. After the war he moved to Augusta, Georgia, where he practiced law, served in the Georgia House of Representatives from 1873 to 1877, and served three terms in the U.S. House of Representatives in the 1890s. "Renowned for elaborate rhetoric, he was in demand as a speaker for over fifty years." Black died in 1928. Callahan, "Black, James Conquest Cross," 81–82.

2. C. R. Wilson, *Baptized in Blood,* 55.

3. Capers, "Address on Memorial Day," 15. Capers was an avid supporter of the Confederate cause, and served for many years as chaplain-general of the United Confederate Veterans. E. J. Warner, *Generals in Gray,* 43–44.

4. Turney, "The South Justified," 25. Turney was elected governor of Tennessee in 1896 and served two terms. He was also a Confederate colonel and was elected to the Tennessee Supreme Court for three eight-year terms, beginning in 1870. Phillips, "Peter Turney," 110–14.

5. C. C. Jones, "Address," 5. Jones, a leading defender of the Confederacy, also established a solid reputation as a historian and archaeologist, publishing over one hundred articles, books, and speeches on Georgia's history and archaeology. Cass, "Charles C. Jones."

6. Waddell, "The Confederate Soldier," 18; McPherson, *What They Fought For,* 4; Boggs, "The South Vindicated," 11.

7. Vedder, "For What did the South Fight?" 3; Turney, "The South Justified," 4. Vedder was pastor of the historic Huguenot church for fifty years. He was a noted preacher, lecturer, and orator who had a national reputation. Born in New York in 1826, he died in Charleston on March 1, 1917. Way, *History of the New England Society of Charleston,* 60–62. This mythology of the South's right to secede is well handled in W. C. Davis, *The Cause Lost,* 186–87.

8. Boggs, "The South Vindicated," 21–22, 24, 28, 29, 32, 35, 45–46; Crump, "Speech at Reunion," 11–12. Boggs was a chaplain in the Sixth South Carolina Volunteers; after the war he was pastor of the Second Presbyterian Church in Memphis and, later, head of a theological college in Georgia. Mathes, "Rev. William E. Boggs," 41.

9. Turney, "The South Justified," 21, 22; F. Lee, "Oration at Jackson's Statue," 29.

10. Vedder, "For What Did the South Fight?" 5, 4, 3; McKim, "Motives and Aims," 15.

11. Turney, "The South Justified," 16, 17, 18, 19; W. M. Hammond, "Address Delivered at Wadesboro," 13. Mr. Rawle's name was brought up by several speakers, such as Rev. McKim, who liked to mention that the political science textbook used by Robert E. Lee and Jefferson Davis at West Point was written by Rawle and St. George Tucker. According to several speakers, it "taught the right of a state to secede." McKim, "Motives and Aims," 17.

12. Boggs, "The South Vindicated," 12, 15, 16, 17, 18, 21.

13. J. H. Martin, "Address," 7, 14.

14. J. Davis, "Address Delivered to the Army of Tennessee," 229.

15. Hoge, "Oration," 14; J. Davis, "Speech at Army of Northern Virginia Banquet," 447. Hoge, pastor of the Second Presbyterian Church in Richmond from 1845 until his death in 1899, had been a fervent supporter of the Confederacy. In 1862 he made a blockade-running trip to England to get Bibles for Confederate troops. For a biographical sketch of Hoge, see Eggleston, "Moses Drury Hoge," 121–22.

16. Capers, "Address on Memorial Day," 10; C. C. Jones, "Georgians during the War," 26–27; Cowles, "Life and Services of Gen'l James B. Gordon," 5.

17. W. H. F. Lee, "Introductory Speech for D. H. Hill," 3; Hoyt, "The Palmetto Riflemen," 37; S. D. Lee, "Laying of the Corner-Stone," 370; Cameron, "Address," 363–64. Stephen D. Lee, originally from South Carolina, had been the youngest Confederate lieutenant general. After the war he settled in Mississippi, served in the state legislature, and was president of Mississippi A&M College. During the last four years of his life he was commander of the United Confederate Veterans. He died in 1908. Hattaway, "Lee, Stephen D.," 920–21.

18. Boggs, "The South Vindicated," 7; Bell, "Address at Johnson's Island," 10, 8; J. Davis, "Address Delivered to the Army of Tennessee," 235; Williams, "Address to Company 'A,'" 9; McKim, "Motives and Aims," 33.

19. Black, "Anniversary Address," 7, 8; Bell, "Address at Johnson's Island," 7, 13.

20. Black, "Anniversary Address," 5; Cowles, "Life and Services of Gen'l James B. Gordon," 4; Bell, "Address at Johnson's Island," 9; Hood, "Oration," 2, 4; Cowles, "Life and Services of Gen'l James B. Gordon," 5; Calhoun, "Memorial Day Address"; Campbell, "Oration," 6; Turney, "The South Justified," 4. Hood, a West Point graduate from Kentucky, resigned his commission in 1861 and joined the Confederate army, where he "quickly established a record as a fighting general." He was wounded at Gettysburg and lost a leg at Chickamauga. Murphy, "Hood, John Bell," 789–91.

21. Wells, "Oration," 6, 27.

22. R. E. Lee, "Speech of Col. Robert E. Lee, Jr.," 5–8.

23. W. R. Cox, "Southern Cause Noble and Just," 10–11. Brigadier General Cox was a U.S. congressman from North Carolina after the war. Reidenbaugh, "Cox, William Ruffin," 422.

24. Gary, "A Vindication of the South," 5, 15–17. Gary served for more than thirty-two years on the bench of the South Carolina Supreme Court, ending his career as its chief justice. He was born August 22, 1854, and died December 10, 1926. "Chief Justice Eugene Blackburn Gary," 494–95.

25. Boggs, "The South Vindicated," 19–20, 52.

26. Eckert, *John Brown Gordon,* 186, 2, 341.

27. J. H. Hammond, "On the Admission of Kansas," 69.

28. Gordon, "The Old South," 143. One example of these pro-slavery sentiments existing for decades after the war is an article by Connie Schultz in *Parade* magazine. "Watching *Roots* in 2010" recounts her story of having a longtime friend from Virginia telling her in 1985 how her great-great-grandfather had "loved the slaves who worked his fields." She went on to say, "Our slaves were happy." Many Lost Cause orators had laid the groundwork for her beliefs. Thanks to my administrative assistant, Fran Scholl, who called this article to my attention. *Parade,* June 27, 2010, 22.

29. Waddell, "The Confederate Soldier," 4; Waddell, "Memorial Day Address." Waddell, from Wilmington, North Carolina, had opposed secession, but supported North Carolina and served the Confederacy as a lieutenant colonel. He was elected to the U.S. Congress in 1870, where he served until 1879. He served as mayor of his hometown at the turn of the century. His "polished eloquence placed him in great demand" as a commemorative speaker. Newsome, "Waddell, Alfred Moore," 300–301.

30. Olmstead, "Confederate Times and Confederate Men," 1; Marshall, "Address," 6–7; Hoyt, "The Palmetto Riflemen," 10. Marshall was born on April 1, 1849, in Columbia, South Carolina. He practiced law and was involved in Palmetto State politics, serving as secretary of state and in the state senate and general assembly. He died in 1908. Bailey, "Marshall, John Quitman," 1058–60.

31. Turney, "The South Justified," 3; J. Davis, "Dedication of the Tomb of the Army of Northern Virginia Association," 219.

32. Gramm, *Somebody's Darling,* 55; Olmstead, "Confederate Times and Confederate Men," 2; J. Davis, "Address Delivered to the Army of Tennessee," 229–30; J. Davis, "Speech at Army of Northern Virginia Banquet," 447.

33. Kershaw, "Address," 6, 7; Lucas, "Response to a Toast," 27.

34. McKim, "Motives and Aims," 31.

35. Hampton, "Address on . . . Robert E. Lee," 15.

36. Black, "Anniversary Address," 5.

37. Lucas, "Response to a Toast," 24; Capers, "Address on Memorial Day," 10; Humes, "Address," 1–2. A recent study points out that "Capers continued to view the southern war effort as having a transcendent purpose and came to see the active commemoration of the Confederate experience as a sacred duty." My reading of several orations and sermons by the South Carolina minister certainly supports this conclusion. Poole, *Never Surrender,* 55. For a biographical sketch of Humes see Pace, "Humes, William Young Conn," 799–800.

38. J. Davis, "Address Delivered to the Army of Tennessee," 230; Young, "Address at Unveiling," 19. Young was commander of the Kentucky division of the United Confederate Veterans. *The South in the Building of the Nation,* 12:582–83.

39. Boggs, "The South Vindicated," 48.

40. Lumpkin, *Making of a Southerner,* 119.

41. Bell, "Address at Johnson's Island," 9; J. W. Jones, "Speech of Dr. J. William Jones," 42–43.

42. Crump, "Speech at Reunion," 5; J. H. Martin, "Address," 4–7.

43. Gary, "A Vindication of the South," 3, 4, 5.

44. Waddell, "Address," 6.

45. J. Davis, "Address Delivered to the Army of Tennessee," 228, 229.

46. Boggs, "The South Vindicated," 55.

47. Black, "Anniversary Address," 9, 11.

48. Carr, "To the Confederate Soldiers," 4. Carr served with the Third North Carolina Cavalry. After the war he became a successful businessman in Durham, North Carolina, where his company made and sold Bull Durham tobacco products. Carr was also involved in banking, textiles, railroads, newspapers, and utility and telephone companies. He was commander of the United Confederate Veterans of North Carolina and had an honorary rank of major general. Carr died in 1924. Biographical sketch in his papers in the Southern Historical Collection, University of North Carolina, Chapel Hill.

49. McKim, "Motives and Aims," 9–11; Gordon, "The Old South," 145; W. R. Cox, "Southern Cause Noble and Just," 8.

50. McCrady, "Address before the Virginia Division," 216. McCrady was an often-wounded Confederate officer from Charleston, South Carolina, who practiced law and wrote historical works on his state. He served in the South Carolina House of Representatives from 1882 to 1890 and was elected president of the South Carolina Historical Society in 1899. He died in Charleston on November 1, 1903. Salley, "Edward McCrady."

51. McCrady, "Address before the Virginia Division," 219.

52. Capers, "Address on Memorial Day," 10–11.

53. R. E. Lee, "Speech of Col. Robert E. Lee, Jr.," 5.

54. Black, "Anniversary Address," 5, 6; Dawson, "Our Women in the War," 5.

55. Weaver, *Southern Tradition at Bay,* 114; McPherson, *What They Fought For,* 6.

Chapter 4

1. Hill, "The Confederate Soldier in the Ranks," 5; Cash, *Mind of the South,* 46.

2. Waddell, "The Confederate Soldier," 9–10.

3. Marshall, "Address," 2–3; Wolfe, "Chickamauga," 179–80.

4. Olmstead, "Confederate Times and Confederate Men," 4.

5. J. H. Martin, "Address," 21; Carr, "To the Confederate Soldiers," 18; C. C. Jones, "Georgians during the War," 33; Daniel, "Memorial Day Address," 1; W. R. Cox, "Southern Cause Noble and Just," 10. Daniel, a Virginia lawyer and wounded Confederate veteran, was elected to the Senate in 1885, where he served until his death in 1910.

6. Faulkner, "The Bear," 288–89.

7. Culberson, "Welcoming Speech," 36.

8. Daniel, "Memorial Day Address," 2.

9. Twain, *Life on the Mississippi*, 319; Graves, "Two Kinds of Heroes," 1; Waddell, "Address," 5. Graves, born in South Carolina in 1856, was a journalist and lecturer in Florida and Georgia for much of his career. Later in life he was editor of the *New York Daily American* and wrote for the Hearst organization of newspapers. He died on August 8, 1925. Pattillo, "Graves, John Temple," 364.

10. Daniel, "Memorial Day Address," 1; Cameron, "Address," 364.

11. Warren, *Legacy of the Civil War*, 15; Mayo, *War Memorials as Political Landscape*, 179; Graves, "Two Kinds of Heroes," 1; Kershaw, "Address," 4. According to the report of the ceremonies, Kershaw's oration was "delivered in a manner that attracted and held the attention of all. While for the most part calm and quiet, the speaker would at times wax eloquent upon some sentiment that touched his heart most deeply, and his words were received with the heartiest approval." Black, "Anniversary Address," 3.

12. Graves, "Two Kinds of Heroes," 1; Hoyt, "The Palmetto Riflemen," 8.

13. Hood, "Oration," 5; Carr, "To the Confederate Soldiers," 20–21, 7–8, 14.

14. J. Davis, "Address Delivered to the Army of Tennessee," 233; Hood, "Oration," 11.

15. Gary, "A Vindication of the South," 19.

16. Kershaw, "Address," 6.

17. Graves, "Memorial Address."

18. Hill, "The Confederate Soldier in the Ranks," 5; Carr, "To the Confederate Soldiers," 15.

19. Marshall, "Address," 3; Crump, "Speech at Reunion," 10–11; Young, "Address at Unveiling," 21, 20, 21, 22.

20. Waddell, "The Confederate Soldier," 2–3.

21. J. H. Martin, "Address," 30.

22. C. C. Jones, "Address," 18–19.

23. "Monument to General Robert E. Lee," 188; Hampton, "Address on . . . Robert E. Lee," 51–52; Anderson, "Robert Edward Lee," 7; "Monument to General Robert E. Lee," 246.

24. Daniel, "Memorial Day Address," 2; Vedder, "For What Did the South Fight?" 7, 8.

25. Hoyt, "The Palmetto Riflemen," 37.

26. "Monument to General Robert E. Lee," 189–90.

27. Ibid., 190–92.

28. Ibid., 194–95.

29. Ibid., 197–217.

30. Ibid., 249–59.

31. Ibid., 303–6.

32. Emerson, *Historic Southern Monuments*, 442–43.

33. Ibid., 153–56; "Historical Sketch of the R. E. Lee Monument Association."

34. Emerson, *Historic Southern Monuments*, 408; *Ceremonies Connected with the Inauguration*.

35. Chaffin, "Daniel's Speech Honoring Robert E. Lee," 312–13.

36. Hill, "The Confederate Soldier in the Ranks," 20; Hood, "Oration," 8, 9; Gary, "A Vindication of the South," 17.

37. Hoge, "Oration"; Moore, "Moses Drury Hoge." 2439; "Jackson's Statue," *Charleston News and Courier,* October 27, 1875; Moger, *Virginia,* 26; Blight, *Race and Reunion,* 80.

38. Eggleston, "Moses Drury Hoge," 121; Moore, "Moses Drury Hoge," 2438; Hoge, "Oration," 5, 7, 8, 9, 11.

39. "Dedication of the Tomb of the Army of Northern Virginia Association," 213, 214, 216, 217.

40. F. Lee, "Oration at Jackson's Statue," 7, 15–16, 31. Lee, a nephew of Robert E. Lee, had been a Confederate major general. After the war he was elected governor of Virginia and served as a major general in the U.S. Army during the Spanish-American War. Rehm, "Lee, Fitzhugh," 914–15.

41. "Dedication of the Tomb of the Army of Northern Virginia Association," 217, 218.

42. J. I. Robertson, *Stonewall Jackson,* 755.

43. Waddell, "Memorial Day Address."

44. Hampton, "Address on . . . Robert E. Lee," 20; Hood, "Oration," 5.

45. For a report on this tour see Towns, " 'To Preserve the Traditions of Our Fathers' "; Gordon, "The Old South."

46. Black, "Anniversary Address," 17.

47. S. D. Lee, "Laying of the Corner-Stone," 366, 367, 368, 380–81.

48. Boggs, "The South Vindicated," 12.

49. Young, "Address at Unveiling," 12, 6–7, 10, 12, 14, 16–17, 18.

50. Carr, "To the Confederate Soldiers," 3.

51. Dawson, "Our Women in the War," 18; Gordon, "Last Days of the Confederacy," 475–76. This speech was given many times around the country; this version was presented in Brooklyn, New York, on February 7, 1901.

52. Vedder. "For What Did the South Fight?" 11; Dawson, "Our Women in the War," 7–8, 9.

53. W. M. Hammond, "Address Delivered at Wadesboro," 22, 23.

54. Dawson, "Our Women in the War," 3, 4, 13, 14, 17, 38; C. C. Jones, "Address," 32.

55. Carr, "To the Confederate Soldiers," 4.

56. Waddell, "The Confederate Soldier," 11; Gordon, "Last Days of the Confederacy," 480.

57. Hampton, "Address on . . . Robert E. Lee," 37.

58. C. C. Jones, "Battle of Honey Hill," 4.

59. Waddell, "The Confederate Soldier," 6.

60. Curry, "Address," 20–22. According to the pamphlet, at least ten thousand copies of the speech were printed and circulated around the South. Buck, in *The Road to Reunion,* describes this speech by the general agent of the Peabody Education Fund, a "masterful address" (251).

61. Hill, "The Confederate Soldier in the Ranks," 20; Capers, "Address on Memorial Day," 15; Carr, "To the Confederate Soldiers," 3.

62. McKim, "Motives and Aims," 33.

63. McCrady, "Heroes of the Old Camden District," 30.

64. Dawson, "Our Women in the War," 18–22.

65. Vance, "Last Days of the War," 9, 11, 14.

66. Hampton, "Address on . . . Robert E. Lee," 32–33.

67. Tyler, "Address of Welcome," 5.

68. C. C. Jones, "General Sherman's March," 14; Vance, "Last Days of the War," 18, 16, 17–18.

69. Vance, "Last Days of the War," 7, 7–8, 10.

70. Olmstead, "Confederate Times and Confederate Men," 7; Cameron, "Address," 364.

Chapter 5

1. Curry, "Address," 24; Bell, "Address at Johnson's Island," 6; Young, "Address at Unveiling," 22; Crump, "Speech at Reunion," 13; Bell, "Address at Johnson's Island," 6; Cobb, *Most Southern Place on Earth*, 60.

2. Vance, "Last Days of the War," 27.

3. Campbell, "Oration," 8, 12, 13; Boggs, "The South Vindicated," 10.

4. Black, "Address of J. C. C. Black," 172–73.

5. W. M. Hammond, "Address Delivered at Wadesboro," 18–19.

6. Williams, "Address to Company 'A,' " 10–11.

7. W. M. Hammond, "Address Delivered at Wadesboro," 19; Daniel, "Oration at Annual Reunion," 408; Walthall, "Address," 17; Graves, "Memorial Address." Walthall was a former Confederate major general and later served as U.S. senator from his home state of Mississippi. Downs, "Walthall, Edward Cary," 1682–83.

8. J. Davis, "Address Delivered to the Army of Tennessee," 229; Vedder, "For What Did the South Fight?" 5–6.

9. Black, "Address of J. C. C. Black," 173.

10. Hoge, "Oration," 12; McKim, "Motives and Aims," 5; Blight, *Race and Reunion*, 22.

11. Boggs, "The South Vindicated," 4–5; Campbell, "Oration," 8; H. S. Thompson, "Anniversary Oration," 6; Goldfield, *Still Fighting the Civil War*, 222.

12. C. C. Jones, "Address," 10; Marshall, "Address," 6.

13. H. S. Thompson, "Anniversary Oration," 14; Black, "Address of J. C. C. Black," 174; Williams, "Address to Company 'A,' " 11.

14. J. Davis, "Address Delivered to the Army of Tennessee," 235; Humes, "Address," 22; E. L. Ayers, *Promise of the New South*, 9.

15. Patrick, *Reconstruction of the Nation*, 150; Franklin, *Reconstruction*, 35.

16. Hood, "Oration," 10–11; Humes, "Address," 22; Black, "Anniversary Address," 19; Carr, "To the Confederate Soldiers," 22.

17. Buck, *The Road to Reunion*, 139; Patrick, *Reconstruction of the Nation*, 250.

18. Hoge, "Oration," 14; Curry, "Address," 26.

19. Daniel, "Oration at the Inauguration," 51; Black, "Address of J. C. C. Black," 171–72.

20. Graves, "Memorial Address"; McKim, "Motives and Aims," 4; Logan, "The Future of the South." For a biographical sketch of Logan see Lund, "Logan, Thomas Muldrup," 2.

21. Daniel, "Oration at the Inauguration," 50, 50–51, 73.

22. Throckmorton, "Speech Delivered at Re-Union of Hood's Soldiers." Throck-morton had been a brigadier general of Texas state troops in the war, and he later served in Congress. Allardice, "James Webb Throckmorton," 221–22.

23. Graves, "Union Decoration Day Speech." The copy of the clipping has penned across the bottom: "This speech was one of the most successful of my life." Graves assessed the event as "a grand affair" in which he spoke to "an immense concourse of people."

24. Curry, "Address," 1.

25. Vedder, "For What Did the South Fight?" 12; W. R. Cox, "Southern Cause Noble and Just," 13.

26. Waddell, "The Confederate Soldier," 22–23; McKim, "Motives and Aims," 28; W. R. Cox, "Southern Cause Noble and Just," 12; Herbert, "To the Confederacy's Sol-diers and Sailors," 219; and Vedder, "For What Did the South Fight?" 13.

27. Buck, *The Road to Reunion,* 310; Carr, "To the Confederate Soldiers," 22. For additional examination of the process of reconciliation and oratory's critical role in promoting it, see Towns, "Ceremonial Speaking"; and Towns, "Ceremonial Orators."

28. Vedder, "For What Did the South Fight?" 12.

29. Graves, "Memorial Address"; Waddell, "Memorial Day Address"; Graves, "Me-morial Day."

30. Black, "Anniversary Address," 18.

31. Carr, "To the Confederate Soldiers," 22; W. R. Cox, "Southern Cause Noble and Just," 12.

32. Olmstead, "Confederate Times and Confederate Men," 7; Daniel, "Memorial Day Address," 2.

33. Hood, "Oration," 10–11; Hoge, "Oration," 14; and Graves, "Memorial Address."

34. Kershaw, "Address," 5–6; Marshall, "Address," 5; Hood, "Oration," 11, 1.

35. C. C. Jones, "Hon. R. M. T. Hunter," 8.

36. Graves, "Memorial Address"; Graves, "Memorial Day."

37. Bauer, "History of the Jefferson Davis Monument Association," 11. For an ex-cellent discussion of the role of children in the Lost Cause efforts, see K. L. Cox, *Dixie's Daughters,* esp. 63–65.

38. Boggs, "The South Vindicated," 11; Turney, "The South Justified," 25; C. C. Jones, "Hon. R. M. T. Hunter," 8; Curry, "Address," 3.

39. Black, "Anniversary Address," 19–20.

40. C. C. Jones, "Georgia during the War," 155, 156; Blight, *Race and Reunion,* 266.

41. Kershaw, "Address," 7, 6; Black, "Anniversary Address," 19; Williams, "Address to Company 'A,'" 14–15.

42. J. W. Jones, "Speech of Dr. J. William Jones," 44; Bell, "Address at Johnson's Island," 6; Gordon, "The Old South," 141–42.

43. Quoted in Osterweis, *Myth of the Lost Cause,* 14.

44. Campbell, "Oration," 15; Williams, "Address to Company 'A,'" 9–10; R. E. Lee, "Speech of Col. Robert E. Lee, Jr.," 15, 9.

45. J. H. Martin, "Address," 18; Gary, "A Vindication of the South," 15.

46. Lumpkin, *Making of a Southerner,* 127–28.

Chapter 6

1. "Memorial Day," *Augusta (GA) Chronicle,* quoted in Towns, "Ceremonial Speaking," 167.

2. Goldfield, *Still Fighting the Civil War,* 40.

3. Poppenheim et al., *History of the UDC,* 92.

4. Lumpkin, *Making of a Southerner,* 111.

5. S. D. Lee, "Speech of Gen. Stephen D. Lee," 3.

6. Williams, "Address to Company 'A,'" 5.

7. J. H. Martin, "Address," 28–29.

8. Barnett, "Strength through Unity," 11; Blight, *Race and Reunion,* 258; Goldfield, *Black, White, and Southern,* 87.

9. Dabbs, *The Southern Heritage,* 128, 263. Dabbs, a native South Carolinian, farmer, college professor, served as president of the Southern Regional Council from 1957 to 1963. A leading southern white liberal on the racial issue, Dabbs died in 1970. For useful articles on Dabbs, see Egerton, *A Mind to Stay Here,* 32–50; Randolph, "James McBride Dabbs"; and Hobson, "James McBride Dabbs."

10. Barnett, "Speech to Louisiana Committee for Free Electors," 5.

11. Faubus, "Speech to Democratic State Convention," 11, 10.

12. Faubus, "Speech of Governor Orval E. Faubus," 255, 261.

13. Barnett, "Mississippi Still Says 'Never,'" 142, 142–43, 144, 145.

14. Barnett, "Speech to Louisiana Committee for Free Electors," 12, 14.

15. Eastland, "We've Reached Era of Judicial Tyranny," 131; Eastland, "Is the Supreme Court Pro-Communist?" 3–4.

16. Thurmond, "A Choice for Americans," 261, 262.

17. Simmons, "Mid-West Hears the South's Story," 3, 6. The pamphlet proclaimed that the "Direct newspaper, radio and television coverage of the address reached an estimated audience of 2,000,000 in Iowa and Nebraska. Wire service coverage was nation-wide." Simmons, from Jackson, Mississippi, organized his hometown chapter of the Citizens' Council in 1954, shortly after the *Brown v. Topeka Board of Education* decision. Later, he devoted himself full-time to the Citizens' Council movement as administrator and editor. He spoke throughout the United States and at one time was president of the Southern Independent School Administration. Simmons was a member of the Sons of Confederate Veterans.

18. Brady, "Segregation and the South," 250, 253.

19. Caskey, "The South's Just Cause," 1, 9; Barnett, "Strength through Unity," 4, 14.

20. Brady, "Segregation and the South," 245–46.

21. Byrnes, "Address at Bennettsville," 90.

22. Simmons, "Mid-West Hears the South's Story," 5, 9.

23. Wallace, "Inaugural Address, 1963," 148, 151.

24. Eastland, "We've Reached Era of Judicial Tyranny," 129; A. C. Thompson, "Speech on Radio and Television," 1; Brady, "Segregation and the South," 250–51; Barnett, "Mississippi Still Says Never," 142.

25. Wallace, "Inaugural Address," 152.

26. Ervin, "Alexander Hamilton's Phantom," 25; Faubus, "Television and Radio Speech," 137; Faubus, "Speech to Democratic State Convention," 6; Eastland, "We've Reached Era of Judicial Tyranny," 131.

27. Barnett, "Speech to Louisiana Committee for Free Electors," 8; Simmons, "Mid-West Hears the South's Story," 15; Brady, "Segregation and the South," 250.

28. Eastland, "We've Reached Era of Judicial Tyranny," 127–28; Brady, "Segregation and the South," 251.

29. Faubus, "Speech to Democratic State Convention," 7; Simmons, "Mid-West Hears the South's Story," 8, 10.

30. Eastland, "Is the Supreme Court Pro-Communist?" 7, 11.

31. Byrnes, "Address at Bennettsville," 90; Simmons, "Mid-West Hears the South's Story," 12; Barnett, "Strength through Unity," 15.

32. Quoted in Coski, "Confederate Battle Flag," 224.

33. "Georgia Next Front for Confederate Flag Battle," *Charlotte Observer*, December 8, 2000, 10-A.

34. Davies, *Patriotism on Parade,* 265.

35. Headquarters S.C. Division, U.C.V., General Order No. 41, Charleston, S.C., April 6, 1899, South Carolina Historical Society Collections.

36. McKim, "Motives and Aims," 4.

37. Williams, "Address to Company 'A,'" 32.

38. Lumpkin, *Making of a Southerner,* 116.

39. Coski, "Confederate Battle Flag," 196.

40. "NAACP Board Approves Boycott of South Carolina," *Pensacola News Journal,* October 17, 1999, 6-A.

41. Firestone, "Bastion of Confederacy."

42. Firestone, "Unfurling a Battle Cry."

43. Eichel, "The Flag Comes Down as Antagonism Rises."

44. "Mfume Visits Boycott Effort," 2B; Page Ivey, "NAACP to Begin 'Border Patrols,'" *Charlotte Observer,* March 2, 2002; "Confederate Flag Supporters Form Own South Carolina Border Patrols," *Charlotte Observer,* March 10, 2002. Even highly successful college football coach Steve Spurrier got into the debate when he remarked in a press conference following the 2007 University of South Carolina Gamecocks spring football game: "My opinion is we don't need the Confederate flag at our Capitol." *Springdale (AR) Morning News,* April 15, 2007.

45. Brent Staples, "South Carolina: The Politics of Barbeque and the Battle of Piggy Park," *New York Times,* September 16, 2002.

46. Emily Wagster, "Few Ripples Follow Flag Decision," *Charlotte Observer,* April 14, 2002, 20-A. See also Reed, "The Banner That Won't Stay Furled," for an excellent overview of this Mississippi flag campaign.

47. Michael A. Fletcher, "Ban on Rebel Flag T-Shirts Opens Old Wounds," *Memphis Commercial Appeal,* January 1, 2003, A6; "Confederate-Flag Shirts Get 13 Students Sent Home," *Charlotte Observer,* March 24, 2004; "Kentucky Teen Sues School over Confederate Prom Dress," *Charlotte Observer,* September 21, 2003, 1B.

48. Dan Huntley, "Should Stars and Stripes Fly over Hunley Crew?" *Charlotte Observer,* September 21, 2003, 1B.

49. Jim Morrill, "Dean Explains, Apologizes for Flag Remark," *Charlotte Observer,* November 6, 2003; Michael Graham, "Democrats Rush to Offend Dixie," *Charlotte Observer,* November 5, 2003.

50. *Chronicle of Higher Education,* November 12, 2004, A75.

51. Various articles in *Charlotte Observer:* October 15, 2004, 11B; November 21, 2004, 2B; January 11, 2005, 1A, 5A; January 22, 2005; March 16, 2005, 12A; March 20, 2005, 2B.

52. "Ceremony to Honor Confederate Deaths," *Arkansas Democrat-Gazette,* April 14, 2006, 2B.

53. Coski, "Confederate Battle Flag," 205; C. N. Wilson, "The Confederate Battle Flag," 271; Forman, "Driving Dixie Down," 272.

54. James K. Flynn, "New Symbol for Southern Pride," *Charlotte Observer,* February 5, 2004.

55. John Stoehr, "Muskets, Cannons Mark Confederate Memorial Day," *Savannah Morning News,* April 28, 2003, 1A.

56. Bill Ward, "Remember Veterans on Other Memorial Day," *Charlotte Observer,* May 5, 2001; Brian McCollum, "Ceremony Spotlights Civil War Warriors," *Pensacola News-Journal,* May 14, 1995, 6B. In 2000, South Carolina legislators approved a compromise that provided for Martin Luther King, Jr. Day to be celebrated as a state holiday along with Confederate Memorial Day; the state had refused to celebrate the former holiday since it was inaugurated in 1986. All state agencies and some county offices close on both days now. The compromise was introduced and pushed through by state senator Robert Ford, an African American South Carolinian who believes it is only proper to recognize those who died in the Civil War. See Prince, *Rally 'Round the Flag,* 238–40, for a discussion of the compromise and its relationship to the Confederate flag controversy in that state.

57. "Columbus Re-enacts First Decoration Day," *Jackson (MS) Clarion-Ledger,* April 23, 1961; "Barnett Speaks at 115th Confederate Memorial Day," *Jackson (MS) Daily News,* April 25, 1978. Clippings in subject file, Mississippi Department of Archives and History, Jackson.

58. Program of Confederate Memorial Day Service, April 25, 1982, copy in subject file, Mississippi Department of Archives and History.

59. Michael Culbreth, "Day Stirs South's Civil War Memories," *Jackson (MS) Clarion-Ledger,* April 26, 1986; Melanie Simpson, "Confederate Heritage Issue Not Forgotten at Oxford Rally," *Jackson (MS) Clarion-Ledger,* April 29, 1997. Clippings in subject file, Mississippi Department of Archives and History.

60. *Civil War News,* May 2003, June 2003.

61. "Maryland Protects Its Military Monuments"; T. Ayers and Yarnall, "Monument to Confederates Unveiled," 1; "Funds Needed for Monument," 48.

62. Stanley, "Confederate Monument Dedicated Memorial Day"; Sears, "General Longstreet and the Lost Cause," 53; Price, "North Carolina Man to Show Battle Monument"; Mitchell, "Monument to Honor Confederate Dead"; B. Smith, "Ghost Can Now Stand Tall Regarding His Monument."

63. "Soldier Whole Again, Reclaims Post," 1B.

64. Lopez, "Ghosts of the South"; C. Smith, "Monument Raises Students' Interest"; Furgurson, "Recalling History," 67.

65. Quoted in Cullen, *Civil War in Popular Culture,* 8.

66. "Beebe Appoints 4 to Panel on Civil War Anniversary," 3B.

67. Horwitz, "Rebel-Flag Battle Opens Old Wounds"; Coski, "Confederate Battle Flag," 216.

68. Warren, *Legacy of the Civil War,* 3.

69. Forts, "Living with Confederate Symbols," 74; Firestone, "The New South"; Carter, "Looking Back," 281, 293.

Bibliography

Speeches

Anderson, Archer. "Address at Dedication of Lee Monument." *Southern Historical Society Papers* 17 (1889): 313–34.

——. "Robert Edward Lee: An Address Delivered at the Dedication of the Monument to General Robert Edward Lee at Richmond, Virginia, May 29, 1890." Richmond: Wm. Ellis Jones, 1890.

Barnett, Ross R. "Mississippi Still Says 'Never.'" Radio and television speech, September 13, 1962. Text in a pamphlet privately printed by the Citizens' Council, Jackson, Mississippi, 1962. Text in University of Mississippi Library. Reprinted in Towns, *Public Address in the Twentieth-Century South*, 141–45.

——. "Speech to Louisiana Committee for Free Electors, Fund Raising Banquet." Monroe, Louisiana, September 3, 1963. Text at University of Southern Mississippi Library, Hattiesburg.

——. "Strength through Unity." Speech to Mississippi Citizens' Council Rally, New Orleans, March 7, 1960. Text in University of Mississippi Library, Oxford.

Bell, Landon C. "An Address at Johnson's Island, in Memory of the Confederate Soldiers Who While Prisoners Died and Are Buried on the Island." May 26, 1929. N.p., 1929.

Black, James C. C. "Address of J. C. C. Black, at the Unveiling of the Hill Statue, Atlanta, Georgia, May 1, 1886." *Southern Historical Society Papers* 14 (1886): 163–79.

——. "Anniversary Address, Confederate Memorial Day, April 26, 1890." Augusta, GA: Chronicle Publishing Co., 1890. Text in University of Georgia Library.

Boggs, William E. "The South Vindicated From the Charge of Treason and Rebellion." Address to the Survivors' Association of the Sixth Regiment, South Carolina Volunteers, Chester, August 4, 1881. Columbia, S.C.: Presbyterian Publishing House, 1881.

Brady, Thomas Pickens. "Segregation and the South." Speech to the Commonwealth Club, San Francisco, October 4, 1957. Reprinted in Towns, "*We Want Our Freedom,*" 244–53.

Byrnes, James F. "Address at Bennettsville, S.C., September 26, 1957." *U.S. News and World Report,* October 4, 1957, 88–90.

Calhoun, Patrick. "Memorial Day Address." Rome, Georgia, May 10, 1880. Text in an unidentified newspaper clipping in author's possession.

Cameron, William E. "Address Presenting a Portrait of Governor James Lawson Kemper, Major-General Confederate States Army." Richmond, Virginia, February 20, 1903. *Southern Historical Society Papers* 30 (1902): 361–68.

Campbell, Josiah A. P. "Oration at the Third Annual Reunion Grand Camp Confederate Veterans, Jackson, Mississippi, July 12, 1892." Pamphlet in Mississippi Department of Archives and History, Jackson.

Capers, Ellison. "An Address on Memorial Day, May 20th, 1890, Greenville, S.C., by Rev. Ellison Capers, D.D." Greenville, S.C.: Daily News Steam Book and Job Presses, 1890. Pamphlet in South Caroliniana Collection, University of South Carolina Library, Columbia.

Carr, Julian S. "To the Confederate Soldiers, of the 'Rank and File,' and to Henry L. Wyatt, the First Hero Who Fell in Defence of the South." Wilmington, North Carolina, May 10, 1894. N.p., n.d.

Caskey, W. M. "The South's Just Cause." Speech delivered on "Mississippi Day" at Valley Forge, Pennsylvania, May 15, 1960. Pamphlet in University of Arkansas Library.

Cowles, William H. H. "The Life and Services of Gen'l James B. Gordon." Address delivered in Metropolitan Hall, Raleigh, North Carolina, May 10, 1887. Raleigh: Edwards, Broughton & Co., 1887.

Cox, Edwin P. "Address to R. E. Lee Camp Confederate Veterans." *Southern Historical Society Papers* 26 (1898): 292–95.

Cox, William Ruffin. "The Southern Cause Noble and Just." Delivered May 10, 1911, Oakwood Cemetery, Richmond, Virginia. Richmond: F. J. Mitchell Printing Corp., 1911.

Crump, S. A. "Speech at Reunion of the North Carolina Confederate Veterans." Greensboro, North Carolina, August 20, 1902. Macon, GA: Macon Evening News, 1902. Pamphlet in University of Georgia Library.

Culberson, Charles A. "Welcoming Speech." Copy in Emory University Library. Reprinted in Philpott, *Sponsor Souvenir Album,* 33–36.

Curry, J. L. M. "Address of Hon. J. L. M. Curry, LL.D., Delivered before the Association of Confederate Veterans, Richmond, Va., July 1, 1896." Richmond: B. F. Johnson Publishing Company, 1896. Copy in Rare Book Collection, University of North Carolina, Chapel Hill.

Daniel, John W. "Address of John W. Daniel, LL.D." In *Ceremonies Connected with the Inauguration of the Mausoleum and the Unveiling of the Recumbent Figure of General Robert Edward Lee at Washington and Lee University, Lexington, Va., June 28, 1883.* Richmond: West, Johnston & Co., 1883.

———. "Memorial Day Address." June 4, 1891, Norfolk, Virginia. Text from *Norfolk Virginian,* June 5, 1891. Text in University of Virginia Library, Charlottesville.

———. "Oration at Annual Reunion of Confederate Veterans at New Orleans, April 9, 1892." In *Speeches and Orations of John Warwick Daniel,* comp. Edward M. Daniel, 383–411. Lynchburg, Va.: J. P. Bell Company, 1911.

———. "Oration at the Inauguration of the Mausoleum and the Unveiling of the Recumbent Figure of General Robert Edward Lee at Washington and Lee University." Richmond: West, Johnston, and Co., 1883.

Davis, Jefferson. "Address Delivered to the Army of Tennessee." Mississippi City, Mississippi, July 10, 1878. In *Jefferson Davis, Constitutionalist,* ed. Dunbar Rowland, 9:227–37. Jackson: Mississippi Department of Archives and History, 1923.

———. "Speech at Army of Northern Virginia Banquet." In *Davis Memorial Volume; or, Our Dead President, Jefferson Davis, and the World's Tribute to his Memory,* ed. J. William Jones, 446–47. Richmond: B. F. Johnson, 1878.

Dawson, Francis W. "Our Women in the War, An Address by Capt. Francis W. Dawson, Delivered February 22, 1887, at the Fifth Annual Reunion of the Association of the Maryland Line at the Academy of Music, Baltimore, Maryland." Charleston, S.C.: Walker, Evans & Cogswell Company, 1887. Pamphlet at the Memphis Public Library.

Eastland, James O. "Is the Supreme Court Pro-Communist?" Speech to U.S. Senate, May 2, 1962. Richmond: The Patrick Henry Group, 1962. Pamphlet in University of Virginia Library, Charlottesville.

———. "We've Reached Era of Judicial Tyranny." Delivered to Association of Citizens' Councils of Mississippi, Jackson, December 1, 1955. Reprinted in Towns, *Public Address in the Twentieth-Century South,* 125–33.

Ervin, Sam J., Jr. "Alexander Hamilton's Phantom." Delivered at Harvard Law School Association of New York City. April 28, 1955. *Vital Speeches of the Day* 22 (October 15, 1955): 23–26.

Faubus, Orval E. "Speech of Governor Orval E. Faubus." Little Rock, September 18, 1958. Text in Special Collections Department, University of Arkansas Library, Fayetteville. Reprinted in Towns, "*We Want Our Freedom,*" 255–64.

———. "Speech to Democratic State Convention." September 5, 1958. Text in Special Collections Department, University of Arkansas Library, Fayetteville.

———. "Television and Radio Speech on the Little Rock Situation." September 1, 1957. Text in Special Collections Department, University of Arkansas Library, Fayetteville. Reprinted in Towns, *Public Address in the Twentieth-Century South,* 135–40.

Gary, Eugene B. "A Vindication of the South." Delivered in Abbeville, South Carolina, May 10, 1917. N.p., n.d. Copy of pamphlet text of speech found in Tennessee State Library, Nashville.

Gordon, John B. "Last Days of the Confederacy." Presented in Brooklyn, New York, February 7, 1901. Reprinted in *Modern Eloquence,* ed. Thomas B. Reed, 5:471–94. Philadelphia: John D. Morris and Company, 1901.

———. "The Old South." Augusta, Georgia, April 26, 1887. Reprinted in Towns, *Oratory and Rhetoric in the Nineteenth-Century South,* 141–48.

Graves, John Temple. "Memorial Address." West Point, Georgia, April 26, 1876. Unidentified newspaper clipping, Graves Scrapbooks, South Caroliniana Collection, University of South Carolina Library, Columbia.

———. "Memorial Day." April 26, 1888. Rome, Georgia. Unidentified newspaper clipping, Graves Scrapbooks, South Caroliniana Collection, University of South Carolina Library, Columbia.

———. "Two Kinds of Heroes." Memorial Day Address, April 26, 1877. La Grange, Georgia. Unidentified newspaper clipping, Graves Scrapbooks, South Caroliniana Collection, University of South Carolina Library, Columbia.

———. "Union Decoration Day Speech." May 30, 1885, Jacksonville, Florida. Unidentified newspaper clipping, Graves Scrapbooks, South Caroliniana Collection, University of South Carolina Library, Columbia.

Hammond, James Henry. "On the Admission of Kansas." U.S. Senate, March 4, 1858. Reprinted in Towns, *Oratory and Rhetoric in the Nineteenth-Century South,* 66–72.

Hammond, W. M. "Address Delivered at Wadesboro, N.C., before the Daughters of the Confederacy and the Confederate Veterans." August 7, 1903. Atlanta: Foote & Davies Company, 1903. Text in University of Georgia Library, Athens.

Hampton, Wade. "Address on the Life and Character of Gen. Robert E. Lee." Delivered October 12, 1871, to Society of Confederate Soldiers and Sailors, Baltimore. Baltimore: John Murphy & Co., 1871.

Herbert, H. A. "To the Confederacy's Soldiers and Sailors." *Southern Historical Society Papers* 26 (January–December 1898): 219.

Hill, Major-General D. H. "The Confederate Soldier in the Ranks." Delivered October 22, 1885, to Virginia Division of the Association of the Army of Northern Virginia. Richmond, Virginia. Richmond: Wm. Ellis Jones, Book and Job Printer, 1885.

Hoge, Moses D. "Oration by Rev. Moses D. Hoge, D.D., at the Inauguration of the Jackson Statue." N.p., n.d.

Hood, John B. "Oration of General J. B. Hood." Delivered to the Annual Meeting of the Survivors' Association of the State of South Carolina, Charleston, December 12, 1872. Charleston, S.C.: Walker, Evans & Cogswell, 1873.

Hoyt, James A. "The Palmetto Riflemen." July 21, 1885. Greenville, S.C.: Hoyt & Keys, 1886. Pamphlet in South Caroliniana Collection, University of South Carolina, Columbia.

Humes, W. Y. C. "An Address Delivered by W. Y. C. Humes at the Unveiling of the Monument over the Graves of the Confederate Dead at Memphis, Tenn., June 6, 1878." Memphis: Price, Jones, & Co., 1878.

Jones, Charles C., Jr. "Address Delivered before Confederate Survivors' Association." Augusta, Georgia, April 26, 1881. Augusta, GA: M. M. Hill & Co., 1881.

———. "The Battle of Honey Hill." Delivered to the Confederate Survivors' Association. Augusta, Georgia, April 27, 1885. Augusta, GA: Chronicle Printing Establishment, 1885.

———. "General Sherman's March from Atlanta to the Coast." Delivered before the Confederate Survivors' Association, Augusta, Georgia, April 26, 1884. Augusta, GA: Chronicle Printing, 1884.

———. "Georgians during the War between the States." Delivered to the Confederate Survivors' Association, Augusta, Georgia, April 26, 1889. Augusta, GA: Chronicle Publishing Co., 1889.

———. "Hon. R. M. T. Hunter: Post-Bellum Mortality among Confederates." Delivered to the Confederate Survivors' Association, Augusta, Georgia, August 2, 1887. Augusta, GA: Chronicle Publishing Co., 1887.

———. "Oration at the Unveiling and Dedication of the Confederate Monument." Augusta, Georgia, October 31, 1878. Augusta, GA: Chronicle and Constitutionalist Job Printing Establishment, 1878.

Jones, J. William. "Speech of Dr. J. William Jones." Reprinted in Philpott, *Sponsor Souvenir Album,* 42–44.

Kershaw, Rev. John. "Address Delivered before the Ladies' Memorial Association and Citizens of Charleston." May 10, 1893. Charleston: Daggett Printing Co., 1893.

Lee, Fitzhugh. "Oration at Jackson's Statue." In *Dedication of Tomb of Army of Northern Virginia, Louisiana Division and Unveiling of Statue of Stonewall Jackson at Metairie Cemetery, New Orleans, May 10, 1881.* New Orleans: M. F. Dunn & Bro., 1881. Source located at Virginia Historical Society, Richmond.

Lee, Robert E., Jr. "Speech of Col. Robert E. Lee, Jr." *Speeches at Richmond Reunion May 30 to June 3, 1907.* N.p., n.d. Pamphlet in Rare Book Collection, University of North Carolina, Chapel Hill.

Lee, Stephen D. "The Laying of the Corner-Stone of the Monument to President Jefferson Davis." Richmond, Virginia, July 2, 1896. *Southern Historical Society Papers* 24 (1896): 364–81.

———. "Speech of Gen. Stephen D. Lee." *Speeches at Richmond Reunion May 30 to June 3, 1907.* N.p., n.d. Pamphlet in Rare Book Collection, University of North Carolina, Chapel Hill.

Lee, William H. F. "Introductory Speech for D. H. Hill." Richmond, October 22, 1885. In D. H. Hill, *The Confederate Soldier in the Ranks,* 3. Richmond: Wm. Ellis Jones, 1885.

Logan, Thomas M. "The Future of the South." Columbia, South Carolina, July 21, 1875. *Columbia (SC) Daily Phoenix,* July 22, 1875.

Lucas, D. B. "Response to a Toast 'Our Dead' at Reunion of the Virginia Division of the Army of Northern Virginia." Richmond, Virginia, October 22, 1885. Richmond: Wm. Ellis Jones, 1885.

Marshall, J. Q. "Address Delivered before the Survivors of the First Regiment of Rifles (Orr's Rifles) at Their Reunion, Held on October 1, 1885 at Sandy Springs, Anderson County." N.p., n.d.

Martin, J. H. "Address of Major-General J. H. Martin at the Reunion of the

Georgia Division United Confederate Veterans." Columbus, Georgia, October 19, 1910. Atlanta: Chas. P. Byrd, 1911. Pamphlet in University of Georgia Library.

McCrady, Edward, Jr. "Address before Virginia Division of Army of Northern Virginia at Their Reunion, October 21, 1886." *Southern Historical Society Papers* 14 (1886): 183–221.

———. "Heroes of the Old Camden District, South Carolina, 1776–1861." An Address to the Survivors of Fairfield County, Delivered at Winnsboro, South Carolina, September 1, 1888. Richmond: Wm. Ellis Jones, 1888.

McKim, Randolph Harrison. "The Motives and Aims of the Soldiers of the South in the Civil War." Delivered to the United Confederate Veterans at their Fourteenth Reunion, Nashville, Tennessee, June 14, 1904. N.p., n.d. Pamphlet in Rare Book Collection, University of North Carolina Library.

Olmstead, Charles H. "Confederate Times and Confederate Men." Delivered to the Confederate Veterans Association. Savannah, Georgia, March 1, 1892. Savannah: Braid & Hutton, 1893.

Rutledge, Col. B. H. "Memorial Day Address." Charleston, South Carolina, May 10, 1875. Printed copy in South Caroliniana Collection, University of South Carolina Library.

Simmons, William J. "The Mid-West Hears the South's Story." Speech to Oakland, Iowa, Farmers-Merchants Annual Banquet, February 3, 1958. Greenwood, MS: Citizens' Councils, 1958.

Thompson, Allen C. "Speech on Radio and Television." May 13, 1963, Jackson, Mississippi. Text in Evers Papers, Tougaloo College, Jackson, Mississippi.

Thompson, Hugh S. "Anniversary Oration before the Washington Light Infantry of Charleston, S.C." February 22, 1879. N.p., n.d.

Throckmorton, James W. "Speech Delivered at Re-union of Hood's Soldiers." Waco, Texas, June 27, 1889. Pamphlet in University of Texas Library, Austin.

Thurmond, Strom. "A Choice for Americans: The Challenge is Yours." Speech to Aberdeen, South Dakota, Chamber of Commerce, January 9, 1965. *Vital Speeches of the Day* 31 (1965): 259–62.

Turney, Peter. "The South Justified." An Address Delivered before Frank Cheatham Bivouac No. 1, of the Association of Confederate Soldiers Tennessee Division, August 18, 1888. Nashville: Albert B. Tavel, 1888.

Tyler, Judge D. Gardiner. "Address of Welcome to the Confederate Veterans." Richmond, June 1, 1915. N.p., n.d. Pamphlet in Rare Book Collection, University of North Carolina Library.

Vance, Zebulon. "The Last Days of the War in North Carolina." Delivered to the Third Annual Reunion of the Association of the Maryland Line, Baltimore, Maryland, February 23, 1885. Baltimore: Sun Book and Job Printing Office, 1885.

Vedder, Rev. Charles S. "For What Did the South Fight in the War of 1861–1865?" A Discourse Preached in the Huguenot Church, Charleston, South Carolina, before Camp A. Burnett Rhett, United Confederate Veterans, November 17, 1901. Monticello, GA: Penn Bros., 1902. Pamphlet in University of Georgia Library.

Waddell, Alfred Moore. "An Address before the Association of the Army of Northern Virginia." House of Delegates, Richmond, Virginia, October 28, 1887. Richmond: Wm. Ellis Jones, 1888.

———. "The Confederate Soldier." An Address Delivered at the Written Request of 5,000 Ex-Union Soldiers at Steinway Hall, New York City, May 3, 1878. Washington, D.C.: Joseph L. Pearson, 1878.

———. "Memorial Day Address." New Bern, North Carolina, May 9, 1879. *The Newbernian*, May 10, 1879.

Wallace, George. "Inaugural Address, 1963." Montgomery, Alabama, January 14, 1963. Reprinted in Towns, *Public Address in the Twentieth-Century South,* 146–52.

Walthall, E. C. "Address of E. C. Walthall, Delivered at the Dedication of the Monument to the Confederate Dead at Jackson, MS, June 3, 1891." N.p., n.d. Pamphlet in Virginia Historical Society Library, Richmond.

Wells, Gen. W. Calvin. "Oration Delivered by Gen. W. Calvin Wells on 6 May 1914." Delivered to the Twenty-Fourth Annual Reunion, United Confederate Veterans, Jacksonville, Florida. Jackson, MS: Jones Printing Co., 1914. Pamphlet in Mississippi Department of Archives and History, Jackson.

Williams, John Sharp. "Address to Company 'A' Confederate Veterans." Memphis, Tennessee, May 31, 1904. Memphis: Paul and Douglass Co., 1904. Pamphlet in Tennessee State Library and Archives, Nashville.

Wise, General Peyton F. "Speech at United Confederate Veterans Reunion." Reprinted in Philpott, *Sponsor Souvenir Album,* 46–52.

Young, Bennett H. "Address at the Unveiling of the Jefferson Davis Monument." New Orleans, February 22, 1911. New Orleans: Jefferson Davis Monument Association, 1911. Pamphlet in Virginia Historical Society Library.

Books and Articles

"200th Anniversary of Lee's Birth." *Civil War News,* May 2003.

Albanese, Catherine L. "Requiem for Memorial Day: Dissent in the Redeemer Nation." *American Quarterly* 26 (October 1974): 386–98.

Allardice, Bruce S. "James Webb Throckmorton." In *More Generals in Gray,* 221–22. Baton Rouge: Louisiana State University Press, 1995.

Allen, W. *Historical Sketch of the Lee Memorial Association.* Richmond: West, Johnston, 1883.

Andrews, James R. "Oaths Registered in Heaven: Rhetorical and Historical Legitimacy in the Inaugural Addresses of Jefferson Davis and Abraham Lincoln." In *Doing Rhetorical History: Concepts and Cases,* ed. Kathleen J. Turner, 95–117. Tuscaloosa: University of Alabama Press, 1998.

"Annual Reunion of the Virginia Division, Army of Northern Virginia." *Southern Historical Society Papers* 6, no. 6 (1878): 283–84.

Aristotle. *On Rhetoric.* Trans. George A. Kennedy. New York: Oxford University Press, 1991.

Ayers, Edward L. *The Promise of the New South: Life after Reconstruction.* New York: Oxford University Press, 1992.

Ayers, Terry, and Wayne Yarnall. "Monument to Confederates Unveiled." *Civil War Courier,* July 2007, 1.

Bailey, N. Louise. "Marshall, John Quitman." In *Biographical Directory of the South Carolina Senate, 1776–1985,* ed. Bailey, 2:1058–60. Columbia: University of South Carolina Press, 1986.

"Barnett Speaks at 115th Confederate Memorial Day." *Jackson (MS) Daily News,* April 25, 1978.

Baskerville, Barnet. *The People's Voice: The Orator in American Society.* Lexington: University Press of Kentucky, 1979.

Bauer, Nicholas. "History of the Jefferson Davis Monument Association." In *Unveiling of the Jefferson Davis Monument,* 11. New Orleans, 1911.

"Beebe Appoints 4 to Panel on Civil War Anniversary." *Arkansas Democrat-Gazette,* October 13, 2007, 3B.

Benning, Ann Caroline. *A History of the Origin of Memorial Day.* Columbus, GA: Thos. Gilbert, 1898.

Bishir, Catherine W. "'A Strong Force of Ladies': Women, Politics, and Confederate Memorial Associations in Nineteenth-Century Raleigh." *North Carolina Historical Review* 77 (October 2000): 455–91.

Bland, Sidney R. "Promoting Tradition, Enhancing Change: The Poppenheim Sisters of Charleston." In *Searching for Their Places: Women in the South Across Four Centuries,* ed. Thomas H. Appleton Jr. and Azela Boswell, 179–95. Columbia: University of Missouri Press, 2003.

Blight, David W. "Decoration Days: The Origin of Memorial Day in North and South." In *The Memory of the Civil War in American Culture,* ed. Alice Fahs and Joan Waugh, 94–129. Chapel Hill: University of North Carolina Press, 2004.

———. *Race and Reunion: The Civil War in American Memory.* Cambridge: Harvard University Press, 2001.

Bodnar, John. *Remaking America: Public Memory, Commemoration, and Patriotism in the Twentieth-Century.* Princeton: Princeton University Press, 1992.

Boorstin, Daniel J. *The Americans: The National Experience.* New York: Random House, 1965.

———. *The Genius of American Politics.* Chicago: University of Chicago Press, 1953.

Braden, Waldo W. "Myths in a Rhetorical Context." In *The Oral Tradition in the South,* 65–82. Baton Rouge: Louisiana State University Press, 1983.

———. *The Oral Tradition in the South.* Baton Rouge: Louisiana State University Press, 1983.

———. "'Repining Over an Irreversible Past': The Ceremonial Orator in a Defeated Society, 1865–1900." In *Rhetoric of the People: "Is there any better or equal hope in the World?"* ed. Harold Barrett, 273–301. Amsterdam: Rodopi, 1974.

Brandt, William J. *The Rhetoric of Argumentation.* Indianapolis: Bobbs-Merrill, 1970.

Brown, William G. *The Lower South in American History.* New York: Macmillan, 1902.

Buck, Paul H. *The Road to Reunion, 1865–1900*. 1937. New York: Vintage Books, 1961.

Callahan, Helen. "Black, James Conquest Cross." In *Dictionary of Georgia Biography*, ed. Kenneth Coleman and Charles Stephen Gurr, 1:81–82. Athens: University of Georgia Press, 1983.

Carleton, William G. "The Celebrity Cult of a Century Ago." *Georgia Review* 14 (Summer 1960): 133–42.

Carter, Hodding, III. "Looking Back." *Southern Cultures* 2, nos. 3–4 (1996): 281–93.

Cash, W. J. *The Mind of the South*. New York: Knopf, 1941.

Cass, Michael M. "Charles C. Jones, Jr. and the 'Lost Cause.'" *Georgia Historical Quarterly* 55 (Summer 1971): 222–33.

Ceremonies and Speeches at the Dedication of the Monument to the Confederate Dead. Alexandria, Va., 1889.

Ceremonies Connected with the Inauguration of the Mausoleum and the Unveiling of the Recumbent Figure of General Robert Edward Lee at Washington and Lee University, Lexington, Va., June 28, 1883. Richmond: West, Johnston & Co., 1883.

"Ceremony to Honor Confederate Deaths." *Arkansas Democrat-Gazette*, April 14, 2006.

Chaffin, William W. "John Warwick Daniel's Speech Honoring Robert E. Lee, Lexington, Virginia, 1883." *Southern Speech Journal* 25 (1960): 305–13.

Charleston (SC) News and Courier, February 20, 1879. Clipping in Holmes Scrapbook on Palmetto Guard. South Carolina Historical Society, Charleston.

Chase, J. Richard. "The Classical Conception of Epideictic." *Quarterly Journal of Speech* 47 (October 1961): 293–300.

"Chief Justice Eugene Blackburn Gary." In *The History of South Carolina: Biographical Volume*, 494–95. New York: American Historical Society, 1935.

Chronicle of Higher Education, November 12, 2004, A 75.

Cobb, James C. *The Most Southern Place on Earth: The Mississippi Delta and the Roots of Regional Identity*. New York: Oxford University Press, 1992.

"Columbus Re-enacts First Decoration Day." *Jackson (MS) Clarion-Ledger*, April 23, 1961.

Condit, Celeste Michelle. "The Functions of Epideictic: The Boston Massacre Orations as Exemplar." *Communication Quarterly* 33, no. 4 (1985): 284–99.

"Confederate Flag Shirts Get 13 Students Sent Home." *Charlotte Observer*, March 24, 2004.

"Confederate Flag Supporters Form Own South Carolina Border Patrols." *Charlotte Observer*, March 10, 2002.

Confederate Pamphlets. Rare Book Collection. University of North Carolina, Chapel Hill.

Corbett, Edward P. J. *Classical Rhetoric for the Modern Student*. New York: Oxford University Press, 1965.

Coski, John M. *The Confederate Battle Flag: America's Most Embattled Emblem*. Cambridge: Belknap Press of Harvard University Press, 2005.

———. "The Confederate Battle Flag in American History and Culture." *Southern Cultures* 2 (Winter 1996): 195–231.

Coulter, E. Merton. *College Life in the Old South.* New York: Macmillan, 1928.

———. "The Confederate Monument in Athens, Georgia." *Georgia Historical Quarterly* 40 (September 1956): 230–47.

Cox, Karen. *Dixie's Daughters: The United Daughters of the Confederacy and the Preservation of Confederate Culture.* Gainesville: University Press of Florida, 2003.

"Crewmen of Recovered Confederate Sub Are Honored at Burial." *New York Times,* April 18, 2004.

Culbreth, Michael. "Day Stirs South's Civil War Memories." *Jackson (MS) Clarion-Ledger,* April 26, 1986.

Cullen, Jim. *The Civil War in Popular Culture: A Reusable Past.* Washington, D.C.: Smithsonian Institution Press, 1995.

Current, Richard N., Paul D. Escott, Lawrence N. Powell, James I. Robertson, and Emory M. Thomas, eds. *Encyclopedia of the Confederacy.* 4 vols. New York: Simon & Schuster, 1993.

Dabbs, James McBride. *The Southern Heritage.* New York: Knopf, 1958.

Dabney, Virginius. *Liberalism in the South.* Chapel Hill: University of North Carolina Press, 1932.

Davies, Wallace Evan. *Patriotism on Parade: The Story of Veterans and Hereditary Organizations in America, 1783–1900.* Cambridge: Harvard University Press, 1955.

Davis, Reuben. *Recollections of Mississippi and Mississippians.* Boston: Houghton, Mifflin, 1890.

Davis, Stephen. "Empty Eyes, Marble Hand: The Confederate Monument and the South." *Journal of Popular Culture* 16 (Winter 1982): 2–21.

Davis, William C. *The Cause Lost: Myths and Realities of the Confederacy.* Lawrence: University Press of Kansas, 1996.

Dedication of Monument to Confederate Dead of Florida. Jacksonville: Da Costa Printing House, 1898.

"Dedication of the Tomb of the Army of Northern Virginia Association and Unveiling of the Statue of Stonewall Jackson at New Orleans." *Southern Historical Society Papers* 9 (May 1881): 213–19.

Dickey, Dallas C., and Donald C. Streeter. "Lucius Q. C. Lamar." In *History and Criticism of American Public Address,* ed. Marie Hochmuth Nichols, 3:175–221. New York: Longmans, Green, 1955.

Downs, Alan C. "Walthall, Edward Cary." In Current et al., *Encyclopedia of the Confederacy,* 4:1682–83.

Eckert, Ralph L. *John Brown Gordon: Soldier, Southerner, American.* Baton Rouge: Louisiana State University Press, 1989.

Edgefield (SC) Advertiser, March 20, 1879. Clipping in Holmes Scrapbook of Palmetto Guard. South Carolina Historical Society, Charleston.

Egerton, John. *A Mind to Stay Here: Profiles from the South.* London: Macmillan, 1970.

Eggleston, Joseph D. "Moses Drury Hoge." *Dictionary of American Biography*, ed. Dumas Malone, 9:121–22. New York: Scribner, 1932.

Eichel, Henry. "The Flag Comes Down as Antagonism Rises." *Charlotte Observer*, July 2, 2000.

Emerson, B. A. C., comp. *Historic Southern Monuments: Representative Memorials of the Heroic Dead of the Southern Confederacy*. New York: Neale, 1911.

Eubanks, Ralph T. "The Rhetoric of the Nullifiers." In *Oratory in the Old South, 1828–1860*, ed. Waldo W. Braden, 19–72. Baton Rouge: Louisiana State University Press, 1970.

Fahs, Alice, and Joan Waugh, eds. *The Memory of the Civil War in American Culture*. Chapel Hill: University of North Carolina Press, 2004.

Faulkner, William. "The Bear." In *Go Down Moses and Other Stories*, 191–331. Birmingham: Oxmoor House, 1983.

———. *The Sound and the Fury*. New York: Modern Library, 1946.

Firestone, David. "Bastion of Confederacy Finds Its Future May Hinge on Rejecting the Past." *New York Times*, December 5, 1999.

———. "The New South: Old Times There Are Not Forgotten." *New York Times*, January 28, 2001.

———. "Unfurling a Battle Cry and Its Last Hurrah." *New York Times*, January 23, 2000.

"The First Confederate Memorial Day." *Richmond Times-Dispatch*, July 15, 1906. Reprinted in *Southern Historical Society Papers* 35 (1907): 369.

Fletcher, Michael A. "Ban on Rebel Flag T-Shirts Opens Old Wounds." *Memphis Commercial Appeal*, January 1, 2003, A6.

Flynn, James K. "New Symbol for Southern Pride." *Charlotte Observer*, February 5, 2004.

Forman, James, Jr. "Driving Dixie Down: Removing the Confederate Flag from Southern State Capitals." *Southern Cultures* 2, no. 2 (1996): 272.

Forts, Franklin. "Living with Confederate Symbols." *Southern Cultures* 8, no. 1 (2002): 60–75.

Foster, Gaines M. *Ghosts of the Confederacy: Defeat, the Lost Cause, and the Emergence of the New South, 1865 to 1913*. New York: Oxford University Press, 1987.

———. "Lost Cause Myth." In *Encyclopedia of Southern Culture*, ed. Charles Reagan Wilson and William Ferris, 1134–35. Chapel Hill: University of North Carolina Press, 1989.

Franklin, John Hope. *Reconstruction: After the Civil War*. Chicago: University of Chicago Press, 1961.

Freehling, William W. *The Road to Disunion*. Vol. 1, *Secessionists at Bay, 1776–1854*. New York: Oxford University Press, 1990.

"Funds Needed for Monument to McGowan's Brigade." *Confederate Veteran*, July/August 2007, 48.

Furgurson, E. B. "Recalling History: Confederate Flags and Monuments in Virginia." *Preservation* 49 (September–October 1997): 62–67.

Gaines, Francis Pendleton. *Southern Oratory: A Study in Idealism*. University: University of Alabama Press, 1946.

Gallagher, Gary W., and Alan T. Nolan, eds. *The Myth of the Lost Cause and Civil War History*. Bloomington: Indiana University Press, 2000.

"Georgia Next Front for Confederate Flag Battle." *Charlotte Observer*, December 8, 2000, 10A.

Goldfield, David R. *Black, White, and Southern: Race Relations and Southern Culture, 1940 to the Present*. Baton Rouge: Louisiana State University Press, 1990.

———. *Still Fighting the Civil War: The American South and Southern History*. Baton Rouge: Louisiana State University Press, 2002.

Graham, Michael. "Democrats Rush to Offend Dixie." *Charlotte Observer*, November 5, 2003.

Gramm, Kent. *Somebody's Darling: Essays on the Civil War*. Bloomington: Indiana University Press, 2002.

Green, Edwin L. *A History of the University of South Carolina*. Columbia: State Company, 1916.

Gronbeck, Bruce E. "The Rhetorics of the Past: History, Argument, and Collective Memory." In *Doing Rhetorical History: Concepts and Cases*, ed. Kathleen J. Turner, 47–60. Tuscaloosa: University of Alabama Press, 1998.

Groppe, John D. "Ritualistic Language." *South Atlantic Quarterly* 69 (Winter 1970): 58–67.

Gross, Doug. "Georgia Keying on Civil War's 150th to Boost Tourism." *Southeast Missourian* (Cape Girardeau), March 5, 2007, 5A.

Haardt, Sara. "Southern Credo." *American Mercury*, May 1930, 102–10.

Hale, Laura Virginia. *Memories in Marble: The Story of the Four Confederate Monuments at Front Royal, Virginia*. N.p., 1956.

Hanley, Ray. "The Gray Reunion." *Civil War Times Illustrated*, January–February 1992, 42–63.

Hariman, Robert. "Afterword: Relocating the Art of Public Address." In *Rhetoric and Political Culture in Nineteenth Century America*, ed. Thomas W. Benson, 163–79. East Lansing: Michigan State University Press, 1997.

Hattaway, Herman. "Clio's Southern Soldiers: The United Confederate Veterans and History." *Louisiana History* 12 (Summer 1971): 213–42.

———. "Lee, Stephen D." In Current et al., *Encyclopedia of the Confederacy*, 2: 921–21.

"The Hero Dead," *Augusta (GA) Daily Chronicle and Sentinel*, April 27, 1875, 3+.

Herrington, Angie. "Civil War History Is an Enduring Tourist Lure." *Chattanooga (TN) Times Free Press*, September 26, 2004, A8.

"Historical Sketch of the R. E. Lee Monument Association." *Southern Historical Society Papers* 14 (1886): 97–102.

Hobson, Fred. "James McBride Dabbs: Isaac McCaslin in South Carolina." *Virginia Quarterly Review* 53, no. 4 (1977): 640–59.

Hollis, Daniel Walker. *University of South Carolina*. Vol. 1, *South Carolina College*. Columbia: University of South Carolina Press, 1957.

Horwitz, Tony. *Confederates in the Attic: Dispatches from the Unfinished Civil War.* New York: Pantheon Books, 1998.

———. "Rebel-Flag Battle Opens Old Wounds, Builds New Alliances." *Wall Street Journal,* February 10, 1995.

Huff, A. V., Jr. "The Democratization of Art: Memorializing the Confederate Dead in South Carolina, 1866–1914." In *Art in the Lives of South Carolinians Nineteenth-Century, Book 1,* ed. David Moltke-Hansen, AH-1–AH-8. Charleston, S.C.: Carolina Art Association, 1978.

Huntley, Dan. "Should Stars and Stripes Fly over Hunley Crew?" *Charlotte Observer,* September 21, 2003, 1B.

Ivey, Page. "NAACP to Begin 'Border Patrols.'" *Charlotte Observer,* March 2, 2002.

Johnson, Samuel R. "The Non-Aristotelian Nature of Samoan Ceremonial Oratory." *Western Speech* 34 (Fall 1970): 262–73.

Jones, Charles C., Jr. *Memorial History of Georgia.* 1900. Reprint, Spartanburg, S.C.: Reprint Co., 1966.

Kammen, Michael. *Mystic Chords of Memory: The Transformation of Tradition in American Culture.* New York: Knopf, 1991.

"Kentucky Teen Sues School over Confederate Prom Dress." *Charlotte Observer,* September 21, 2003, 1B.

Kilmer, Kenton. "The Origin of Memorial Day." Washington, D.C.: Library of Congress Legislative Reference Service, 1963. Copy of typescript in Mississippi State Archives.

Kinney, Martha E. "'If Vanquished I Am Still Victorious': Religious and Cultural Symbolism in Virginia's Confederate Memorial Day Celebrations 1866–1930." *Virginia Magazine of History and Biography* 106 (Summer 1998): 237–66.

Lawton, Christopher R. "Constructing the Cause, Bridging the Divide: Lee's Tomb at Washington College." *Southern Cultures* 15 (Summer 2009): 5–39.

Letter to the editor. *Atlanta Constitution,* April 26, 1887, 4.

Lewis, Bernard. *History: Remembered, Recovered, Invented.* Princeton: Princeton University Press, 1975.

Lopez, Steve. "Ghosts of the South." *Time,* April 30, 2001.

Lumpkin, Katherine Du Pre. *The Making of a Southerner, with an Afterword by the Author.* Athens: University of Georgia Press, 1981.

Lund, Jennifer. "Logan, Thomas Muldrup." In Current et al., *Encyclopedia of the Confederacy,* 2:942–43.

Martin, Sharron. "Confederate Memorial Day." *UDC Magazine* 62 (March 1999): 8–10.

"Maryland Protects Its Military Monuments." *Civil War News,* May 2003.

Mathes, J. Harvey. "Rev. William E. Boggs." In *The Old Guard in Gray: Researches in the Annals of the Confederate Historical Association,* 41. N.p., n.d.

Mayo, James M. *War Memorials as Political Landscape: The American Experience and Beyond.* New York: Praeger, 1988.

McCollum, Brian. "Ceremony Spotlights Civil War Warriors." *Pensacola News Journal,* May 14, 1995, 6B.

McMichael, Kelly. *Sacred Memories: The Civil War Monument Movement in Texas.* Denton: Texas State Historical Association, 2009.

McPherson, James M. *What They Fought For, 1861–1865.* Baton Rouge: Louisiana State University Press, 1994.

Meaders, Margaret Inman. "Postscript to Appomattox: My Grandpa and Decoration Day." *Georgia Review* 24 (Fall 1970): 297–304.

"Memorial Day." *Augusta (GA) Chronicle,* April 22, 1887.

"Memorial Day." *Augusta (GA) Daily Chronicle and Sentinel,* April 25, 1875.

"Memorial Day." Editorial. *Raleigh News and Observer,* May 10, 1887.

"Memorial Day." *Newbernian* (New Bern, NC), May 17, 1879.

"Mfume Visits Boycott Effort." *Charlotte Observer,* April 20, 2002, 2B.

Mills, Cynthia, and Pamela H. Simpson, eds. *Monuments to the Lost Cause: Women, Art, and the Landscapes of Southern Memory.* Knoxville: University of Tennessee Press, 2003.

Mitchell, Hannah. "Monument to Honor Confederate Dead." *Charlotte Observer,* May 11, 2001.

Moffatt, Frederick C. "A Tale of Two Monuments: Civil War Sculpture in Knoxville." *East Tennessee Historical Society's Publications* 50 (1978): 3–20.

Moger, Allen W. *Virginia: Bourbonism to Byrd, 1870–1925.* Charlottesville: University Press of Virginia, 1968.

"Monument Dedicated." *Civil War News,* June 2003.

"Monument to General Robert E. Lee." *Southern Historical Society Papers* 17 (1889): 188–216.

Moore, Walter W. "Moses Drury Hoge." In *Library of Southern Literature,* ed. Edwin A. Alderman and Joel Chandler Harris, 6:2435–39. New Orleans: Martin and Hoyt Co., 1910.

Morrill, Jim. "Dean Explains, Apologizes for Flag Remark." *Charlotte Observer,* November 6, 2003.

Murphy, Terrence V. "Hood, John Bell." In Current et al., *Encyclopedia of the Confederacy,* 2:789–91.

"NAACP Board Approves Boycott of South Carolina." *Penscola News Journal,* October 17, 1999, 6-A.

Neff, John R. *Honoring the Civil War Dead: Commemoration and the Problem of Reconciliation.* Lawrence: University Press of Kansas, 2005.

Negri, Paul, ed. *Civil War Poetry: An Anthology.* Mineola, N.Y.: Dover, 1997.

Newsome, A. R. "Waddell, Alfred Moore." *Dictionary of American Biography,* 19:300–301. New York: Scribner, 1936.

Nolan, Alan T. "The Anatomy of the Myth." In *The Myth of the Lost Cause and Civil War History,* ed. Gary W. Gallagher and Alan T. Nolan, 11–34. Bloomington: Indiana University Press, 2000.

Norfolk Virginian, June 5, 1891. Text in University of Virginia Library, Charlottesville.

"Orr's Rifles Reunion." *Charleston (SC) News and Courier,* July 24, 1875.

Osterweis, Rollin G. *The Myth of the Lost Cause, 1865–1900*. Hamden, Conn.: Archon Books, 1973.

Owsley, Frank. *Plain Folk of the Old South*. Baton Rouge: Louisiana State University Press, 1948.

Pace, Robert F. "Humes, William Young Conn." In Current, *Encyclopedia of the Confederacy*, 2:799–800.

Patrick, Rembert. *The Reconstruction of the Nation*. New York: Oxford University Press, 1967.

Pattillo, John W. "Graves, John Temple." In *Dictionary of Georgia Biography*, ed. Kenneth Coleman and Charles Stephen Gurr, 1:364. Athens: University of Georgia Press, 1983.

"Pensacolians Decorate Graves of the Blue and Gray." *Pensacola Journal*, April 26, 1983.

Perelman, Chaim. *The Realm of Rhetoric*. Trans. William Kluback. Notre Dame, Ind.: Notre Dame University Press, 1982.

Perelman, Chaim, and Lucie Olbrechts-Tyteca. *The New Rhetoric: A Treatise on Argumentation*. Notre Dame, Ind.: University of Notre Dame Press, 1969.

Phillips, Margaret I. "Peter Turney." In *The Governors of Tennessee*, 110–14. Gretna, La.: Pelican Publishing Co., 1978.

Philpott, William Bredsoe, ed. *The Sponsor Souvenir Album and History of the United Confederate Veterans' Reunion 1895*. Houston: Sponsor Souvenir Company, 1895.

Piehler, G. Kurt. *Remembering War the American Way*. Washington, D.C.: Smithsonian Institution Press, 1995.

Poole, W. Scott. *Never Surrender: Confederate Memory and Conservatism in the South Carolina Upcountry*. Athens: University of Georgia Press, 2004.

Poppenheim, Mary B., et al. *History of the United Daughters of the Confederacy, 1894–1955*. Raleigh, N.C.: Edwards and Broughton, 1956.

Porcher, F. A. *A Brief History of the Ladies' Memorial Association of Charleston, S.C., from Its Organization in 1865 to April 1, 1880*. Charleston: H. P. Cooke, 1880.

Price, Mark. "North Carolina Man to Show Battle Monument." *Charlotte Observer*, October 17, 2003.

Prince, K. Michael. *Rally 'Round the Flag, Boys!* Columbia: University of South Carolina Press, 2004.

Randolph, Robert M. "James McBride Dabbs: Spokesman for Racial Liberalism." In *From the Old South to the New: Essays on the Transitional South*, ed. Walter J. Fraser Jr. and Winifred B. Moore Jr., 253–64. Westport, Conn.: Greenwood Press, 1981.

Reed, John Shelton. "The Banner That Won't Stay Furled." In *Minding the South*, 201–17. Columbia: University of Missouri Press, 2003.

Regenstein, Lewis. Letter. *New York Times Book Review*, April 24, 2005, 6.

Rehm, Karen G. "Lee, Fitzhugh." In Current et al., *Encyclopedia of the Confederacy*, 2:914–15.

Reidenbaugh, Lowell. "Cox, William Ruffin." In Current et al., *Encyclopedia of the Confederacy,* 1:442.

Robertson, James I., Jr. *Stonewall Jackson: The Man, the Soldier, the Legend.* New York: Macmillan, 1997.

Robertson, James O. *American Myth, American Reality.* New York: Hill and Wang, 1980.

Salley, A. S., Jr. "Edward McCrady." *South Carolina Historical and Geneological Magazine* 5 (1904): 62–67.

Schultz, Connie. "Watching *Roots* in 2010." *Parade,* June 27, 2010, 22.

Scott, Anne Firor. *The Southern Lady: From Pedestal to Politics, 1830–1930.* Chicago: University of Chicago Press, 1970.

Sears, Stephen W. "General Longstreet and the Lost Cause." *American Heritage* 56 (February/March 2005): 53.

Seigler, Robert S. *A Guide to Confederate Monuments in South Carolina: "Passing the Silent Cup."* Columbia: South Carolina Department of Archives and History, 1997.

"Shall Memorial Day Be Changed?" *Atlanta Constitution,* April 22, 1887, 4.

Shuptrine, Hubert, and James Dickey. *Jericho: The South Beheld.* Birmingham: Oxmoor House, 1979.

Simpson, Melanie. "Confederate Heritage Issue Not Forgotten at Oxford Rally." *Jackson (MS) Clarion-Ledger,* April 29, 1997.

Smith, Bruce. "Ghost Can Now Stand Tall Regarding His Monument." *Charlotte Observer,* December 2, 2004.

Smith, Celeste. "Monument Raises Students' Interest." *Charlotte Observer,* November 16, 2004.

"Soldier Whole Again, Reclaims Post." *Arkansas Democrat-Gazette,* August 13, 2002, 1B.

The South in the Building of the Nation. Vols. 9 and 12. Richmond: Southern Historical Publication Society, 1909.

Springdale (AR) Morning News, April 15, 2007.

Stanley, Dennis. "Confederate Monument Dedicated Memorial Day." *Smithfield (TN) Record,* May 28, 1997.

Staples, Brent. "South Carolina: The Politics of Barbeque and the Battle of Piggy Park." *New York Times,* September 16, 2002.

Stoehr, John. "Muskets, Cannons Mark Confederate Memorial Day." *Savannah Morning News,* April 28, 2003, 1A.

"Suggested by the Day." *Atlanta Constitution,* April 26, 1887, 4.

Sullivan, Dale L. "The Ethos of Epideictic Encounter." *Philosophy and Rhetoric* 26, no. 2 (1993): 113–33.

Sydnor, Charles S. *Gentlemen Freeholders.* Chapel Hill: University of North Carolina Press, 1952.

Tallahassee (FL) Daily Democrat, April 27, 1922.

Taylor, Rosser H. *Ante-Bellum South Carolina: A Social and Cultural History.* Chapel Hill: University of North Carolina Press, 1942.

Towns, Walter Stuart. "Ceremonial Orators and National Reconciliation." In *Oratory in the New South*, ed. Waldo W. Braden, 117–42. Baton Rouge: Louisiana State University Press, 1979.

———. "Ceremonial Speaking and the Reinforcing of American Nationalism in the South, 1875–1890." Ph.D. diss. University of Florida, 1972.

———. "Honoring the Confederacy in Northwest Florida: The Confederate Monument Ritual." *Florida Historical Quarterly* 57 (October 1978): 205–12.

———. *Oratory and Rhetoric in the Nineteenth-Century South: A Rhetoric of Defense*. Westport, Conn.: Praeger, 1998.

———. *Public Address in the Twentieth-Century South: The Evolution of a Region*. Westport, Conn.: Praeger, 1999.

———. "'To Preserve the Traditions of Our Fathers': The Post-War Speaking Career of Jefferson Davis." *Journal of Mississippi History* 52 (May 1990): 111–24.

———. "*We Want Our Freedom*": Rhetoric of the Civil Rights Movement. Westport, Conn.: Praeger, 2002.

Turner, Victor, ed. *Celebration: Studies in Festivity and Ritual*. Washington, D.C.: Smithsonian Institution Press, 1982.

Twain, Mark. *Life on the Mississippi*. New York: Penguin Books, 1984.

"The Unveiling of the Statue of General Robert E. Lee, at Richmond, VA, May 29th, 1890." *Southern Historical Society Papers* 17 (1889): 262–335.

Van Zelm, Antoinette G. "Virginia Women as Public Citizens: Emancipation Day Celebrations and Lost Cause Commemorations, 1863–1890." In *Negotiating Boundaries of Southern Womanhood: Dealing with the Powers That Be*, ed. Janet L. Coryell et al., 71–88. Columbia: University of Missouri Press, 2000.

Wagster, Emily. "Few Ripples Follow Flag Decision." *Charlotte Observer*, April 14, 2002, 20-A.

Walker, Jeffrey. "Aristotle's Lyric: Re-Imagining the Rhetoric of Epideictic Song." *College English* 51 (1989): 5–28.

Ward, Bill. "Remember Veterans on Other Memorial Day." *Charlotte Observer*, May 5, 2001.

Warner, Ezra J. *Generals in Gray: Lives of the Confederate Commanders*. Baton Rouge: Louisiana State University Press, 1959.

Warner, W. Lloyd. *American Life, Dream and Reality*. Rev. ed. Chicago: University of Chicago Press, 1962.

Warren, Robert Penn. *The Legacy of the Civil War: Meditations on the Centennial*. New York: Random House, 1961.

Way, William. *History of the New England Society of Charleston, South Carolina, for One Hundred Years, 1819–1919*. Charleston: New England Society, 1921.

Weaver, Richard M. *The Southern Tradition at Bay: A History of Postbellum Thought*. Ed. George Core and M. E. Bradford. New Rochelle, N.Y.: Arlington House, 1968.

Wheeler, Frank. "'Our Confederate Dead': The Story behind Savannah's Confederate Monument." *Georgia Historical Quarterly* 82 (Summer 1998): 382–97.

Wheeler, Marjorie Spruill. *New Women of the New South: The Leaders of the Woman Suffrage Movement in the Southern States*. New York: Oxford University Press, 1993.

Whites, Lee Ann. "'Stand by Your Man': The Ladies Memorial Association and the Reconstruction of Southern White Manhood." In *Women of the American South: A Multicultural Reader*, ed. Christie Anne Farnham, 133–49. New York: New York University Press, 1997.

Widener, Ralph W., Jr. *Confederate Monuments: Enduring Symbols of the South and the War Between the States*. Washington, D.C.: Andromeda Associates, 1982.

Wilson, Charles Reagan. *Baptized in Blood: The Religion of the Lost Cause, 1865–1920*. Athens: University of Georgia Press, 1980.

Wilson, Clyde N. "The Confederate Battle Flag: A Symbol of Southern Heritage and Identity." *Southern Cultures* 2, no. 2 (1996): 271.

Winberry, John J. "'Lest We Forget': The Confederate Monument and the Southern Townscape." *Southeastern Geographer* 23 (1983): 107–21.

Wolfe, Thomas. "Chickamauga." In *Thomas Wolfe's Civil War*, ed. David Madden, 173–202. Tuscaloosa: University of Alabama Press, 2004.

Wyatt-Brown, Bertram. *Southern Honor: Ethics and Behavior in the Old South*. New York: Oxford University Press, 1982.

Index